d.
house with fully dedicated details | London loft design of
the unexpected but logical | house focussed on perfectly
E
frau und fortschritt 11/82
ff
Kundenzeitschrift der
Stadtwerke Neustadt a. Rbge.
erdgas
D1918879
Hallenbäder:
Alles klar zum Schwimmen
Energie:
Mehr Sowjetgas - mehr Sicherheit?
Energiesparen:
Wärmereserven in Dämmung und Heizung
JEUNE & JOLIE
SPECIAL BEAUTE
KUNSTZEITSCHRIFT
K
Lecturas
525 ptas.
3,16 €
ESPECIAL MODA
COLECCIONES PRIMAVERA VERANO 1999
París
Milán
COLOR Y HUMOR LA MODA MÁS D VERTIDA
BAÑO SABROSO
PALAVRA
P
Edu Lobo
Cinema na internet
Carla Camurati
E mais...
DAS COMPAQ MAGAZIN
Q
Web-Orakel
Prognosen bis 2010
NO:15
R
ROCK KÜLTÜRÜ DERGİSİ
V
W
In Your Face
Clothes That Startle
The Artist Who's Shocking London
x height

SURPRISE ME

EDITORIAL DESIGN

EDITORIAL DESIGN

HORST MOSER

SURPRISE ME

MARK BATTY, PUBLISHER

Leica
LEICA
1/02
LEICA
1/02

IMAGES 12
ILLUSTRATORS 22
ILLUSTRATORS 33
Illustration Index II
AMERICAN ILLUSTRATION
ILLUSTRATORS 29
ILLUSTRATORS 21
VERVE
GRAPHIS MAGAZINE DESIGN
MOHOLY-NAGY
EL LISSITZKY
Der Schriftatlas

CONTENTS

PREFACE

Surprise Me: A designer's ultimate magazine collection

Every graphic designer tends to collect magazines. Not just ones on design, but anything from the thick slick glossy presenters of style to curious goofy one-off zines. The collection tends to grow with our endless need to be visually turned on. The task of managing the increasing piles and deciding what to keep and what to throw becomes dreadful – surely we'll need to refer to them for a project in the future, right?

Years ago, when I was in the process of moving from San Francisco to New York, I could not afford to cart cross-country my vast collection of European and American magazines, neither could I resign myself to dump them altogether. I resolved to find someone – anyone – who would enjoy my back issues of Italian *Vogue*, British *Tattler*, French *Actuel*, and German *The Manipulator*. A couple of phone calls later, I found out that the local jail took magazine donations for their prisoners' recreation room. Why not, I thought. I filled up the back of my car with 12 cardboard boxes weighing a ton each – 350 magazines, about the equivalent of one giant redwood tree – and headed for the detention center on the outskirts of the city. There, I was instructed to unload my gift in the waiting room where the prison chaplain would inspect them to make sure that their content would contribute to the edification of the convicts.

Leafing through *Surprise Me* reminded me of this amusing episode. Surprise was indeed the emotion I read on the face of the pious man as he perused through issue after issue of some of the most avant-garde publications of the previous decade. I held my breath as he scrutinized the salacious photo spreads and the daring typographical layouts. I prayed silently that the sense of surprise he was experiencing – the very same thing that compels designers like me to collect magazines regardless of their topics – would override his religious objections. "I'll take your magazines," he said at last. "The pictures might encourage our prisoners to learn a foreign language."

Horst Moser, designer and author of *Surprise Me*, didn't wait for a priest to give him permission to share with others some of the best examples of editorial design in the world. He did what I wish I had done: He offered his extensive collection of contemporary magazines to readers in the form of a book. Written to appeal to designers as well as non-designers – editors, entrepreneurs, marketers – *Surprise Me* is not encumbered with insider's jargon. Moser, who creates corporate magazines for his German clients (*Leica World*, *Das Microsoft* magazine, *Compaq Computer* magazine), wanted to explain in layman's terms how real magazines are put together. His thorough understanding of the process, combined with intriguing juxtapositions of layouts, no-nonsense comments, and original insight make for an entertaining read – as surprisingly fresh as the subject matter he is presenting. And unlike my captive audience, the only crime you have to commit to have access to this editorial treasure trove is to indulge your curiosity.

Véronique Vienne

FOREWORD

A stimulus for the exchange of ideas

Looking back, magazines are an indispensable source of cultural history, providing a very vivid and compact record of the Zeitgeist. This applies not only to the big names like *Life, Berliner Illustrierter, National Geographic, The New Yorker, Vu, The Economist*, and so on, but also to those relatively short-lived and apparently unimportant magazines in which a valuable and original voice may have been recorded. Great designers have lifted this medium to lofty heights – you've only got to think of names like El Lissitzky, László Moholy-Nagy, Alexey Brodovitch, Alexander Liberman and Willy Fleckhaus. The Dada and Expressionist movements also spawned countless manifesto-type magazines, generally with a very small circulation.

Magazines have changed the world. Einstein's Theory of Relativity, which forms the basis of our world view, first saw the light of day in a magazine. And we mustn't forget the artists and writers who have worked for magazines – Picasso, Warhol, Dalí, Kandinsky, Klee, Matisse, Beardsley, Schwitters, Rodtschenko, Miró, Braque, Chagall, Poe, Schmidt, Tucholsky, Hemingway, Joyce, Kraus, Sartre, the list goes on.

Compared to books, magazine design is more flexible, often more elaborate, more expensive, and more experimental. Photography, typography and illustration all work together. Art directors, like their colleagues in the cinema and theatre – though on far smaller budgets – can create a complete work of art. But in more recent times magazines have had to compete ever more fiercely with other media to gain the public's attention. For a while it even seemed as if the industry was in terminal decline. But after the initial euphoria of the Internet had appeared to herald the death of the printed page, there has been an extraordinary upsurge in the number of highly ambitious magazines – not from the major publishing houses, where the paths of decision-making appear to be too tortuous, but from the smaller firms and the domain of corporate publishing. In the world of science there's now a much more intensive exchange of current ideas. It would be unthinkable for a molecular biologist or an astrophysicist not to be totally up to date with all the latest discoveries.

Some magazines are internationally famous for their editorial design, but there are also many outstanding developments within a narrower, national framework.

This book aims to present the very best, state-of-the-art magazine design from all over the world and, by doing so, to provide a fruitful source of ideas. In order to capture the true spirit of contemporary design, I've chosen examples that stem almost exclusively from the new century. Only when dealing with basic themes, or when there are no current examples because other trends have taken over, have I gone back to older specimens.

The book is divided into sections: basic and theoretical issues are followed by practical and technical themes, with the main body devoted to what may be called the grammar of magazine design. The last section presents international treatments of specific subjects, with virtuoso examples of how the basic elements can be applied. As the book had to be kept within manageable proportions, many good examples have unfortunately had to be sacrificed, but perhaps sufficient interest will be generated for further volumes to be published, enabling an even wider range of topics to be embraced.

It's well worth while examining the whole spectrum of magazines published. Before the first edition of a new magazine hits the stands, all those involved are sworn to secrecy. But as soon as the first issue shows its face, it gives away all its own secrets – the format, the typeface, the print, the quality of paper. The whole concept is thrown open to public scrutiny. Even the photographers and illustrators are named in the credits, and everyone can profit from this public revelation.

Every new development may influence international design. These ideas can work on all levels, and their influence doesn't necessarily have to be confined to the obvious highlights. But anyone who merely imitates what they've seen will never be content with the results. Every task has its own particular problems, and so the solutions must always be tailored accordingly.

This book presents a broad spectrum of design and encourages the development of an extensive repertoire, since it's only through a wide range of ideas that the appropriate language of design can consistently be found.

Horst Moser

The foundations of modern magazine design were laid sixty years ago

He worked for twenty-five years as the art director of *Harper's Bazaar*, and during that time he laid the foundations for modern magazine design. This archetypal art director came to New York from Russia, via Paris, and his name was Alexey Brodovitch. If you look at his magazines today, you'll be struck by the fact that even after sixty years the photographers and illustrators are still familiar names: Richard Avedon, Lillian Bassman, Martin Munkácsi, Henri Cartier-Bresson, Erwin Blumenfeld, Man Ray, and Andy Warhol, who made his mark then as a young illustrator with his drawings of shoes. Brodovitch's sureness of touch when it came to choosing quality photographers and illustrators is astonishing. At the time, nearly all of these people were unknown beginners. Just as Griffith, Eisenstein, Chaplin and Hitchcock brought the cinema to a peak, Brodovitch raised his chosen medium to a pinnacle of achievement. Of course there have been new steps forward right through to the present, but never on that scale. There are countless features of outstanding design in the double-page spreads created by this great innovator: his revolutionary use of photographs, asymmetrical layout of pages, three-dimensional effects, breaking the framework of the grid, classic typography, combinations of text and picture, free arrangement of picture material, the design of the unprinted area, rhythmic repetition of pictures, black and white photographs tinted with colour, and so on. His 'Design Laboratory' became a legend, but it was not confined to theory; he was always at pains to get his students to think and act practically and independently, with each one seeking and finding their own way. Nearly three and a half thousand creative talents attended these highly unconventional courses, including such photographers as Irving Penn, Lillian Bassman, and Hiro and Diane Arbus. It was Brodovitch who invested the post of art director with total responsibility for the visual impact of the magazine, and it was he who issued the all-embracing challenge to his colleagues in magazine design: Astonish me!

Harper's Bazaar, November 1935, Photo: Martin Munkácsi

Harper's Bazaar, March 1936, Photo: Man Ray

Harper's Bazaar, March 1950, Photo: Lillian Bassman

Harper's Bazaar, March 1945, Photo: George Hoyningen-Huené

Harper's Bazaar, September 1955, Photo: Richard Avedon

Harper's Bazaar, October 1944, Photo: Martin Munkácsi

Harper's Bazaar, April 1948, Artwork: Henri Matisse

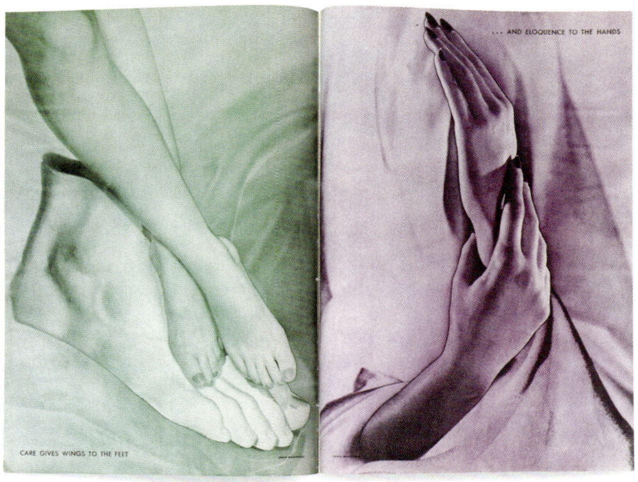

Harper's Bazaar, April 1942, Photo: Erwin Blumenfeld

Sketch

ART DIRECTORS

Three basic types of magazine art director

Art directors are responsible for the visual elements of a magazine. They can be divided into three basic types: the artistic art director, the virtuoso editorial art director, and a third, special creature that's evolved within the large publishing houses, best identified as an art director whose decisions are all heavily influenced by market research.

Examples of the first category are Neville Brody and David Carson. Their magazine concepts are dominated by their own personal style, and the fact that a magazine is designed by Carson will override all other aspects. This can be an advantage when the designer meets the demand for originality and inventiveness, but of course it can also be a disadvantage.

The second category places emphasis on service, technique, teamwork – this designer is the conductor of an orchestra, bringing out all the essential harmony, counterpoint and rhythms of photography, typography, composition, the blending of black and white with colour, illustrations, charts, and so on. Head and heart have to work together if intellect and emotion are to be correctly balanced, and laws both written and unwritten must be known and observed. What effect do we want to achieve, on whom, and by what means? How can we surprise, provoke, entertain and inform our readers? How can we ensure that our author's text will be read? The virtuoso art director will have mastered a wide variety of design languages and be able to cater for a wide variety of target groups, bringing out all the subtle differences between one concept and another.

With our third category of art director we find the smallest degree of individuality. Their magazines are like the artificial products of chemistry laboratories, emerging from their test-tubes with all the 'right' ingredients. Sometimes these instant packages may even be successful, if your criteria for success are sales figures and income from ads.

Raygun, No. 26, 1995, USA

Form, No. 3, 1995, Germany

Neville Brody and David Carson had a huge influence on design in the 1990s. They were prime examples of artistic art directors and all the magazines they designed carry their own personal touch. They both avoided using normal headline fonts. In some issues of *Raygun* Carson distorted the letters to the point of illegibility, and even sought out weathered inscriptions in public places to inspire a degree of amateurishness in his presentation. Brody designed his own fonts, based on examples from the 1930s and 1940s. His characteristic sign systems enable readers to find their way round his magazines.

Per Lui, February 1990, Italy

Actuel, November 1990, France

Tempo, December 1988/January 1989, Germany

Max, May 1996, Germany

Arena, No. 16, 1989, Great Britain

The Face, No. 69, 1986, Great Britain

SKETCHING

The precondition for good design is conceptual thinking

One of the attractions of the computer screen is that whatever you put on it will somehow look good. It's also easy to try out countless variations, shifting your images back and forth, making them bigger, making them smaller – it's all really helpful. Or is it? There's a danger that you'll be tempted to begin without knowing exactly where you want to go. Of course, it's not easy to just force yourself to start sketching, and you do normally have some idea of what you're aiming at. But it's far better and far less time-consuming to have a precise concept. First of all, read the text that's to be designed. Then consider the visual elements that are available or that will have to be devised. For instance, if you're dealing with a report that's already accompanied by photographs, you'll have to make a careful selection: which pictures should you put first, are there others that follow on logically, how will these others be grouped, do the colours go together, is the sequence too repetitive, does it add something new to what we already know? If the overall design leaves you freedom of choice regarding the font, which one do you choose, and why? For the sake of everyone who works on the magazine there should be good reasons for this choice, which must also be practical. If it's merely a matter of personal taste, then the decision-making process becomes arbitrary and even arrogant.

The designer is also usually the first reader of the article, and may feel that there are questions to be asked about one aspect or another; these may find their way into a box or a margin in the form of additional information. The designer must have a total grasp of the content if they're to work in partnership with the editor, and if together they're to find the optimum form of presentation. Supposing, for instance, the text is too long-winded, the designer should suggest ways of dividing it up into palatable sections. Or if a factual description is not clear enough, the designer has to devise other means of animating the presentation.

Peter Knapp, former art director of the French magazine *Elle*, drew designs for most of his magazines and books on large sketch pads. This is the best way to get a feeling for the rhythm of a section, or indeed of a whole issue.

There are many different views on what constitutes the perfect sequence of subjects or the rhythm of a magazine as it emerges during the compilation and structural planning of the material. The classic form is quite like that of a grand opera. You whet the appetite with the overture, which offers a short introduction to all the main themes – the magazine equivalent being the editorial and the list of contents. Next the opera may introduce us to shorter passages and fragments of melodies, building up to the climax of a great aria – here the magazine equivalent is a sequence of short announcements or articles, before embarking on the major theme. There are, of course, many possible variations on this structure. The editor of the German edition of *Wiener* came up with the idea of beginning a red-hot feature on page two – even before the editorial and contents – and stretching it over several pages in order to grab the reader's attention straight away, like a front door opening straight into a living-room. Fashion magazines tend to begin with a big block of ads, with the main bulk of editorial material found later on. You could argue that many readers don't actually read from beginning to end, but open up at random or even flick through backwards, and this is definitely true. Even so, the structure should be as logical and comprehensible as possible, so that even the casual browser is aware of what they're disregarding.

In order to explain their own principles of design and methods of composition, many designers compare their work to other fields. Brody, for instance, refers to examples from architecture, and says that he tried to base his design for *The Face* on town planning, guiding his reader through the magazine with signposts and, at particular points, with open spaces. These are always at the beginning of a piece, where the white space is used to denote the entrance. If you have a large building, he argues, you're not going to place its entrance down a little alley.

Alexey Brodovitch compared his double-page spreads in *Harper's Bazaar* to film sequences, and used the term 'flow' to describe the narrative and rhythmic qualities of his designs. He would lay all the pages in their original size out on the floor, and then shuffle and juxtapose them until he'd established the best order.

Willy Fleckhaus used the image of a well-stocked table, a buffet from which readers could serve themselves. In particular he visualized it as Italian cuisine – the art of the simple. The basic menu of hors d'oeuvre, main dish, and dessert is certainly appropriate for the layout of many magazines.

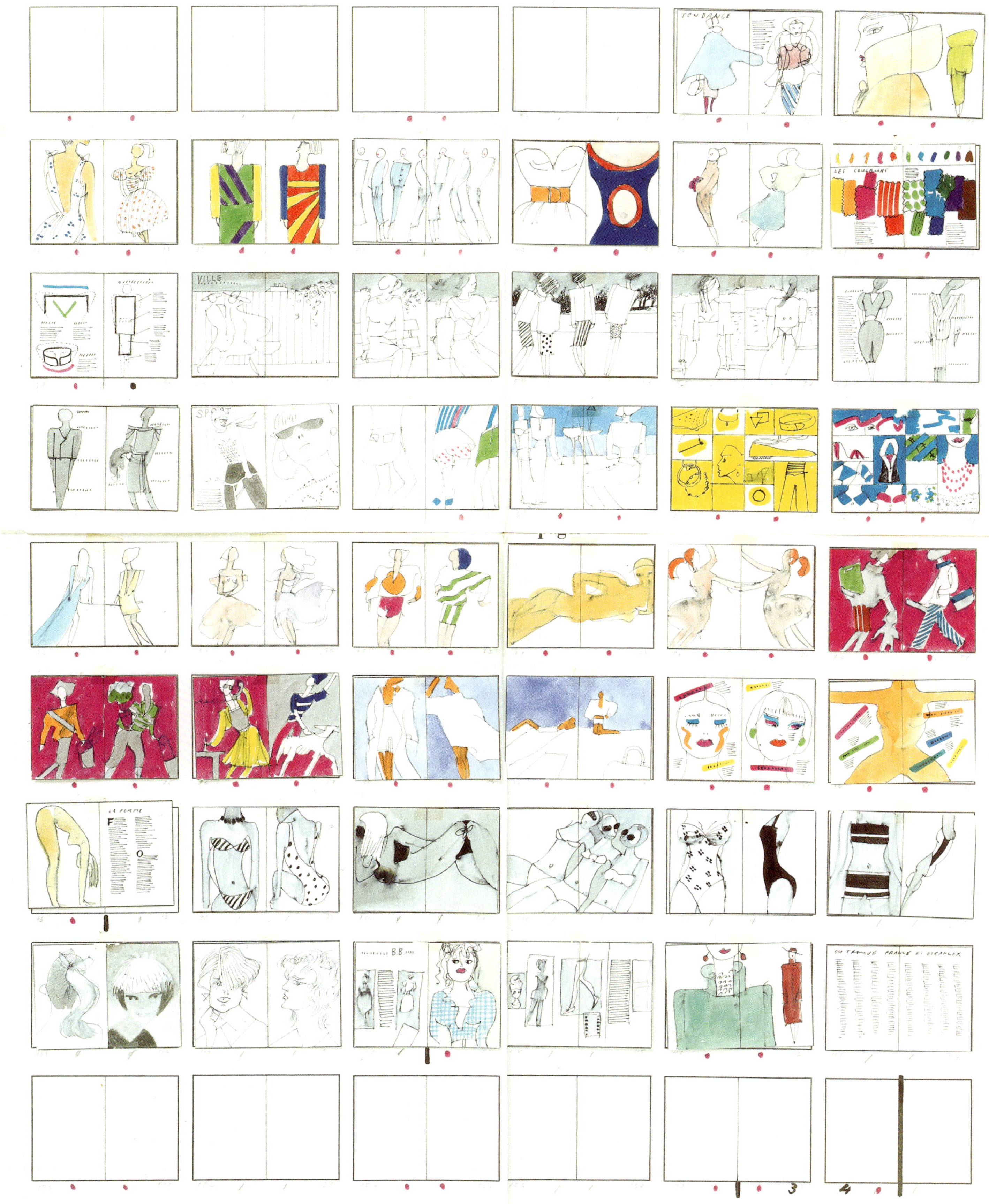

Peter Knapp, sketches

LAYOUT VARIATIONS

A secret competition between Neville Brody's *The Face* and Lo Breier's *Wiener*

The vast number of possible variations in magazine design is not self-evident from the finished products. The publishing firms and design studios may try out lots of things, but most of the results remain hidden from the public. Nevertheless, every variation in design gives a different slant to the actual material, changing the appearance – and message – of any given article to a greater or lesser extent. The choice of opening picture sets the mood for the rest, and the typography has a decisive influence on this mood. An exemplary case from 1983 illustrates these influences perfectly: eight European magazines – *Actuel, Wiener, The Face, Oor, El Vibora, Frigidaire, ETC,* and *Tip* – got together on a joint project with the theme of Europe. For their November editions all eight tackled the same subjects, with each editorial board making its own contributions. They all worked with the same material, though not all the contributions were printed in every magazine. Some themes, though, were published in several magazines, and it's through these that you can compare the different presentations. In some cases,top quality art directors were at work, and so there are very clear differences in standards. Taking the story about Boy George for example, *Tip* opens with a typical, garish publicity photo accompanied by deadly dull typography, while *Wiener* opens with a large black and white picture that promises a personal and exclusive story. In any article on pop stars, the promise of exclusive revelations inevitably arouses far more curiosity than the usual PR material. The interviewer asks his questions on behalf of the reader, and the more original and probing these questions are, the closer the reader feels to the star concerned. In this respect, the design has a very positive effect. Even though it cannot influence the actual text, it can certainly effect the atmosphere and the impact. In *The Face,* Brody uses a similar picture to the one used in *Tip*, but the accompanying typography makes all the difference. It creates a completely modern mood, arousing interest in the story itself.

Another theme from this Europe project offers a pot-pourri of new ideas from all areas of culture. While the choice of different artists naturally gave each issue its own special character, they all used the same cover photo, taken by the Austrian photographer Margit Marnul: a child in jeans. Here too we can see very clearly how the context, logo and typography can influence the overall impact of the photograph. A similar experiment took place in 1999, though on a smaller scale: the different provincial editions of *Max* agreed to combine operations, but since they were already very similar in their overall concepts, the differences turned out to be far less striking.

Tip, No. 23, 1983, Germany

Wiener, No. 11, 1983, Austria

The Face, No. 43, 1983, Great Britain

In 1983, eight contemporary magazines got together on a joint project. For their Europe edition, each editorial board thought up themes relating to their own country but also connected in some way with Europe. The texts were identical, but the layout of each magazine – sometimes using the same pictures – was done independently. The differences demonstrate the wide variety of possible forms of expression through design.

EUROPA MOBIL
BOY GEORGE:
DAS UNMÖGLICHE SEX-SYMBOL

Tip, No. 23, 1983, Germany

SAMTWEICHES SEXSYMBOL

Boy George, Chef der Londoner Soul- Funk-Gruppe Culture Club, ist die liebenswerteste Tunte, die dieses Geschäft je hervorgebracht hat. Die Redaktionen von acht Zeitungen können nicht anders, als ihm einen dicken Kuß zu geben.

Wiener, No. 11, 1983, Austria

EUROPE
A BOY FOR EUROPE

The Face, No. 43, 1983, Great Britain

EXPO
EUROPE

The Face, No. 43, 1983, Great Britain

80 NEUE IDEEN FÜR DIE 80ER

Eine Leistungsschau junger europäischer Kreativität. Präsentiert von 8 Zeitschriften aus 8 Ländern.

SIE ERFINDEN BIO-SCHALLPLATTEN, GEBEN SICH WIE COMICS-FIGUREN, TANZEN WIE DIE ROBOTER, PFEIFEN AUF DIE AVANTGARDE UND BLEIBEN WILD, SELBST WENN ALLE LÄNGST DOMESTIZIERT SIND – DIE KREATIVEN EUROPAS.

Wiener, No. 11, 1983, Austria

The role of the art director in the editing process

The first step for every issue of a magazine is a conference on subject matter. Here the lines are laid down for the whole issue, with editors and heads of department putting their proposals to the board, who discuss and decide. It's important for the various creative talents involved to take part in this first phase of the process. Their ideas can have a powerful influence on the direction an individual article will take, as well as on the final stages of planning once the themes have been selected from the different proposals. But it's especially in the overall composition of the magazine that the visual aspect will be of vital importance.

At the next conference, individual contributions are discussed and visual ideas formulated. In addition to the senior editor, the authors of the different articles (or the editors responsible) and the art directors and picture editors should also take part. Unfortunately at this stage there are very rarely any completed texts available – only bare summaries. It would, of course, be ideal if the texts were already finished, as the language and the atmosphere they create can themselves inspire visual conceptualizations. The more fragmentary the text, the more general and vague the pictorial concept will be. With many editorial boards these conferences can place an intolerable burden on the art directors, who are expected to come up with a whole range of spontaneous ideas there and then. Creativity needs time. For this reason, most proposals made at such meetings relate to pictures that are already in existence, although it should be the ambition of every editorial team to create something new, or to reveal something that has never been seen before.

'The future of the art director' – a conversation between Horst Moser and Mike Meiré

HM: Magazine design is very similar to other phenomena like fashion and furniture design – one revival takes the place of another. Way back in the 1940s a magazine genius like Brodovitch solved a vast number of design problems for ever. Why are there now fewer and fewer formal innovations?

MM: I don't find it at all frustrating that everything's already been done. In fact ultimately I see it as a kind of liberation, because it enables me to concentrate on more fundamental things. The art director is evolving more and more into a sort of producer, who brings together various disciplines and areas of design. When all is said and done, we magazine-makers are the creators of new desires or even perhaps of new forms of consciousness, and as I see it, this is a very different and much more complex challenge. I don't regard myself as an art director or designer in the conventional sense. What interests me isn't the question of formal innovation but the need to realize that we must get to grips with our own identity, and I think that will have an influence on the future design of magazines. As a designer, you can channel and inspire people, like a theatre director, but then you're no longer just a designer who's presented with texts and photos that he's supposed to make something beautiful out of. Incidentally, in Paris there's an agency where you can hire art directors just like photographers and models. This means that the art director is taking up an ever more important position in the whole chain of information processing, and of course that heightens the profile and makes the job more demanding – which I think is an exciting development.

HM: Of course this development requires the exact opposite of your ordinary graphic designer, who sets the text as greyscale.

MM: That's something which imposes its own limitations. It seems to me at the moment that there's a development towards deceleration, a slowing down that's not trying to suppress complexity – that's something that can't be done, it would be stupid, a step backwards – but we need to settle the media disciplines, calm them down. But I could just as easily imagine that there'll be a counter movement to promote cross cultures and bring about an increase in complexity. That would lead to a sort of collage, pictures being stuck onto or fading into one another. Pictures seen as different levels of information, interwoven with texts, so that spaces and depths arise on the paper, where everything is blended together. You could almost talk of communication architects.

HM: In between floods of hectic innovation there have always been quiet patches, where innovation – in design too – has been seen as completely unnecessary or even absurd. For instance, in medieval icon painting. The master would pass on all his knowledge to his pupil who would use it in precisely the same way as his predecessors. No one thought of expressing himself in his own way, and diverging from the paths of tradition. In the Egyptian Museum in Cairo you can see sandals whose design hasn't varied for the last three thousand years. Even in really fashion-conscious fields like hairstyles there are classics that don't change – like the Julius Caesar style.

MM: Archetypes are always being produced, and I could imagine creating a classic magazine even now. But that doesn't mean that I'm an out-and-out classical man. I can surf the Internet, and zap between three hundred programmes, though at the same time I like to sit in front of a fire on a winter's night and drink a glass of mulled wine and maybe read a good magazine. That's not a contradiction – I think there's something nice about that.

HM: The idea of deceleration of course runs counter to the credo of many magazine makers, who think you should always strive to be topical.

MM: Even a weekly magazine can never really be bang up to date, and of course that's even more true of monthlies. As far as quarterlies are concerned, the question of topicality never even arises. If I want information on current affairs, I turn to the daily newspaper, the TV or the Internet.

HM: What functions will be left for magazines to perform in the future?

MM: I think you can only keep trying to create a forum, or communicate identities and attitudes that will run right through the magazine. I imagine that there'll be a lot more special interest magazines in the future, filling particular niches.

HM: The business magazine *Brand eins* has dispensed with all the conventional measuring devices like charts and tables, and compared to what the normal reader would expect, the texts are very long.

MM: The craze for only allowing short snippets, as apparently we're no longer able to read long sentences, means that ideas discussed in interviews get badly rehashed, because we have to reduce them to extracts that simply can't reproduce the full substance of what's actually been said. I can't accept that in a world that's become increasingly complex, we're supposed to pretend that it can all be described in three words. With *Brand eins* I only want to see text, because at the moment I'm not interested in the form but in the content. I know that these new subjects or new ideas will also give rise to new patterns on the formal level. I'm a designer who designs content – and there the first priority is the word. The content is the word, and the word is the content – full stop. And if people don't want to read it, because maybe it's too long for them... well, OK, there's plenty of other things to do. I don't have to please everybody.

The number and width of columns influence the character of a magazine

The right layout of columns is immensely important for the structure of a magazine page. How many columns there are depends on the format and on the length of the lines, which should contain approximately sixty characters each for optimal readability. But there are many factors at work here. First of all, the choice of font and the space between the letters. Coloured lettering has a different effect from black, and the leading also makes a difference. Of course you need to know the rules, but in the end, after you've tried out the various settings, sizes and spacings, you'll have to decide for yourself which combination is the easiest to read. Another important factor is the paper you intend to use: matt and glossy surfaces affect readability in different ways.

Apart from these material considerations, the content also influences the choice of layout. If, for instance, you know that a particular section is going to contain a lot of addresses, you'll need to ensure that the column is wide enough to prevent awkward breaks. Another important element is the format of your ads. Very few magazines only allow full- or double-page ads; those which take up half, two-thirds, or three-quarters of the page require different column divisions. A vertical, half-page ad will need a two- or four-column grid, whereas an ad that occupies two-thirds of the page can only be accommodated in a three-column layout. The four-column system has certain disadvantages (the shortness of the lines, for instance, and a tendency towards quite a monotonous symmetry) and so a mixture of grids within the magazine is advisable. The choice, though, naturally needs to fit in with the content. Sections containing long texts can be divided into two or three columns and the appropriate ads can be inserted in those pages. Small sections can use the four-column system, and can incorporate half-page and quarter-page ads. A well-composed page can also allow for marginal columns. Originally, this narrow border was used for snippets of text, but in modern magazines it now accommodates small pictures, captions, quotations, and illustrations that overshoot the width of the column. The wandering margin is a special form, and this narrow column frequently changes its position, facilitating a rich variety of page layouts.

In some magazines the column widths are completely irregular – *Leica World*, for instance. In this magazine, it's impossible to shorten or lengthen the text of the exclusive interviews, and so the only corrective is the length and breadth of the columns. When a system changes within a single text, the impact of that text also changes. In some cases, the layout of the opening double-page spread may differ from that of the pages that follow, and clever variation of these grid systems can influence the whole character of a magazine: it may appear pleasantly calm and relaxed, or it may generate a feeling of pace and excitement. Both have their uses, but of course it's vital that the choice isn't arbitrary. The system must always fit in with the nature of the content.

INVESTIGATION

"Watch and learn, mate. I've had every performance car on the road. Once you've driven one Aston Martin, you've driven them all"

"It's not opportunism. To be a good con man, you've got to read up. You've got to have a good memory so you can remember what lies you told"

Esquire, March 2002, Great Britain, flexible margins

In the magazine *Leica World* there's no fixed grid because it's impossible to change the length of the exclusive interviews. The width and number of columns therefore depends on the amount of text.

Leica World, No. 1, 2000, Germany

»Mir ging es nicht um einen Stil«

Leica World, No. 1, 1998, Germany

Leica World, No. 1, 1998, Germany

NORBERT ROSING

Natur pur

Leica World, No. 2, 1997, Germany

Leica World, No. 2, 2000, Germany

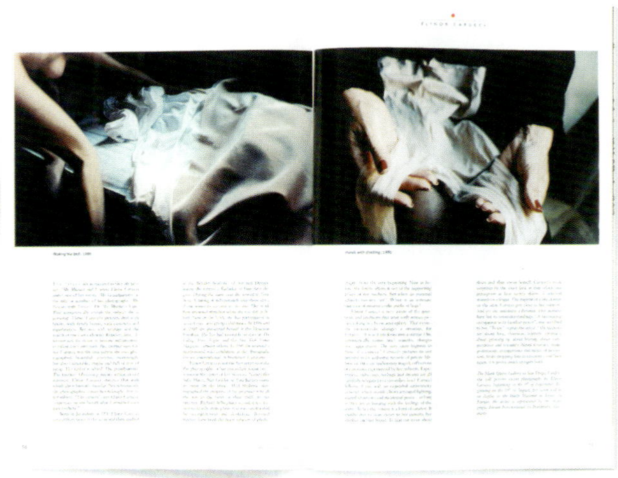

Leica World, No. 2, 2000, Germany

Mini International, No. 1, 2001, Germany

1/4 nach 5, No. 5, 2002, Germany

Lucky, No. 9, 2001, USA

Jalouse, November 2001, France

Martha Stewart Living, March 2002, USA (see index for credits)

Esquire, March 2002, Great Britain

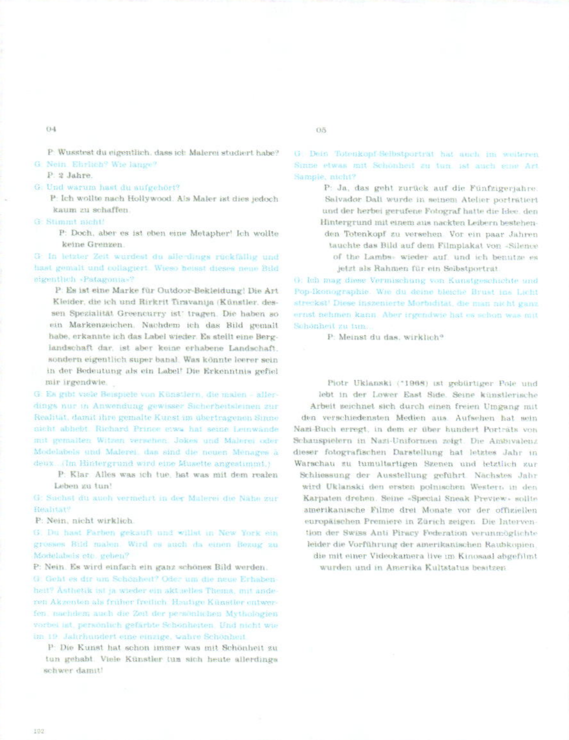

Soda, No. 17, 2001, Switzerland

RE, No. 3, 1998, Netherlands

Frame, No. 19, 2001, Netherlands

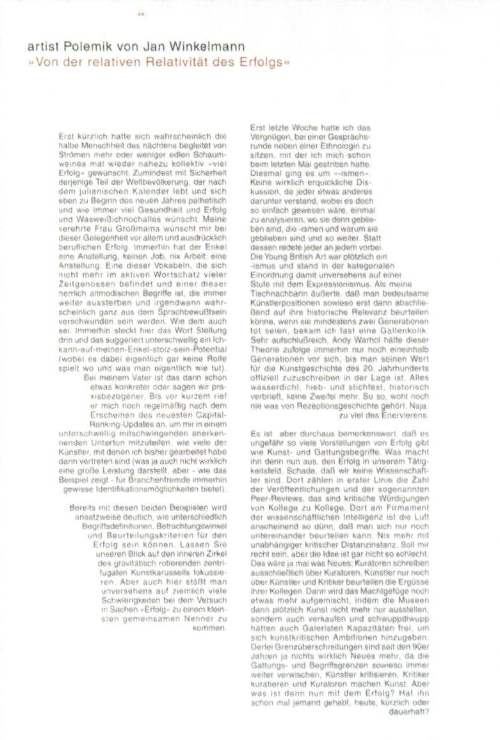

Artist, No. 1, 2002, Germany

How rigid or flexible should the instructions be?

As soon as the concept of a magazine has been settled, the composition of sample pages or of a design manual follows. It's always important to bear in mind who's subsequently going to be responsible for the layout. Sometimes the proprietor will leave the actual compilation of the magazine to people who have no training in design, and in such cases provision has to be made within the original concept for a correspondingly straightforward layout. When the staff don't have specialist knowledge of magazine design, it's a good idea to set out all the desired variations on the sample pages, and to give precise definitions of any exceptions. But this would be inappropriate for magazines that are produced by experts, since too much regulation removes the vital element of surprise and results in monotony. In all cases, you have to allow for the working methods of those responsible for the layout. Should everything be defined by way of existing stylistic models, or should only the most important elements be preserved? There are always going to be different solutions to every problem, but even when detailed instructions are necessary, you should always bear in mind that too much information can actually be a hindrance.

When can the sample pages be regarded as finished with? Definitions must first be tested in practice, and two or three issues are generally needed before the process of development can be seen as complete. There may still be elements that need modification or extension, and it's important that the experiences and suggestions of those who work daily with these sample pages are taken into account.

Unfortunately, most firms have now dispensed with the printing of manuals, and the sample pages are generally only available in digital form. One example, though, that was not only a manual but was also intended as a book of ideas for designers, was published in 1992 for the German edition of the magazine *Forbes*.

Forbes Manual, 1992, Germany, cover and inside pages (right)

Inhalt
BUSINESS
!Forbes
INHALT OKTOBER 1992

Trixie Plain
ABCDEFGHIJKLM
NOPQRSTUVWXYZ
abcdefghijk
lmnopqrstvwxyz
1234567890
Erik van Blokland
Der Dadaist
aaaa

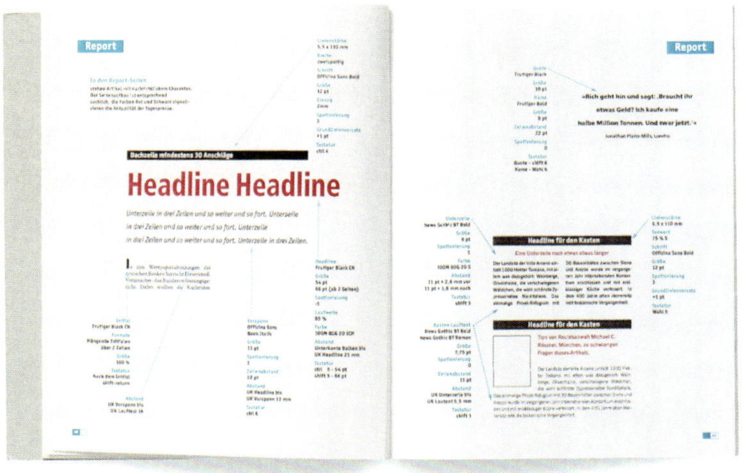
Report
Headline Headline
Report

Infonauten

Leserbriefe
Hilfe für Hamburg

Different factors to be considered in the choice of format

If you're starting up a new magazine, you'll soon be confronted with the problem of the format. Your choice will be influenced by a number of different factors: when and where will the magazine be read? Plane, train, café, underground, study or living room? Does it need to fit into a handbag or briefcase? If it's to be distributed by post, will it need a special-sized envelope? How important will the ads be? Will you need to take into account the clients' existing advertising format so that you don't lose them? What will be the impact of the format when the magazine is opened? Is it nice to handle? The content will also influence the format. If, for example, every edition is to contain thirty recipes, with each dish being photographed on a round plate, the best format will be more or less square. If there are going to be lots of oblong photos of snowboarders, you don't want a narrow, vertical format. The basic format of *Leica World*, for example, is that of the 35 mm photograph, and so a vertical picture suitably enlarged covers the entire page. As the magazine has glued binding, there's always a narrow unprinted strip – the gutter – so that no detail of the picture will be lost.

The format and the paper, as well as the strength of the paper (g/m^2), are all interdependent, and so before embarking on production, it's worth while creating a dummy. This will enable you to test whether the paper and its strength go together with the format and the thickness planned, and whether the magazine will be too rigid or too floppy. Even the relative strengths of the cover and the inside pages can be important for the overall feel. The German magazine *Max* has a very thin cover which can easily be torn off the staples. The same is true of the American editions of *Rolling Stone* and *Interview*. There are also issues relating to printing technology: does the chosen format fit in with the formats normally created by the paper manufacturer? Which printing press would be the most economical to use for the quantities required? Inappropriate formats can very quickly lead to spiralling costs. In other words, with close attention to the correct use of technology, and with sometimes very minor adjustments, you can often make far better use of paper and machinery and avoid unnecessary expense.

Mare has a standard format of 21 × 28 cm, while *Glamour's* 'handbag' format suits the mobility of its target group. *The Manipulator*, at 49.5 × 70 cm, is the largest magazine so far to appear on the market.

Mare, No. 25, 2001, Germany, 21 × 28 cm (8¼ × 11 in.)

Glamour, October 2001, Italy, 17 × 22.5 cm (6¾ × 8¾ in.)

The Manipulator, June 1986, Germany, 49.5 × 70 cm (19½ × 27⅝ in.)

McK Wissen, No. 1, 2002, Germany, 28 × 19.5 cm (11 × 7⅝ in.)

Colors, No. 49, 2002, Italy, 23 × 14 cm (9 × 5½ in.)

Mutabor, No. 10, 2002, Germany, 22.2 × 39 cm (8¾ × 15⅜ in.)

Room, April – July 2002, Germany, 27 × 28 cm (10⅝ × 11 in.)

Max, August 1997, Germany, 33.6 × 23 cm (13¼ × 9 in.)

Matador, Vol.D, 1999, Spain, 30 × 40 cm (11¾ × 15¾ in.)

A new feel to the pages: instead of turning them from right to left, you turn them from bottom to top in *McK Wissen*. The reader of *Colors* is transported around the world in an oblong format, while the special cinema edition of *Max* uses an appropriate 'widescreen' format. There are no limits to the range of shapes and sizes: they may be tall and slim like the lady on the cover of *Mutabor*, virtually square like *Room*, or a classic rectangle like *Matador*.

Cut-outs, indentations, gloss, holograms and picture puzzles

There's a virtually infinite variety of effects that can be used to attract attention in the marketplace, and to distinguish your product from the opposition. They're only available, though, to high-priced magazines with lofty aesthetic ambitions, because the more outlandish the special effect, the more expensive it will be to produce. Even so, current trends suggest that for the sake of originality, this is a risk that's frequently being taken.

One method of getting your magazine to stand out from the crowd is to use cut-outs. *Flaunt* makes particularly creative use of this device. There may be gaps in the page through which you catch a glimpse of a woman's face, or you may be invited to open a window. They keep coming up with new variations that add new twists to this game of visual hide and seek. But the cut-outs are limited to the cover and front page, and the rectangular format of the magazine remains conventional. This is not so with the magazine *Nest*, which uses a completely new shape, the normal rectangular edge of the pages being broken up by irregular curves. The rounded corners of *Designers Digest* seem relatively conservative by comparison; the designer, Marko Thiele, adapted this outline to fit in with his playful typographical experiments.

Other popular devices are reflective surfaces, holograms, transparent paper, indentations and gloss. These special effects are strengthened if they actually coincide with and complement a particular idea. A classic example of this was the cover of *Das Büro* that was made from a piece of carpet. This would certainly have elicited the desired 'Wow!' from its readers – but such successes are the exception rather than the rule. Effects for their own sake may be striking at first glance, but they make no lasting impact. In one edition of *Visionaire*, Stephen Gan used a picture puzzle that revealed a different picture depending on the way you held it up. In this case the effect corresponded perfectly with the subject: supermodel Kate Moss sitting on a swing whose movement was recreated by moving the picture. Transparent or glossy materials are less expensive than some other refinements, and a wide variety of interesting aesthetic effects can be created through the interplay of dull and shiny.

Ausdruck, No. 2, 1997, Germany

Brett, No. 8, 2000, Germany

RE, No. 23, 1997, Netherlands

Tank, Best of Tank Magazine 1998 – 2000, Great Britain

Apart from conventional staple and glue bindings, there are various ways of holding the pages together: a simple spiral binding (*Ausdruck*), a single screw (*Brett*), string or rivets (*Form+Zweck*), or an elastic band (*RE*). In 2002 a collection of the Best of Tank appeared in the form of a cigarette packet.

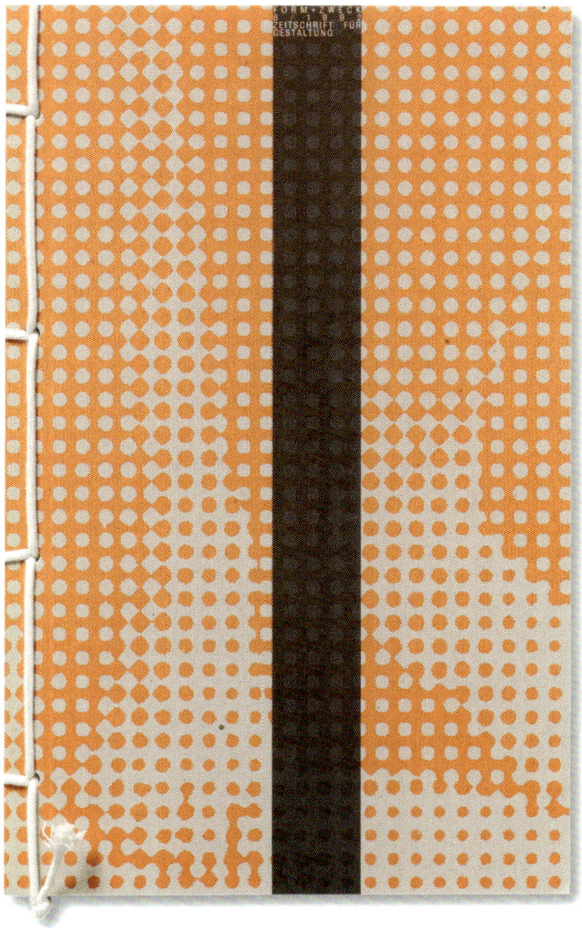

Form+Zweck, No. 6, 1992, Germany

Form+Zweck, No. 11, 1995, Germany

The whole magazine may be rounded off at the edges (*Designers Digest* and *Nest*), or just the cover may be perforated, punched or cut out, as in the peekaboo style of *Flaunt*.

Designers Digest, No. 77, 2001, Germany

Nest, No. 12, 2001, USA

Nest, No. 16, 2002, USA

Flaunt, May 1999, USA

Flaunt, September 2001, USA

Flaunt, June/July 1999, USA

Annabelle Création, April 2002, Switzerland

Another Magazine, No. 2, 2002, Great Britain

Ecuad, 1999/2000, Singapore

Rosebud, No. 2, 2001, Germany

Typographic, No. 58, 2002, USA

If you want to attract attention in the marketplace, you need to come up with new ideas: a simple paper band draws the eye to *Annabelle Création*; a purple lace bookmark does the same for *Another Magazine*; Singapore's *Ecuad* has a transparent cover; the US magazine *Typographic* is in the form of a poster; *Rosebud* is wrapped in silver foil.

Visionaire, No. 29, 1999, USA

Visionaire, No. 28, 1999, USA

Gum, No. 5, 1999, Germany

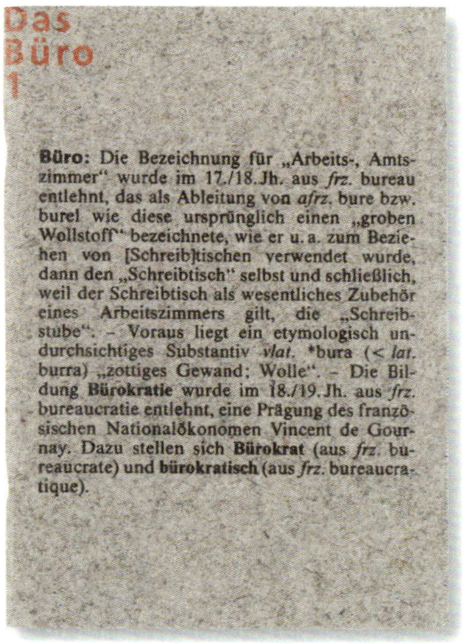

Das Büro 1, No. 10, 1996, Germany

Tactile magazines: rough felt (*Das Büro*); fine silk (*Visionaire*); sandpaper (*Gum*); indentations and gilt edging (*Visionaire*).

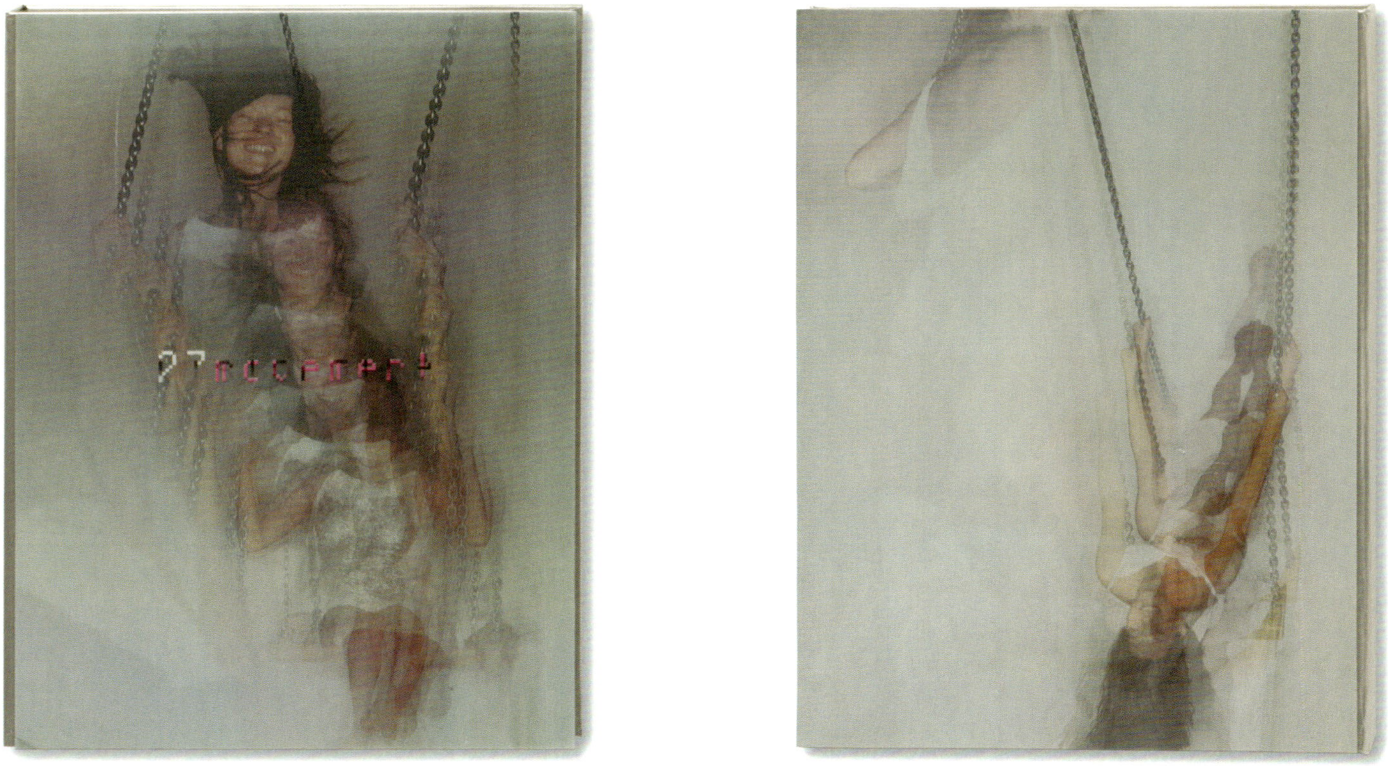

Visionaire, No. 4232, USA

Jalouse, May 2000, France

Kate Moss on a swing in *Visionaire*, and an ad for the Chanel perfume 'Allure' in *Jalouse* – two effective attention-grabbers.

Embrace, No. 1, 2002, Finland

Vogue, December 1999, Great Britain

Style, No. 50, 20C2, Germany

Domus, No. 788, 1996, Italy

The trend for reflective surfaces: partial, as with the mirror in *Embrace*; total, with the rich silver of *Vogue*; iridescent in *Domus*; a bronze effect in *Style*.

THE AVENUE BOX

A magazine becomes a box of surprises

Magazines are not read like novels, from beginning to end. People tend to leaf through, and they start reading when their eye alights on something that catches their attention. That is, assuming you *can* leaf through. It's not always easy. In a lot of fashion and design magazines, there are so many samples, inserts and supplements that you just keep getting stuck in the same places. Many readers help themselves out by getting rid of all the intruders before they even start reading, but there's an interesting alternative to the stuffing technique: the Dutch magazine *Avenue* launched itself onto the market as a box. The box contained the magazine, together with the whole collection of samples and supplements. A great idea, since it allows the advertiser to promote his products without obstructing the reader's access to the magazine itself. Still, from the point of view of cost and handling, this form isn't without its problems.

Avenue, No. 1, 1994, Netherlands

Avenue, No. 4, 1994, Netherlands

Avenue, No. 3, 1995, Netherlands

Avenue, No. 5, 1994, Netherlands

Avenue, No. 1, 1995, Netherlands

Avenue, No. 3, 1994, Netherlands

Avenue, No. 5, 1995, Netherlands

Avenue, No. 6, 1995, Netherlands

Avenue, No. 2, 1995, Netherlands

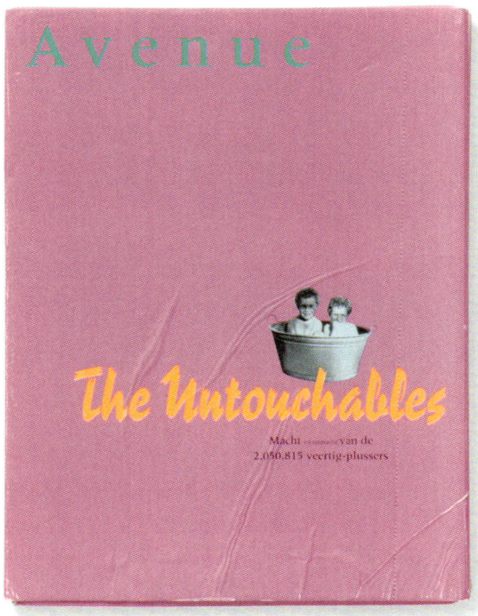

Avenue, No. 2, 1994, Netherlands

PICTURE FRAMES

From the work of art to games with frames

A lot of people don't even think of picture-framing as an aspect of design, and when it comes to layout, all too often no consideration is given to how an illustration is to be enclosed. It seems to be taken for granted that photos will be cut into rectangles without borders. But different forms of enclosure can create striking effects. Ideally, there should be a link between the picture and its frame. One of the commonest devices is the irregular border that surrounds enlarged photos, and this serves to emphasize the aesthetic craftsmanship of the photographer's art. It also suggests a certain stylistic level which would not be appropriate for, say, a football report. The conventional photo frame is redolent of the museum or gallery, where framed paintings hang at some distance from each other in order to avoid any sort of distraction. This enables them to live their own lives. In magazines, the decision on whether to bleed pictures or provide them with identical frames will have a major influence on how they are perceived. In the one case, the result will be an increased dynamism; in the other, uniformity will tend to create more detachment.

Harper's Bazaar, July 1994, USA

Rails, July/August 2000, Netherlands

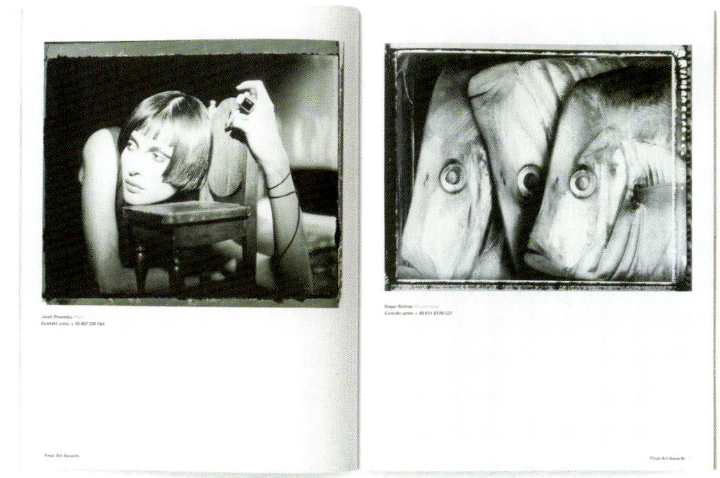

P, No. 17, 1999, Germany/Great Britain

Rails, March 2001, Netherlands

Harper's Bazaar, April 1994, USA

Harper's Bazaar, April 1994, USA

Rails, No. 4, 2001, Netherlands

Harper's Bazaar, April 1994, USA

Harper's Bazaar, February 1996, USA

NRC Handelsblad, April 2001, Netherlands

VISUAL METASYSTEMS

When there's a spontaneous overview, reading plays a secondary role

A well-thought-out magazine has an identity of its own. It's distinguished from other magazines by certain special qualities both of written content and of visual presentation – the texts and the design. The first impression, of course, will be made by the cover, which combines the different elements of logo, picture and typography in such a way as to create a totally individual and unmistakable identity. This image must be coherent and consistent to guarantee repeated recognition in the marketplace. If every edition were to look different, the reader wouldn't have any precise image in mind: a memorable appearance distinct from all the opposition is integral to commercial success. Still, it must be said that very few magazines could be safely identified if the title were covered up.

The extent of information that can be conveyed by the metasystems becomes clear if we experiment with a blurred, unreadable page from a newspaper. The moment we look at this page, the typographical system already gives us a feeling of familiarity. By a process of visual elimination, we can easily establish what kind of page it is not: we can see that it's not a cover, a collection of facts and figures from the financial pages, an illustrated report, or part of the arts section. Sport would also look quite different. Once you've eliminated all the rest, you're left with the classified section, and in particular recruitment. There's no doubt about this, and you can even say with a degree of certainty what kind of jobs are being advertised. They're not for high fliers, and even ads for middle management would be in a different format. Anyone really familiar with this type of recruitment ad would probably even be able to recognize individual firms. And yet we've not been able to read a single letter. If we'd not learned these formal systems, we'd never be able to skim through the pages of magazines, to select or ignore particular sections. If you were now to imagine the ads on this page presented as continuous text, without distinction, set in the same font and the same size, you would get some idea of the time and effort that goes into the typography of such a section, regardless of its quality. With any magazine that we know or recognize, we can name the components that give it a particular character. In this context, covers with some overall concept are the easiest to analyse. The less precise the concept, or the more flexible and variable the design, the more difficult it will be to identify the magazine. Every designer has to be aware of the rules that govern the overall image, and this should be part of their basic training. When it comes to a new concept, or to redesigning an old one, the extent to which these rules should be applied or broken will then, of course, be up to them, but either way, the process can only work if the designer is fully conscious of what they're doing. The Swiss designer Hans-Rudolf Lutz gave an extraordinary demonstration of this in 1977, when he experimented with the covers of the magazine *Typografische Monatsblätter*. When you see the covers, you think they belong to other, well-known magazines. Only when you look and read more closely do you realize that you've been misled: the letters give the name 'Typografische Monatsblätter', but the strikingly familiar visual components of the other magazines – typography, logos, colours and pictures – suggest a different identity. This demonstrates that our first impression is through general perception rather than through reading. The reverse of this experiment can be seen from the aftermath of Princess Diana's death: her picture appeared on countless magazine covers, and although she was one of the most photographed people of all time, there were not so many photos available at that particular moment for every journal to use a different one. As a result, many of the covers contained the same picture, and this uniformity unquestionably meant that each magazine had to sacrifice a degree of its own identity. At first sight it's extremely difficult to make any distinction between them. A closer inspection, though, reveals interesting differences in the typography and other minor details. In some cases, the black and white photo has been coloured to give it greater popular appeal.

Typografische Monatsblätter, May 1977, Switzerland

Typografische Monatsblätter, June/July 1977, Switzerland

Typografische Monatsblätter, December 1977, Switzerland

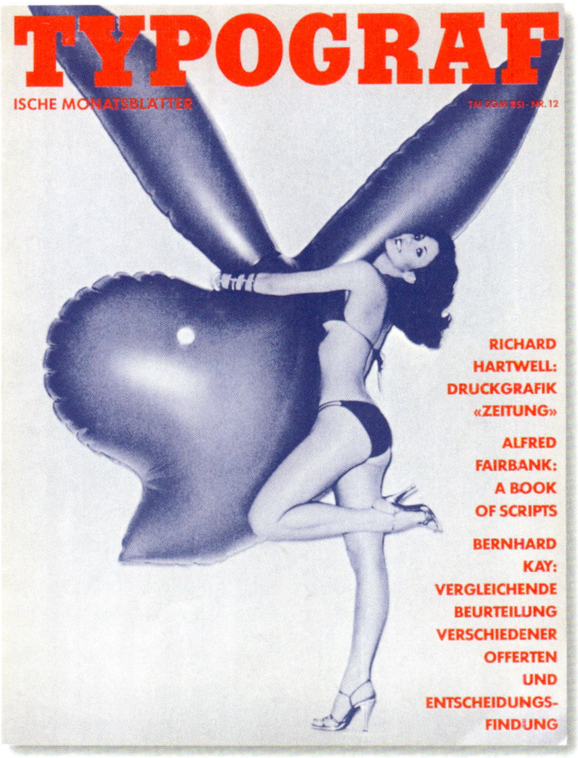

Typografische Monatsblätter, December 1977, Switzerland

First impressions may deceive: 1970s editions of *Typografische Monatsblätter* imitated the covers of other well-known magazines.

Who, September 1997, Australia

People, September 1997, Great Britain

Gioia, September 1997, Italy

Stern, September 1997, Germany

Nokta, September 1997, Turkey

Point De Vue, August 1998, France

Intimità, September 1998, Italy

Facts, September 1997, Switzerland

Neue Revue, September 1997, Germany

Visual metasystems function only through an individual pictorial language. With global media events like the death of Princess Diana, the use of the same pictures cancels out individual identities. It's interesting that even though the same photo is on every cover, there are still many variations possible through size and position, background, reversal, colour, and so on. The different effects of the typography on the picture are also very clear.

The role of the avant-garde in magazine design

Not many people would ask why *Time* magazine looks completely different from, say, *Die Gartenlaube* – and that's a pity. The power of innovation is vital to the very existence of magazines. There's about a hundred-year gap between *Die Gartenlaube* and *Time*, and both are deeply rooted in their own period, totally mainstream and anything but avant-garde. But their covers could not be more different. *Die Gartenlaube* is rather like one of those late nineteenth-century, stucco-ceilinged old houses, rampant with the eclectic ornamentation typical of the period. *Time* has a single, full-page picture, and a classical logotype, with all the normative power of the tried and tested. While the differences between the covers are very marked, those on the inside are only minor. The layout of the columns and the positioning of the illustrations are structurally quite similar, and considering the vast array of artistic 'isms' that separate the two – Impressionism, Expressionism, Cubism, Dadism, Futurism, the Bauhaus and New Functionalism, Art Nouveau, Art Deco, Art Informel, Tachisme, Pop Art and all its derivatives – remarkably little has changed.

When and where do innovations – even if not particularly radical ones in this case – actually spring from, and who initiates them? Looking at the current situation, the fact is that every new initiative by the big publishing firms is under the shadow of a 'me too' mentality, with any trace of innovation being wiped out by the germ-killers of market research. Anyone involved in the development of magazines will have experienced this painful process, and if they have a dozen designers on the payroll, any revolutionary proposal will need to be modified with an evolutionary sweetener. This trend is reflected in the vast majority of magazines found on sale at the news-stand. And quite apart from the cold-feet mentality of most proprietors, the tiny budget allocated to development means that there's neither time nor resources available for the sort of visual research that might produce practicable innovations. The task of promoting the new falls to those magazines that exist within more independent structures. They are free from the 'that's how we've always done it' syndrome, and thanks to their short and swift decision-making processes, which are not always based on the lowest common denominator, they're the ones who are able to charge their printing presses with the unconventional. And from the work of these magazines, which act as a kind of research laboratory, the big publishing houses then proceed to profit.

Die Gartenlaube (illustrated family journal), 1897, Germany

Die Gartenlaube (illustrated family journal), 1897, Germany

Time, May 2000, USA

Time, March 1991, USA

Raygun, No. 10, 1995, USA

Raygun, No. 11, 1994, USA

INTRODUCTION TO COVER DESIGN

A balancing act between surprise and familiarity

The cover is crucial to the success of any magazine and must encapsulate its whole character. Virtually every genre has developed its own forms, which of course are heavily dependent on the tastes of the time: covers of top contemporary fashion magazines, for instance, mostly offer a very narrow range of variations on the portrait theme. Even the form of these portraits is usually very similar: faces in close-up, head and shoulders, or half-length. Eye contact is almost universal, although this has always been pretty general and is not a specifically modern trait. Though if you look at the covers of *Harper's Bazaar* or *Vogue* from the 1930s or 1940s, you're struck by the extraordinary variety and inventiveness of the ideas.

Computer magazines have developed their own aesthetics to which the majority conform. Once again, there's a 'me too' mentality instead of any attempt to create an original, independent brand that will distinguish itself from the opposition.

On the other hand, the covers of some business magazines are astonishingly unconventional. *Fast Company, Quote, Red Herring* and *Business 2.0* have all come up with highly distinctive designs that leave the old norms far behind. *Fortune* was the progenitor of this breed, and during the first few decades of its existence came up with quite outstanding covers. Since then its quality has plummeted.

If you try to call magazine covers to mind, the memorable ones are those that offer a powerful image or striking individuality. They're the ones your eyes alight on, and of course that's their purpose – the one means they have of shining forth from the news-stand. Of the thousands of covers we see, though, the vast majority will be instantly forgettable. This is of little importance to subscribers, who receive their favourites through the post and are therefore no longer spoilt for choice, but what's the secret of the attention-grabbers? Certainly not the 'me too' principle. Brodovitch's challenge of the 1930s and 1940s is just as valid today as it was then: astonish me! Astonishment, though, should not degenerate into shock.

Whoever buys a magazine expects to find something new in it. The cover must also be new, but at the same time, familiar enough to be recognized and easily found at the news-stand. This may limit the range of possibilities, yet within that range you can always come up with something new – maybe in the photography, the illustrations, the typography. Usually what does the trick is an intelligent interplay between words and picture. If we're to believe the media analysts, the average attention span at the news-stand is two to three seconds, and so the message must be clear and immediate. Of course this also depends on how the magazine is presented – whether in piles or displayed on the shelf – where it's essential that the message is visible. If the whole cover is displayed, this isn't a problem, but you have to allow for a worst case scenario, and so many magazines have now taken to repeating their logo in small print at the top of the spine.

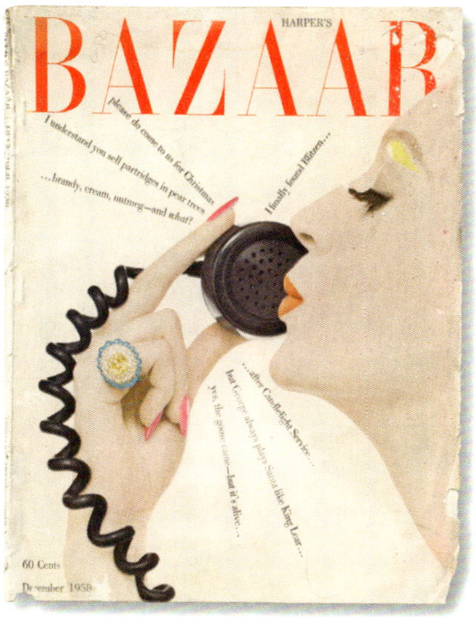

Harper's Bazaar, No. 2965, 1958, USA

Harper's Bazaar, August 1940, Great Britain

Harper's Bazaar, July 1958, USA

Vogue, March 1945, USA

Vogue, January 1950, USA

Vogue, February 1953, USA

Harper's Bazaar, October 2000, USA

Vogue, November 2001, France

Madame, June 2001, Germany

COPIES AND QUOTES

From pure plagiarism to intelligent allusion

Good ideas are a wonderful thing, and everybody loves them. But what happens when problems arise and no one can come up with an original solution? For many, the simplest way out seems to be battening on to others. Regardless of whether a licence fee has or has not been paid, the rehash always leaves an unpleasant taste in the mouth. Many of these cases are only known to those on the inside, but even if the general public has no idea what's going on, the copy-cat with a conscience will still feel guilty at having failed to find his own solution. The spectrum runs from quoting, through adapting, to outright pinching. All the same you have to admit that, apart from the question of ethics, there's a lot to be learned from comparing similar covers. Even when exactly the same picture is used, there are always differences brought about by the particular design, with logos and text automatically affecting the impact of the picture. The two Jack Nicholson covers for *Männer-Vogue* and *GQ* are a good illustration of the point. In the first one the close-up is hemmed in by the typography, in the other the face is left with room to breathe. The extent to which the pictures themselves have become the subject matter can be seen from the cover of *TV Spielfilm*, in which three models fill the whole page. A few years earlier the same company had used the same photo for the cover of *Max*, but the new version omitted Naomi Campbell. The missing parts of Tatjana Patitz's body were supplied by Photoshop.

Photos were already being tampered with seventy years ago. You only have to think of how they were touched up during the Communist era and also under the Nazis. In those days the process was done by hand and was still pretty clumsy, but today even experts can no longer detect the best work. This, of course, has repercussions on the perception of the truthfulness of the medium, which is increasingly losing the one vital quality it seeks to achieve – its credibility. There is another negative aspect to these modern developments: the widespread use of agency photographs and of CD-ROMs that are free from copyright has resulted in a flattening of their impact. If the same photos appear in ads and brochures and on magazine covers, they'll all inevitably lose a proportion of their individuality. A feeling of 'take it or leave it' rather than 'look how special we are' is produced. The exchange of ideas can go in different directions, with the editorial side influencing the advertising and vice versa, while the vast reservoir of picture material can serve everyone, from record and CD covers to billboards.

THE CASE OF CAPITAL

Capital was the second biggest publication, after *Twen*, to be developed by the giant of the German magazine world, Adolf Theobald. This new business magazine first appeared in 1961, and like the American *Fortune* its overall concept could be summed up as describing business in human terms, and humans in business terms. The first issues were in a larger format than today, with a black cover and a clear, uncluttered design by Karl Gerstner. In keeping with the content, for decades the cover showed a prominent figure from the business world. In the 1990s *Capital* went international, and it's interesting that in France and Italy, where so many cultural features are held in common, the same subject matter was given a totally different visual treatment. The French edition dispensed entirely with a cover figure and worked only with typographical designs in a popular, almost tabloid style, a bit like posters for a supermarket. The cover of the early Italian *Capital* is the exact opposite: extremely dignified, with a black and white picture of a gentleman in a dark suit. The choice of an elegant, classical font underlines the elitist touch. This noble concept obviously failed to last the course, and in time the vulgarity of the Italian cover came to exceed even that of the French. In order to appeal to the masses, it now parades naked women on the premise that sex sells. Fortunately, the long-serving editor and publisher of the German *Capital*, Johannes Gross, one of the most intelligent people ever to grace the German press, was not there to suffer this humiliation. A Turkish edition is now published under licence, and while the German *Capital* has undergone profound changes in recent years, the Turkish cover continues to follow precisely the same design of coloured areas that marked the German version at the time when the licence was first granted.

Helpline booklet

Focus, No. 44, 1997, Germany

Börse Online, No. 11, 1999, Germany

GQ, January 1996, USA

Männer Vogue, March 1996, Germany

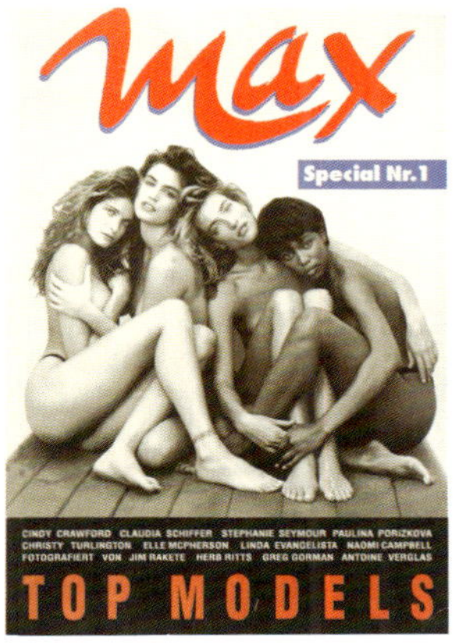

Max Special, No. 1, 1991, Germany

TV Spielfilm, No. 9, 1998, Germany

Der Spiegel, No. 23, 1992, Germany

Focus, No. 19, 1993, Germany

Advertising campaign for milk (from 1996), USA

Men's Health, June 1996, Germany

Bob Dylan, 'Blowin in the Mind' 1966, Luxembourg (Great Britain)

Adrenalin, No. 9, 2001, Great Britain

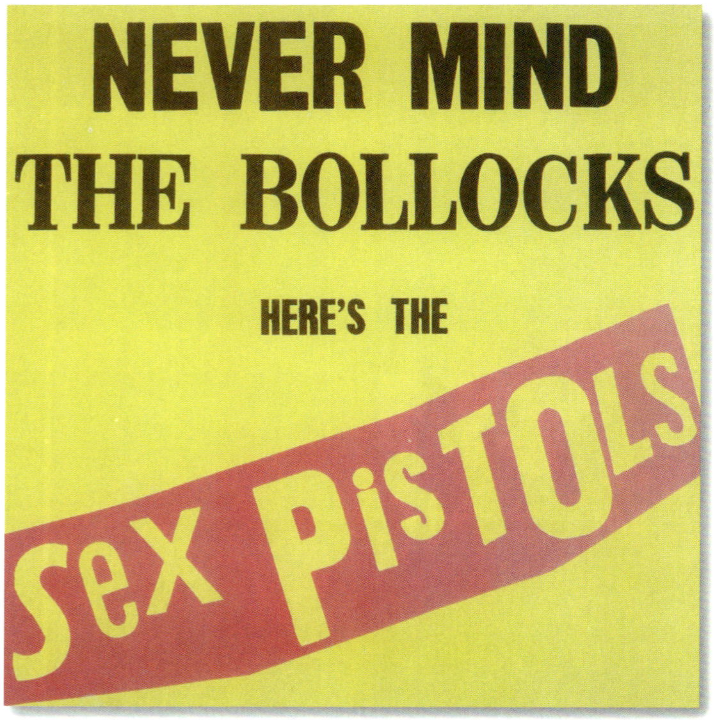

Sex Pistols, 'Never Mind the Bollocks, Here's the Sex Pistols' 1977, Great Britain

Brand eins, No. 7, 2000, Germany

Right: Comparing the covers of international editions of *Capital*. Following the precepts of its founder, Adolf Theobald, the cover always showed figures from various sections of the business world. The international licensed editions are sometimes totally different from one another. The biggest contrast is between the French and Italian versions: top right is the supermarket, tabloid-style design of the French, and second row left the elegant, dignified Italian. This dignity seems to have lost out, and since 2001 the Italian *Capital* has followed the principle that sex sells (second row, centre). The Turkish cover design (bottom row right) has preserved the German design that was in existence when the licence was first granted (bottom row, centre).

Capital, April 1976, Germany

Capital, No. 8, 2000, Germany

Capital, February 1996, France

Capital, April 1997, Italy

Capital, April 2001, Italy

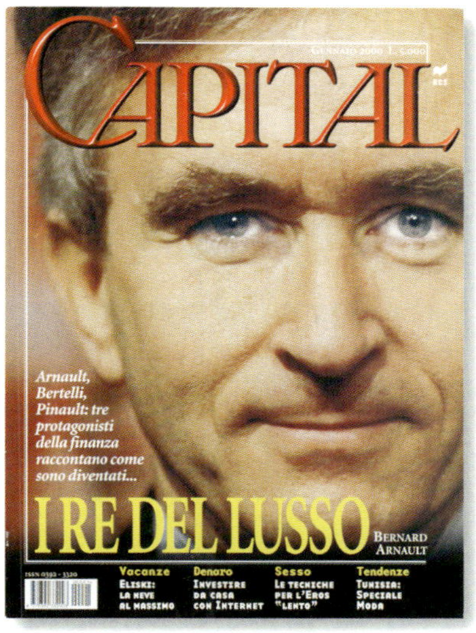

Capital, January 2000, Italy

Capital, No. 12, 1999, Japan

Capital, October 1993, Germany

Capital, June 2000, Turkey

JURASSIC PARK

A film that became a global media event

The film *Jurassic Park* was first released in 1993 and was a worldwide phenomenon that dominated all the headlines. The subject itself was not new, but never before had extinct creatures, in this case, dinosaurs, been brought back to life so realistically.

As always, editors sat down with their editorial boards to discuss the theme of the next edition. For film and video magazines it was blindingly obvious that the cover would mark the opening of the film, but amazingly the rest – quite independently of one another – followed suit: news, science, illustrated, nature, esoteric and satirical magazines all went dinosaur crazy. As picture material was limited, a lot of editors commissioned expensive artwork, but curiously these were not the scientific journals, who mostly made do with stills, but the popular magazines like *Stern* and *Max*. Some tried to grab the reader with cheap horror effects, while others were content to display textbook-style illustrations. Only one magazine rose to the challenge of what in fact was a very complex theme: the cover of *Focus* showed a computer-generated dinosaur climbing out of a screen and mutating into a real creature.

Cinema, September 1993, Germany

Studio Hors Serie, 1993, France

Videoplay, September 1993, Germany

Premiere, November 1993, France

Geo, September 1993, Germany

Dinosaurier, 1993, German special edition, USA

Discover, September 1993, USA

Earth, September 1993, USA

Focus, August 1993, Germany

Stern, September 1993, Germany

Paris Match, October 1993, France

Panorama, September 1993, Italy

Max, September 1993, Germany

Le Figaro, September 1993, France

Epoca, September 1993, Italy

Libération, October/November 1993, France

Prisma News, November/December 1993, Germany

Journalist, November 1999, Germany

BZ Das Magazin, August 1993, Germany

Bild+Funk Spezial, 1993, Germany

Cambio 16, September 1993, Spain

2000 Magazin für Neues Bewusstsein, October/November 1993, Germany

Jurassic Park Comic, No. 2, 1993, Germany

Titanic, September 1993, Germany

RUNNING JOKES

Variations on a self-imposed theme

Readers can sense what motivates a magazine. They know if it has serious political, cultural or social aims, and they know if it's been thrust onto the market to make a quick buck out of a momentary sensation. Journalists have even been known to go to prison for their principles.

But it's the subject matter that dictates how interests are communicated to the reader. The rules that govern political magazines, for instance, are quite different from those applicable to the entertainment variety, in which you often find the technique of the running joke. We all know this from Alfred Hitchcock, who always made a very brief appearance at the beginning of his films to ensure his audience concentrated right from the start so as not to miss his little cameo. The classic equivalent in the field of magazines is *Playboy*. The world-famous bunny turns up on every cover in all sorts of variations and disguises. Sometimes he hits you in the eye, and sometimes he's very hard to find, but he's always there, challenging the reader to solve the visual puzzle. Once you've let yourself in for this device, you've got to be certain you can keep it going, and that requires a great deal of ingenuity. The problem is evident with *Playboy*. After a highly creative early phase, in which no expense was spared in the construction of, say, bunny-shaped chairs or guitars, there have been times when the powers that be have tightened the corporate belt and banished the little fellow to buttons and earrings. Another example is *i-D*. Through all the changing times, it's a remarkable feat to have maintained the running joke of the winking eye – whether in photos or comic illustrations – right through to the present day. The magazine *George* couldn't keep it up. The idea was to make a reference to George Washington on every cover, and this certainly spawned some original ideas, but evidently inspiration soon flagged and the joke stopped running. The gag need not be visual. *Loaded* has applied it to the subtitle. The standard version goes: 'For men who should know better', and each new cover story creates a variation on this theme.

Playboy, April 1980, Germany

Playboy, August 1968, USA

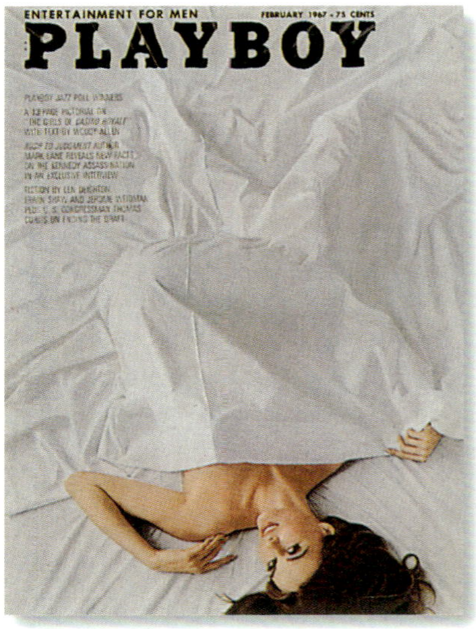

Playboy, February 1967, USA

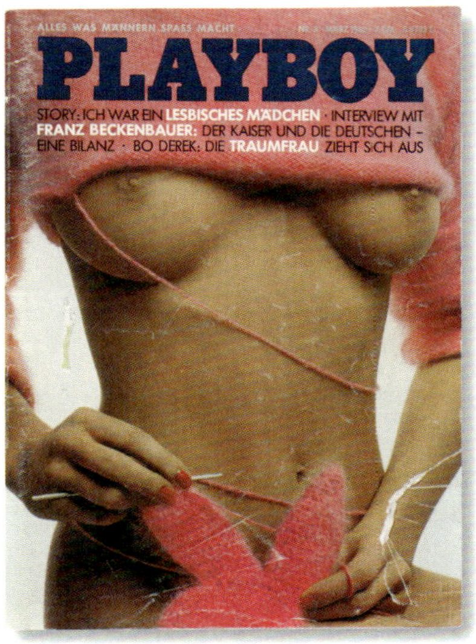

Playboy, March 1980, Germany

Playboy, October 1971, USA

Playboy, July 1980, Germany

Playboy, November 1970, Germany

Playboy, April 1973, Germany

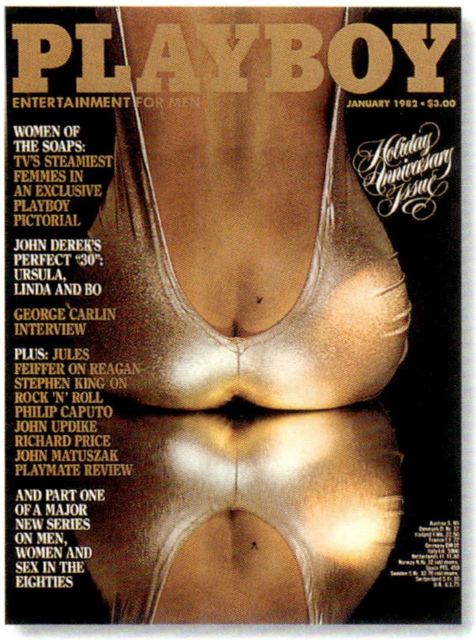

Playboy, January 1982, USA

Playboy, February 1968, USA

Playboy, October 1965, USA

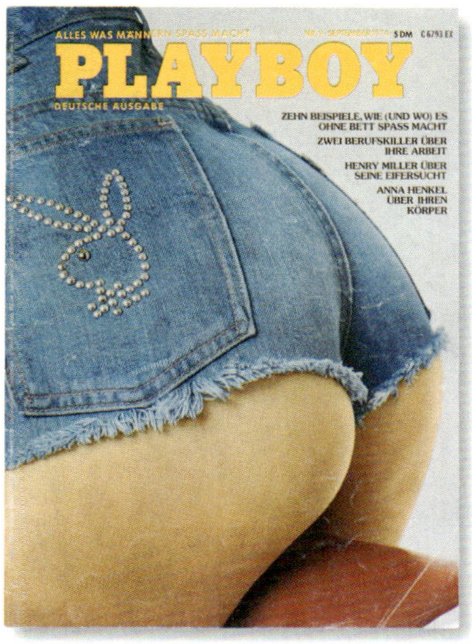

Playboy, September 1974, Germany

I-D, September 1985, Great Britain

I-D, December 1988, Great Britain

I-D, May 1990, Great Britain

I-D, October 1990, Great Britain

I-D, January 1993, Great Britain

I-D, May 1995, Great Britain

I-D, June 1995, Great Britain

I-D, February 1996, Great Britain

I-D, July 1996, Great Britain

I-D, January 1997, Great Britain

I-D, September 1997, Great Britain

-D, December 1997, Great Britain

I-D, May 1998, Great Britain

I-D, April 1998, Great Britain

I-D, June 1998, Great Britain

I-D, September 1998, Great Britain

I-D, June/July 2002, Great Britain

I-D, May 2000, Great Britain

Loaded, June 2000, Great Britain
'for men who should know britters'

Loaded, January 2000, Great Britain
'for girls hugh should know better'

Loaded, October 2000, Great Britain
'for men who should know b'

Loaded, June 2001, Great Britain
'for men who should have butlers'

George, October/November 1995, USA

George, April 1997, USA

George, December 1995/January 1996, USA

George, June 1997, USA

George, June/July 1996, USA

George, February/March 1996, USA

COVER PHOTOS. Portraits

Cover design with the evocative power of the human face

In order to catch the eye, most magazine covers use pictures – generally photos, but occasionally also drawings. The covers reflect the huge range of styles and subjects, and the focal point of interest is humanity, whether in the form of portraits and full-length figures, or in relation to various environments such as architecture or nature. The evocative power of the face is certainly at its strongest when eye contact is made with the reader, and so the magazine strategists naturally make full use of this device. Nearly all women's and fashion magazines design their covers along these lines, and so do those that specialize in erotica. The face is often almost life-size, but there are extreme cases in which the camera has zoomed in to fill the whole page just with the eyes and lips. Another way of attracting attention is to focus on unusual details, or on sophisticated composition. Colour and black and white photographs are used in equal measure. Coloured portraits, so long as they're straightforward, are best suited to popular, more fashionable magazines, while those that are more culturally orientated lean towards black and white. When the subject is someone well known in public life, the choice of picture depends on the type of story to be told. If it's about their unusual life, for instance, the familiar mass-produced press agency photograph won't be suitable, because here the emphasis should be on the unfamiliar, hidden side of the person concerned.

This does not apply to fashion or lifestyle magazines. They use professional models who can change their identity, with the help of subtle make-up and styling, to achieve any desired effect and fit in with any theme. These faces can convey all nuances and moods, ranging from the romantic to the inaccessible, from an infectious 'joie de vivre' to irradiating eroticism – all of which are evident, for instance, in the collection of Claudia Schiffer covers.

In the sphere of political or financial magazines, there's far less flexibility in the portraits of politicians and high-profile businessmen. Only in exceptional cases will these busy people grant the time for a photo session, and so even the best-known magazines have to make do with stock material. Some opt for a montage or collage in order to convey their message. But even when an exclusive session is granted, the interests of the VIP often clash with those of the photographer or art director. The subject may wish to hide behind the mask of responsibility, while the photographer may seek openness. In any case there's often not enough time for the photographer to form any sort of relationship with their subject. It's entirely the opposite with personalities from show business. Film stars and pop stars live and thrive on the media, and are happy to use photo sessions as a means of establishing their image.

So far only single photographs have been mentioned, but there's also the multi-picture principle. This form of serial presentation is best suited to subjects that deal with a variety of different aspects. The division into small sections may detract from the immediate impact of the cover, but in terms of form it can lead to quite intriguing effects. Typographically, though, such covers pose tricky problems, and the cover lines need to be reduced to a bare minimum.

Vanidad, March 2002, Spain

Zeit Magazin, No. 8, 1991, Germany

The New York Times Magazine, No. 3, 1998, USA

The New York Times Magazine, No. 8, 1991, USA

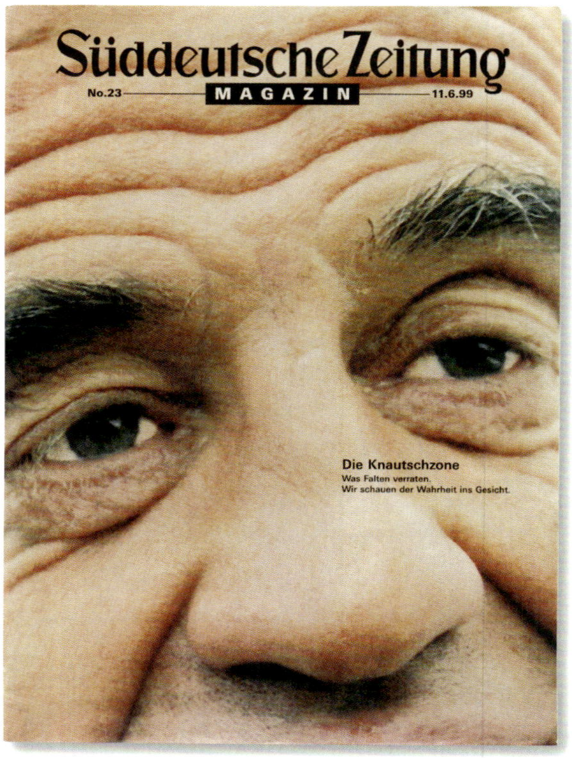

Süddeutsche Zeitung Magazin, June 1999, Germany

Skim.com, No. 2, 2000, Switzerland

Jetzt, No. 7, 2001, Germany

I-D, July 1999, Great Britain

Allegra, January 1996, Germany

Domus, October 1998, Italy

Arena, November 1999, Great Britain

Max, June 1997, France

Tempo, March 1986, Germany

Jetzt, No. 35, 1998, Germany

Die Zeit Magazin, October 1998, Germany

Süddeutsche Zeitung Magazin, November 1994, Germany

Donna, March 2002, Italy

Colors, No. 13, 1995 – 1996, Italy

Style, October 2001, Great Britain

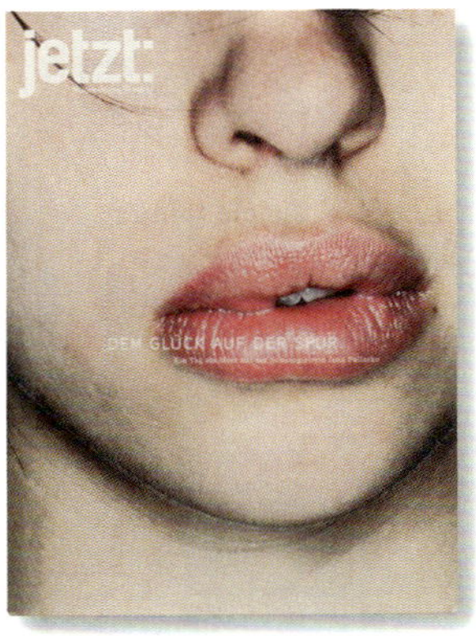

Jetzt, No. 42, 2001, Germany

Dutch, No. 24, 1999, Netherlands

Lux, August 1994, Germany

Jetzt, No. 22, 2000, Germany

Jeunes Créateurs, No. 127, 2001, France

V Magazine, May/June 2000, USA

Brand eins, August 2000, Germany

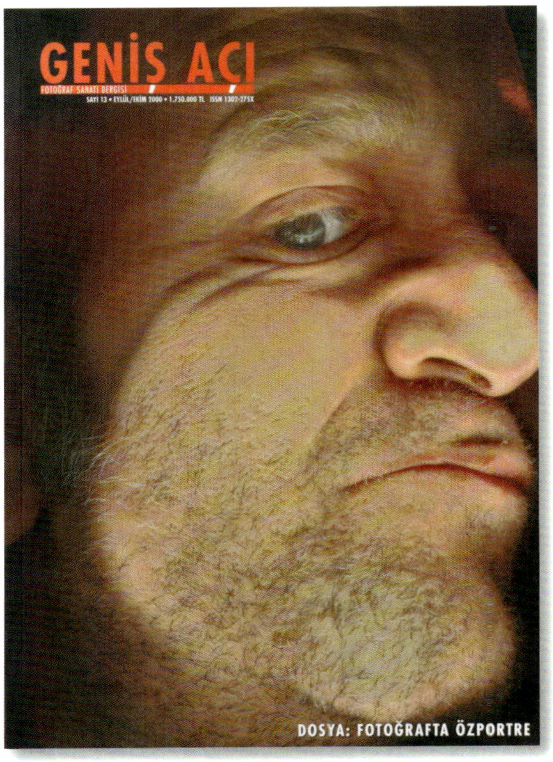

Genis Açi, No. 13, 2000, Turkey

Form, No. 182, 2001, Germany

L' uomo Vogue, February 2001, Italy

Big, No. 28, 2000, USA

Photo, April 2002, France

Tank, June 2001, Great Britain

Spoon, October 2002, Great Britain

Photo, No. 292, 1992, France

Stern, No. 15, 1990, Germany

Lei, No. 138, 1989, Italy

Tempo, October 1989, Germany

Vanity Fair, December 1994, Great Britain

Moda, December 1991, Italy

Wallpaper, May 2001, Great Britain

GQ, September 2000, Italy

Madame Figaro, No. 681, 1997, France

Spiegel Spezial, No. 4, 1999, Germany

Stern, No. 39, 1998, Germany

Vanity Fair, January 1993, Great Britain

The range of expressions covered by one model, Claudia Schiffer.

Tomorrow, No. 26, 2000, Germany

TV Spielfilm, No. 25, 2001, Germany

Gala Life & Style, August 2000, Germany

Max, August 1991, Italy

Amica, September 1999, Germany

JJ Jeune & Jolie, No. 88, 1994, France

Mademoiselle, November 1989, USA

Marie Claire, November 2001, France

Harper's Bazaar, March 1995, USA

Arena, October 1999, Great Britain

W, June 1989, USA

W, October 1995, USA

Rolling Stone, December 1999, USA

P, No. 17, 1999, Germany/Great Britain

Brett, No. 14, 2001, Germany

Süddeutsche Zeitung Magazin, No. 49, 1998, Germany

O, The Oprah Magazine, May 2002, USA

FAZ Magazin, October 1998, Germany

Jetzt, No. 8, 2000, Germany

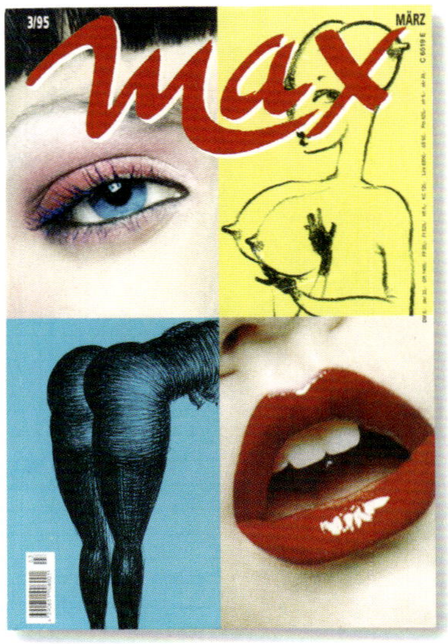

Max, March 1995, Germany

Die Zeit Magazin, No. 35, 1998, Germany

Print, January/February 1995, USA

Zeit Magazin, No. 8, 1981, Germany

Martha Stewart Living, March 2002, USA

Juice, May 2002, Germany

Life, No. 56, 1995, USA

Econy, No. 3, 1999, Germany

Stern, No. 49, 1983, Germany

Der Spiegel, No. 13, 2001, Germany

Max, December 1998, Germany

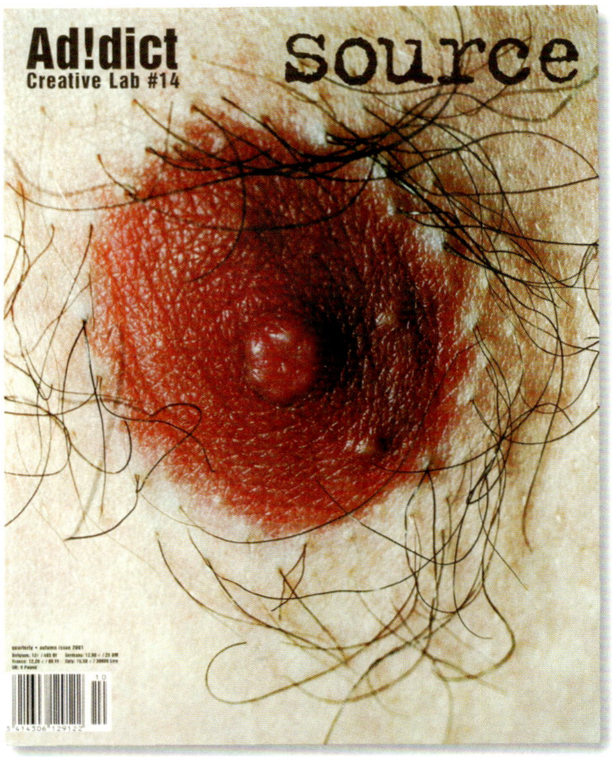

Ad!dict, No. 14, 2001, Belgium

Das Magazin, No. 4, 2000, Switzerland

Pur, Spring 2001, Germany

Dae, No. 3, 2001, Great Britain

Jetzt, No. 13, 2002, Germany

Loewe, No. 1, 2002, Germany

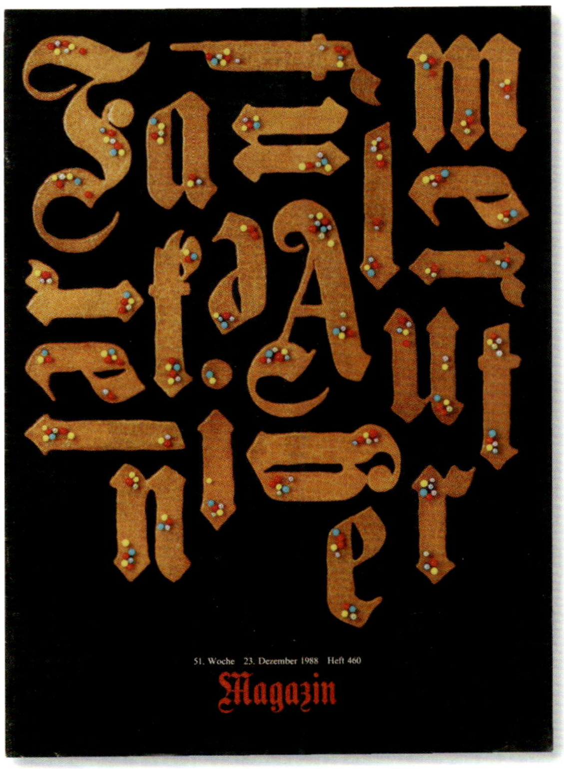

FAZ Magazin, No. 460, 1988, Germany

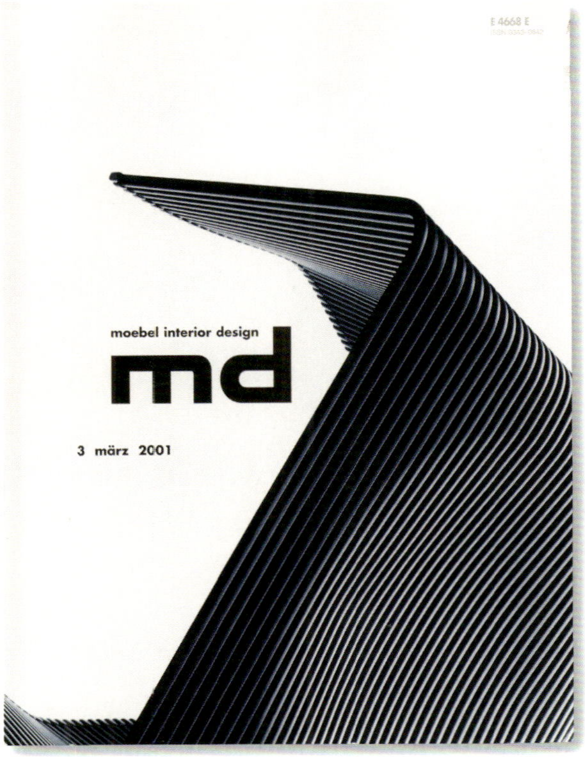

Md, March 2001, Germany

Domus, June 2000, Italy

Domus, July/August 1999, Italy

Domus, February 1995, Italy

Domus, November 2000, Italy

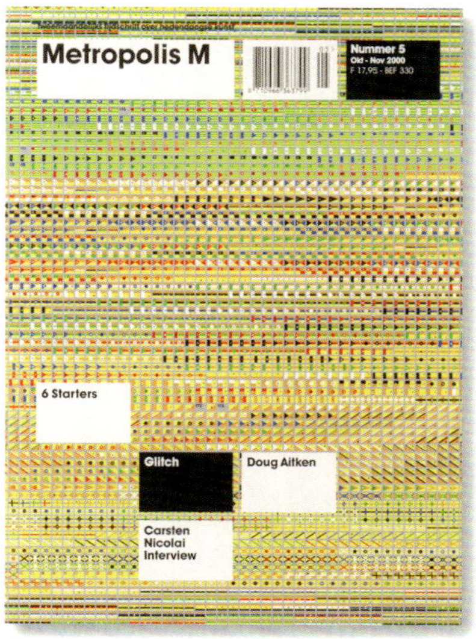

Metropolis M, October/November 2000, Netherlands

British, No. 1, 2001, Netherlands

Life, January 2002, Great Britain

Raveline, No. 4, 2002, Germany

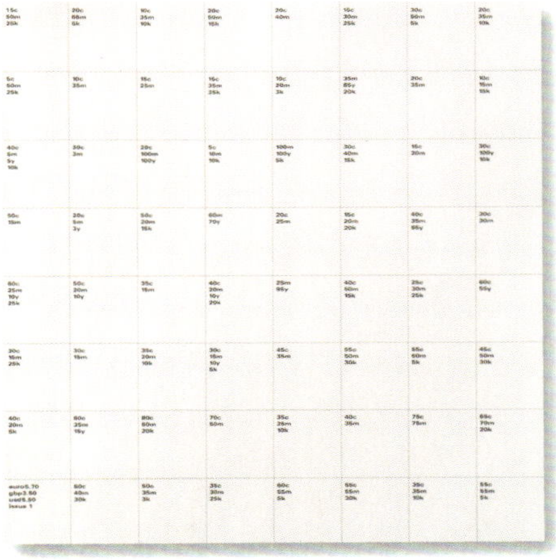

M-real, No. 1, 2000, Finland

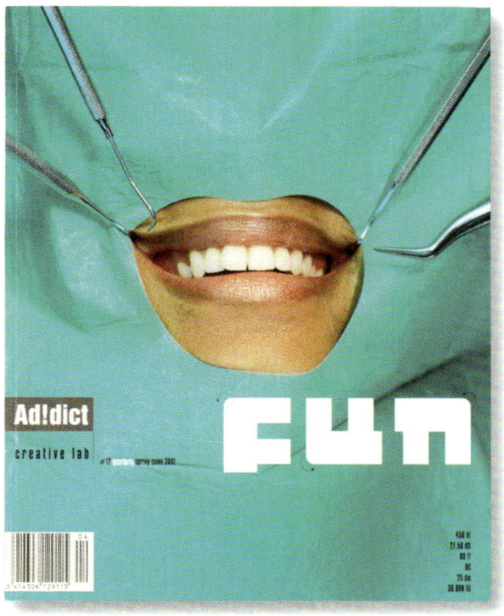

Ad!dict, No. 12, 2001, Belgium

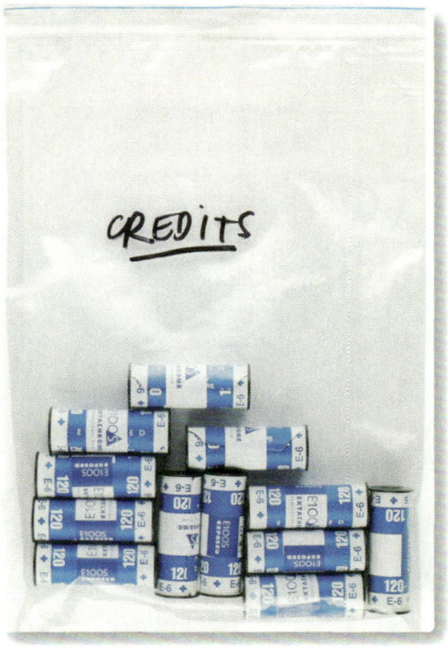

Credits, 1999, Netherlands

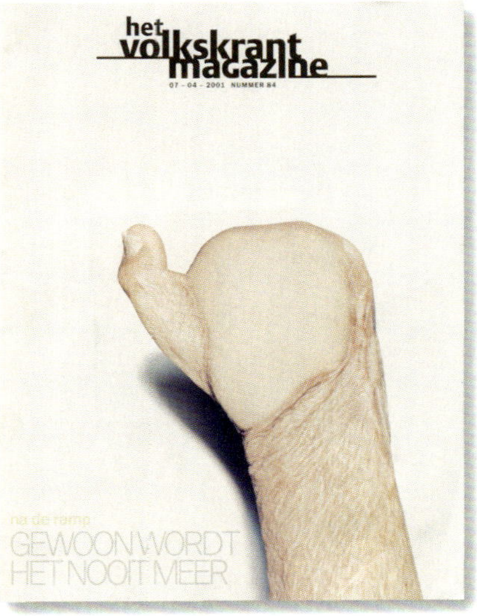

Het volkskrant magazine, No. 84, 2001, Netherlands

Gardens Illustrated, December. 2001/ January 2002, Great Britain

TYPOGRAPHICAL COVERS

The wide range of typographical designs

Magazine covers don't necessarily have to be pictorial. It's also possible to create interesting designs just by using typography. The impact may not be quite so popular, but a wide range of styles are available. Certain filigree forms can have a very intellectual effect, and big, colourful lettering can arouse strong emotions. Computer magazines have become more and more inclined to use nothing but text on their covers, though there's little sign here of typographical sophistication. In this field, the covers are becoming almost indistinguishable, and the only competitive element is the number of subjects they each try to cram in. Character and individuality are nowhere to be seen. One happy exception is the Dutch business magazine *Quote*, which over the years has shown that typography and colour alone can be used to create an attractive cover. Simply by varying the size of the letters, cleverly juxtaposing the lines, and changing the colours, an astonishingly rich range has been created.

Emigre, No. 54, 2000, USA

Ampers & ND, No. 2, 2001, Great Britain

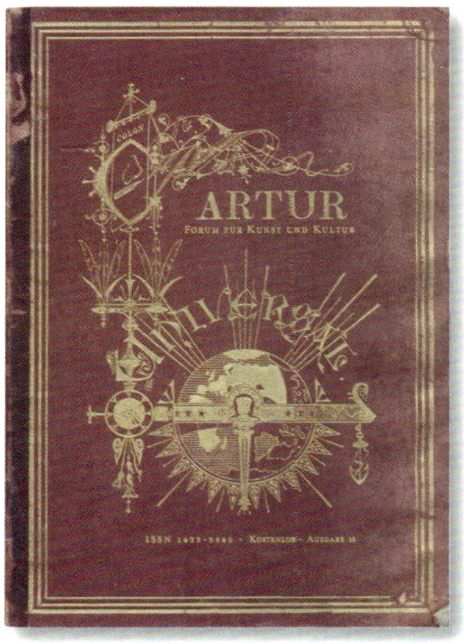

Artur, No. 16, 1998, Germany

Fast Company, 1997, USA

Vogue 3W, No. 615, 2001, Italy

Rolling Stone, No. 855, 2000, USA

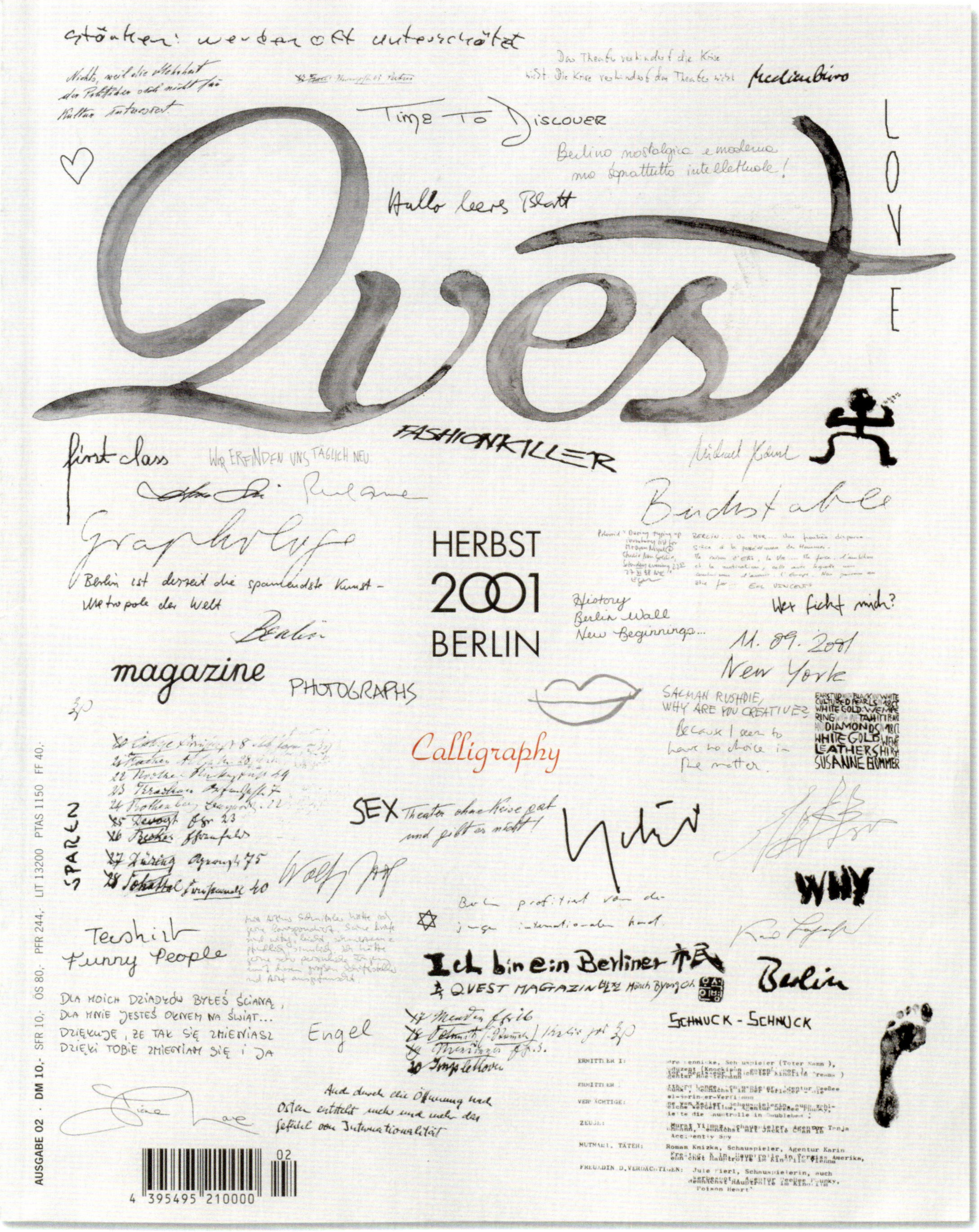

Quest, No. 2, 2001, Germany

Print, May/June 2000, USA

Wired, October 2001, USA

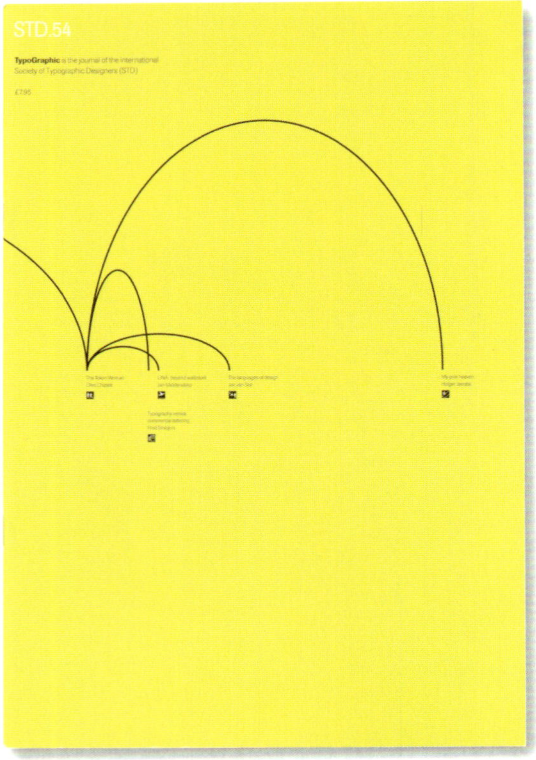

Typographic, No. 54, 1999, Great Britain

Greenpeace Magazin, No. 6, 2001, Germany

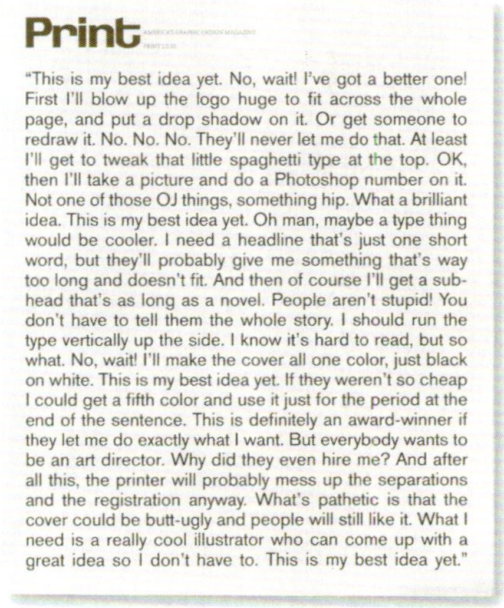

Print, May/June 1998, USA

Material, No. 5, 2001, Switzerland

Exhibit:a, June/July 2001, Great Britain

28832 Berlin, October 1999,

Der Spiegel, No. 7, 2001, Germany

Jpside, March 2001, USA

Wallpaper, January/February 2000, Great Britain

The World of Interiors, April 2002, Great Britain

Items, May/June 2002, Netherlands

Quote, April 1998, Netherlands

Quote, November 2000, Netherlands

Quote, December 1999, Netherlands

Quote, October 1999, Netherlands

Quote, April 2000, Netherlands

Quote, November 1999, Netherlands

Quote, March 2000, Netherlands

Quote, August 1999, Netherlands

Quote, May 1999, Netherlands

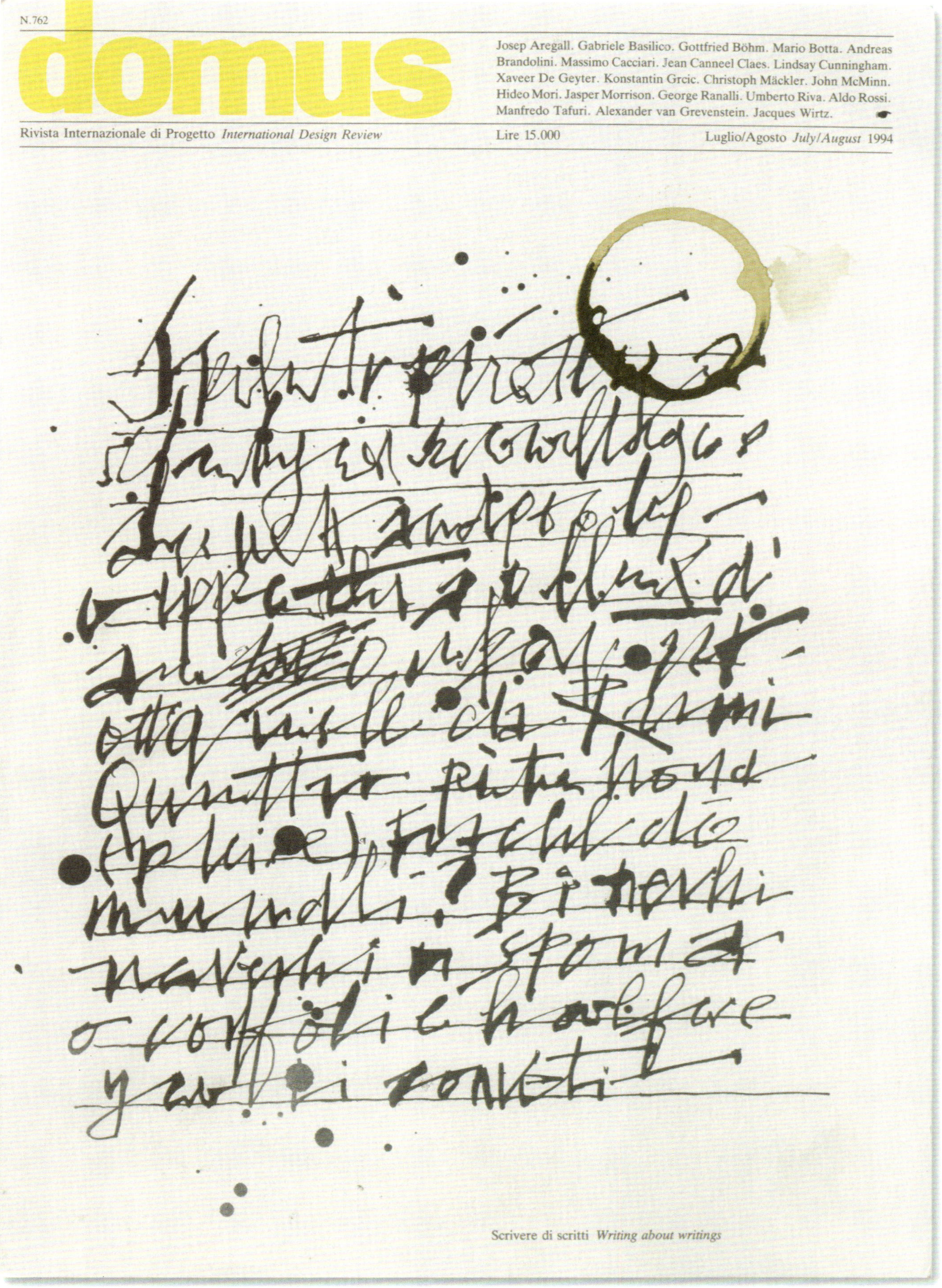

Domus, July/August 1994, Italy

ILLUSTRATED COVERS

From the realistic drawing to the artistic illustration

The flood of pictures and the levelling effect of photography have meant that anyone who wants to stand out from the crowd has to look for different means of expression. Illustrations are the perfect way to counter the conventional. They're always suffused with an artistic, personal element, and are particularly suited to matters of individual interpretation. An illustrated cover automatically adds a touch of class, and its succinctness of expression makes it more memorable. But the aesthetic elitism of a good illustration doesn't endear itself to the masses, and so this form remains exceptional. In the 1950s and 1960s there were some extremely popular illustrated magazines with very realistic drawings – the *Saturday Evening Post* in USA and *Hörzu* in Germany, for instance – but nowadays photography is deemed to be more effective. Illustrations are also made use of in political magazines, but they're exceptional and are only there to make comments on particular issues.

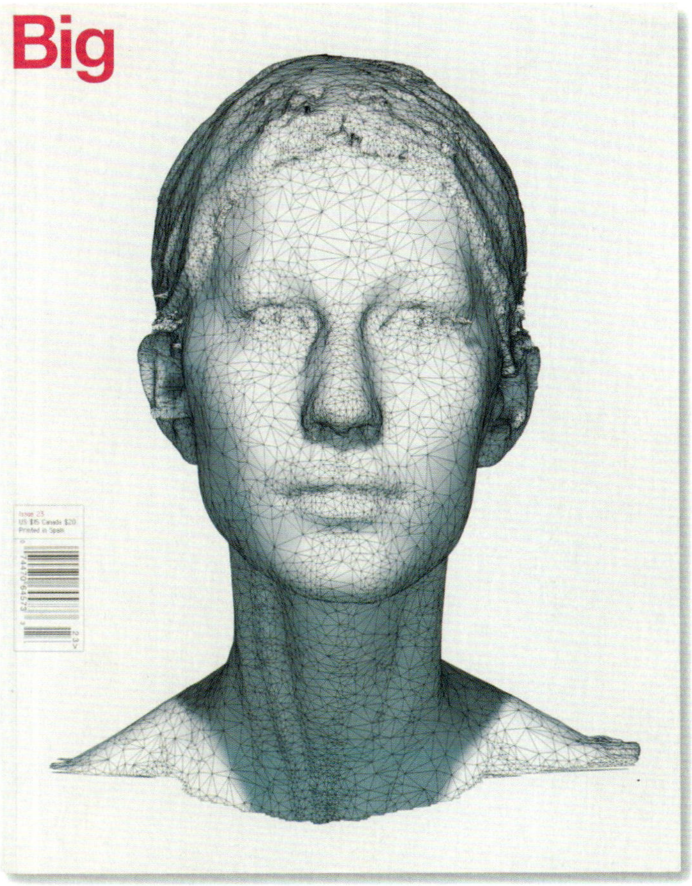

Big, No. 23, 1999, USA

Kunst & Kultur, February 2001, Germany

Der Spiegel, No. 33, 1999, Germany

Brett, No. 10, 2001, Germany

Brand eins, March 2000, Germany

Artbox magazine, No. 1, 2002, Netherlands

Eye, No. 11, 2002, Great Britain

Designer, No. 2, 2001, Singapore

Jalouse, No. 35, 2000, France

Eye, No. 39, 2001, Great Britain

Wired, June 1997, USA

IdN, No. 2, 2002, China

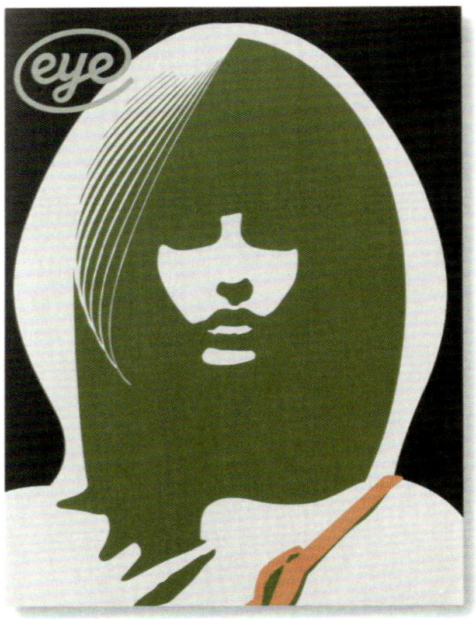

Eye, No. 42, 2001, Great Britain

Vogue, No. 662, 1985/1986, France

Adrenalin, No. 10, 2001, Great Britain

Ad!dict, No. 11, 2001, Belgium

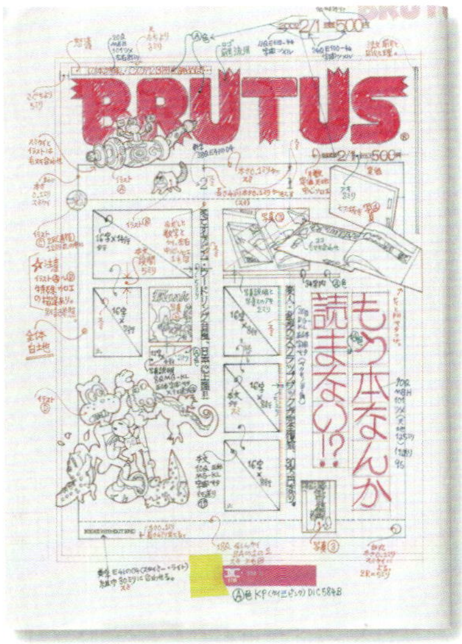

Brutus, Nos. 1–2, 2002, Singapore

Dada, No. 25, 2000, Netherlands

Greenpeace Magazin, No. 3, 2001, Germany

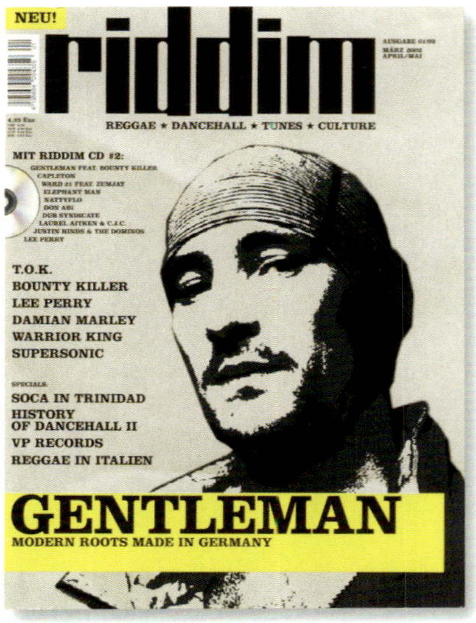

Riddim, March/April/May 2002, Germany

Brand eins, September 2001, Germany

The Face, January 2000, Great Britain

Magazines with different covers

If you're a creative designer and want to experiment with a magazine cover, you're better doing it with one of the leisure variety rather than with an earnest issue on current affairs. Innovative magazines are nowadays indulging in more and more experiments. The most popular is the creation of a link between front and back covers – for instance, the front showing the front of the model, and the back showing the back. Another interesting variation is to get the same edition displayed at the news-stand with different covers, either quite independent of each other or complementing each other like a kind of puzzle. The object can be to test readers' reactions, or simply to get them to buy more than one copy. *Domus* had a chameleon cover in several different colours to imitate the animal's ability to camouflage itself. One edition of *Rolling Stone* printed five different covers to feature the five members of the band NSync. This method of displaying different covers on the shelf can even be used as a democratic means of influencing public opinion. Liz Jones, editor of the British *Marie Claire*, was concerned about the health risks entailed in the current trend of employing very thin models. For one edition she used two different covers, one with a fuller figure, and one with the usual waif. Apparently it was the fuller figure that sold more copies, but this seems to have had no lasting effect on the modern concept of beauty.

Marie Claire, June 2000, Great Britain (Pamela Anderson)

Marie Claire, June 2000, Great Britain (Sophie Dahl)

Rolling Stone, August 2001, USA

Rolling Stone, August 2001, USA

Rolling Stone, August 2001, USA

Rolling Stone, August 2001, USA

Domus, July/August 2000, Italy

Domus, July/August 2000, Italy

Domus, July/August 2000, Italy

Harper's Bazaar, February 2002, USA

Harper's Bazaar, February 2002, USA

Rails, December 2001/January 2002, Netherlands

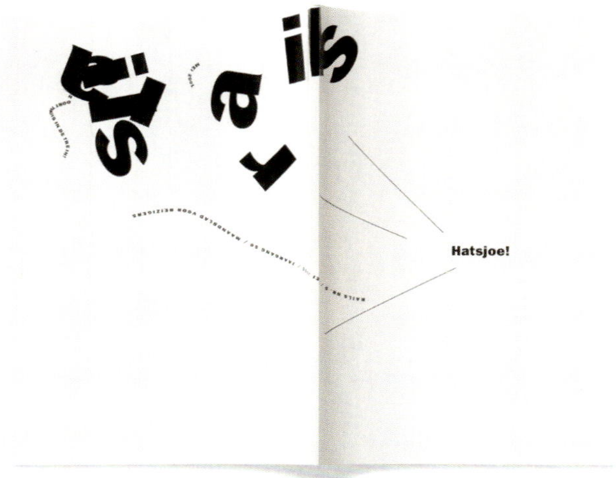

Rails, May 2001, Netherlands

Rails, August/September 2001, Netherlands

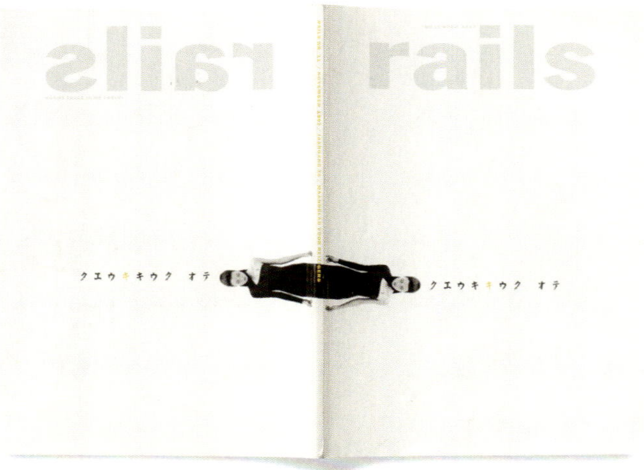

Rails, November 1997, Netherlands

Rails, July/August 2000, Netherlands

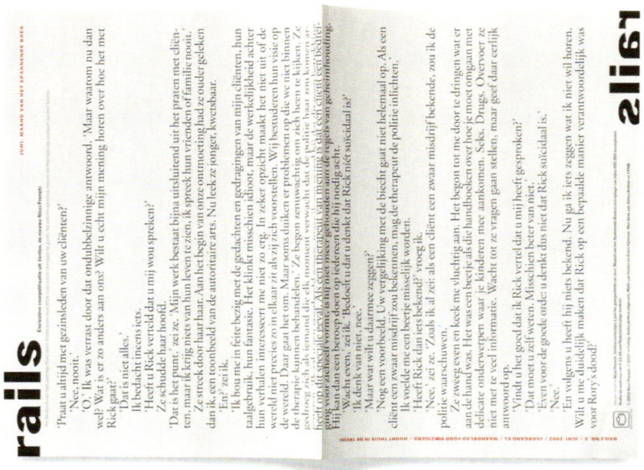

Rails, June 2001, Netherlands

Nanyou/Nüyou, February 2002, Singapore

Spruce, No. 1, 2001, Great Britain

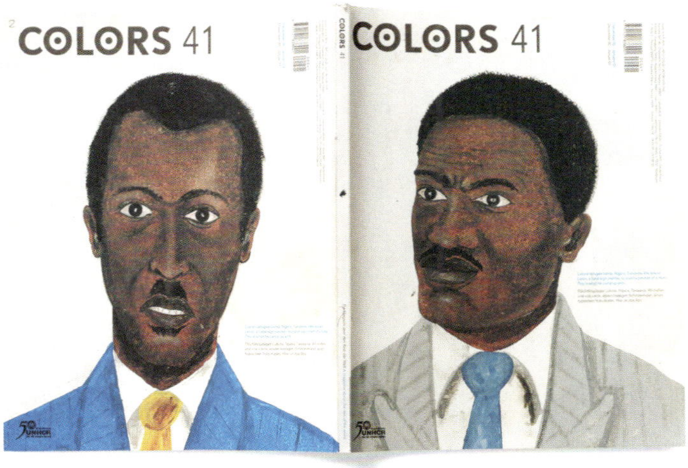

Colors 41, December 2000/January 2001, Italy

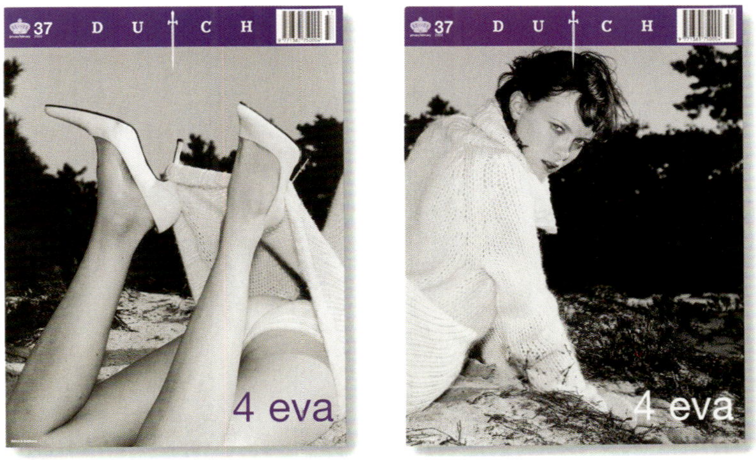

Dutch, January/February 2002, Netherlands

Esquire, March 2002, Great Britain

Surface, No. 14, 1998, USA

Magazines are brands just like other consumer goods

An essential feature of magazines is regularity of publication – whether at weekly, fortnightly, monthly, bimonthly, quarterly or half-yearly intervals. What matters to the reader is that the magazine is recognizable, and the prime responsibility for this falls to the trademark, or logo. A classic example is the red masthead with white lettering which, ever since it was started in 1936, made *Life* magazine instantly identifiable all over the world. This form of logo is still the most common to be seen at the news-stand. The original idea was to send out a clear, strong signal, but of course when everyone's sending out similar signals, the effect is drastically reduced. With the great flood of magazines now on the market, logos have undergone a large number of mutations. The masthead, which stands out from the rest of the cover, is now to be seen in all shapes and colours. Its normal position is in the top left-hand corner, because that's the section guaranteed to be visible at the news-stand, no matter how densely the magazines are displayed. Even so, there are variations: at the bottom, in the middle, or even vertical along the left or right-hand sides. The letters are often combined with a symbol, an obvious example being that of the German magazine *Stern*, meaning 'Star', whose masthead consists of a red panel with a stylized white star to complement the title.

Although the rules of the advertising game say that, for psychological reasons, trademarks should never be changed, there are some magazines that make a virtue out of ignoring the rules. A well-known example is *Raygun*, which, during the design reign of David Carson, appeared with a different logo for every issue. The design of the cover was always so different that its very unconventionality became the hallmark of its identity. The mutations of the logos were an integral part of this creative rule-breaking, and in such cases the desire to be original and innovative can justify the slaughter of commercially sacred cows. Of course the rules are not an end in themselves, but are only there as an aid to building and preserving an identity. If this can be achieved by other methods, then no one will complain at the widening of the repertoire.

The masthead, which needs to be clear and concise, usually stands on a different coloured surface to the rest of the text. But even here there are exceptions. If there's no masthead, it's particularly important to choose lettering that will distinguish the logo from the cover lines, which announce the subject matter inside and must be easy to read. A logo is not read, but simply recognized, and since logo and cover lines perform quite different functions, it makes sense to separate them typographically. Many magazines nowadays are quite happy to use existing fonts for logos, although in the past there were periods when they were specially made to measure. There was a rule that one letter in the logo had to be 'wrong', or odd, so that it would be noticed and imprinted on the memory. Anything unobtrusive, uniform, or easily overlooked generally disappears at once from our recollection. Logos that are handwritten or drawn are sure to be individualistic. Of course, they fulfil none of the requirements of objectivity or timelessness, but instead they offer personality and emotion. It's always difficult to find the right balance between the modern and the classical, but generally the more modern or fashionable the logo, the shorter its life will be, while the more classical or neutral it is, the less striking and expressive it will be. The classical solution is always stigmatized with a sort of wishy-washiness, and can never endow its magazine with any sort of individual character. One significant criterion for the effectiveness of a logo is the link between form and content, and this can be vividly illustrated by the following example of two logos that follow the same principle – that of *Blond* and that of the German film magazine *Schnitt*, which means 'Cut'. The letters of both logos are cut off at the bottom. In the first case, the device simply plays with form and has nothing to do with the content; in the second, a typographical equivalent is created for the cutting of the roll of film which gives the magazine its title. The parallel here between logo and subject matter is therefore far more striking.

Blond, March 2002, Germany

Schnitt, March 2000, Germany

The device of sliced letters applied to logo design: in *Blond* it's purely decorative, while in *Schnitt* it directly complements the title.

Internet World, March 1996, USA

Focus, May 1997, Germany

Using nothing but conventional fonts for a logo can cause problems. Ideally, the logo should be so unique that it cannot be used in a different context by another magazine.

Arena, Jan./Feb. 1988, Great Britain

Arena, December 1997, Great Britain

Arena, December 2001, Great Britain

Arena, June 2002, Great Britain

The mutating logo of *Arena*: originally it sprang from a font designed for *The Face* and later transformed into 'Typeface six' by Neville Brody. In time, only the characteristic A remained from the original.

DOS, No. 8, 1996, Germany

DOS, No. 10, 1996, Germany

PC Magazin DOS, No. 12, 1996, Germany

When computer magazines are named after a particular system, their existence is naturally bound up with that system. An interesting case is the magazine *DOS*. Once the system had become obsolete, the name had to undergo a process of modernisation. The change took place in stages, with 'DOS' getting ever smaller, until *PC Magazin* took over entirely.

PC Magazin DOS,
No. 1, 1997, Germany

PC Magazin DOS,
No. 3, 1997, Germany

PC Magazin DOS,
No. 5, 1997, Germany

PC Magazin DOS,
No. 2, 1998, Germany

PC Magazin,
No. 7, 1998, Germany

Life, April 1954, USA

Sowjetunion, No. 7, 1979, Russia

Star Revue, October 1957, Germany

Paris Match, No. 500, 1958, France

Bunte Illustrierte/Münchner Illustrierte, No. 50, 1960, Germany

Triumfo, June 1963, Spain

Hayat, May 1966, Turkey

Wienerin, Autumn 1985, Austria

Magma, June 1987, Switzerland

The Face, June 1990, Great Britain

Spy, March 1992, USA

Man, January/February 1997, Netherlands

Baby, April 2001, Netherlands

AD Architectural Digest, April/May 2002, Germany

Doin' fine, November/December 2000, Germany

AM7, No. 7, 2001, Germany

Frame, January/February 2002, Netherlands

Design Report, April 2002, Germany

H.O.M.E., No. 4, 2000, Germany

Edit, No. 27, 2002, Germany

Massiv, January 2002, Switzerland

Frame, No. 10, 2002, Germany

Wallpaper, December 2000, Great Britain

Feel Good, No. 3, 2002, Germany

Raygun, March 1994, USA

Raygun, February 1994, USA

Raygun, November 1994, USA

Raygun, April 1993, USA

Raygun, September 1996, USA

Raygun, September 1993, USA

Raygun, June/July 1994, USA

Raygun, May 1994, USA

Raygun, November 1993, USA

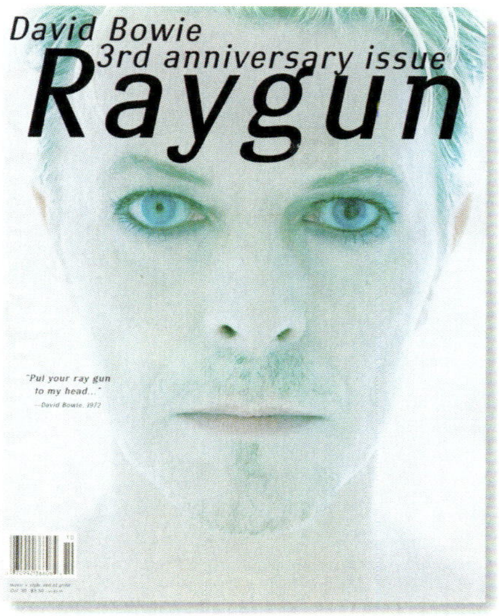

Raygun, October 1995, USA

Raygun, October 1993, USA

Raygun, April 1995, USA

Raygun, March 1993, USA

Raygun, March 1993, USA

Raygun, September 1995, USA

Raygun, October 1994, USA

Raygun, February 1993, USA

Raygun, June/July 1993, USA

Big, No. 33, 2000, USA

Big, No. 26, 1999, USA

Details, February 1989, USA

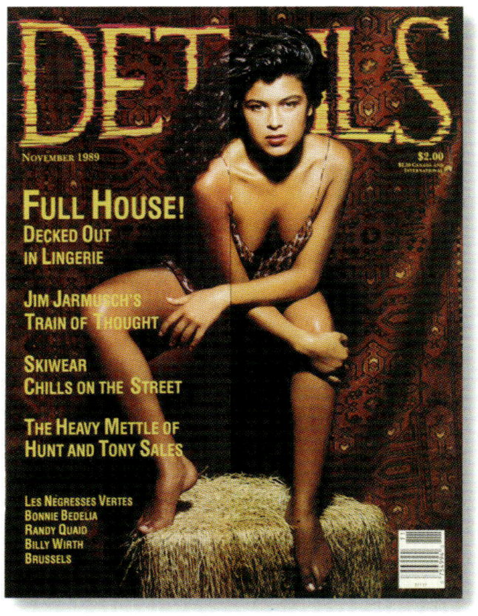

Details, November 1989, USA

Details, December/January 1990, USA

Big, No. 35, 2001, USA

Big, No. 40, 2001, USA

Details, February 1990, USA

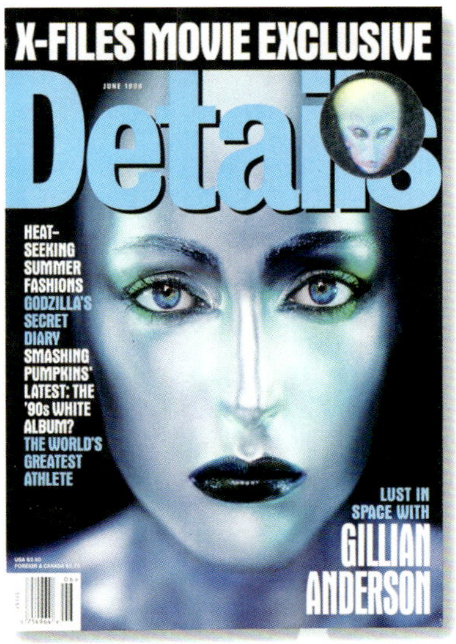

Details, June 1998, USA

Details, March 2002, USA

Interview, January 1990, USA
(see index for credits)

Madison, January/February 2000, USA

Backspin, March 2002, Germany

Flaunt, No. 5, 2000, USA

Bloom, June 2001, France
Cover photo by Sarah Allen

M-real, Winter 2001, Great Britain

Big, No. 39, 2001, USA

Blvd., April 2000, Netherlands

Polaroid, No. 13, 1997, Germany

Super Lodown, No. 30, 2002, Germany

Massiv, No. 6, 2000, Switzerland

Street, January/February 2001, Austria

High Potential, April/May 2001, Germany

Nest, October 2000, USA

Speak, Winter 1998, USA

h4, January – March 2000, Singapore

Seventh Sky, November 1999, Switzerland

Passport, September 2000, Switzerland

Trans-form, 2001, Great Britain

Constructional aspects of a magazine feature

In designing the layout of a magazine feature that's to cover several pages, you first have to decide what visual elements (photographs, illustrations, charts, and so on) are to be used to accompany the text. Naturally, the selection must fit in with the content, and here the ideal example is a report illustrated with photos by a single photographer. It's more difficult when the pictures stem from different sources, and in this case you need to choose photos that have plenty of stylistic features in common. The more heterogeneous the pictures, the less harmonious the layout will be. Is it possible to combine coloured photographs with black and white? They might complement each other, but only if they can still be related to elements of the text – for instance, with a recipe, in which the preparations are shown in black and white, and the finished dish in colour. If there's no logic behind the choice, the effect will be messy. With articles on politics or business, the mixture of photos and charts is often unavoidable. An article might begin with a large-scale portrait – photo or drawing – and then continue with various charts, which would then create a good balance. Magazines on current affairs generally have to use a wide variety of picture material, but the priority here lies with the information and not with purely aesthetic considerations.

As soon as you know how the feature is going to be constructed and what pictures are available, you can design the opening section. With longer articles, it makes sense to begin with a double page to set the right tone. This spread should touch on as many aspects as possible so the reader can decide whether or not they want to read the rest. If you want to open with a large picture, you'll obviously go for the best one you've got, but it must be representative of the whole article and not just one tiny aspect that will be irrelevant later on. To what extent it should be a teaser depends on the designer, but again it's important to strike a balance between arousing the reader's curiosity and not giving the whole game away at the same time. Mike Meiré often begins with rear views in order to get his reader to turn the pages until they finally see the face.

The vital typographical element at the beginning of any article or story is the combination of headline and standfirst. This form has found favour all over the world. Ideally, the headline should be exciting, but it must tie in with the opening without merely duplicating what's about to be said. The standfirst, which forms a link between headline and text, will be more informative, but again it must arouse curiosity without telling the whole story. The headline/standfirst format is both binding and liberating, and can also be supplemented by other forms of heading. Where justified, the author and photographer can be given due prominence after or even in the standfirst. Whether the actual text should begin on the opening page or not depends on the overall composition, but it's certainly better to launch the reader into the feature straight away, rather than having a break in continuity before they turn the page.

Econy, No. 2, 1999, Germany

Econy, No. 1, 1998, Germany

HOW NOT TO GET STARTED

A few dos and don'ts

1. OFF THE PEG

After the winner of an open competition has turned down the job because the conditions are totally unacceptable, a young pair of graphic designers, 'SunnyMoonMouse', are commissioned to design a visual concept for a brand new in-store magazine. They have to come up with the following: one editorial page, one double-page list of contents (but single-page if they like), a double-page of reports, and a longer feature that opens with a double-page spread and continues for two more pages. The proprietor wants to have a three- and four-column format, three types of chart (one pie, one bar and one graph), and of course two cover designs with variations, including a logo and sample pages complete with stylistic models. The typefaces must be delivered along with all of these. The designers can go ahead and copy the banderole idea proposed by the sixth-placed competitor because, in the words of the marketing director: 'You can't copyright things like that.' A total of eight working days will be allotted, and all rights will be the proprietor's. With the first issue, the design team should just 'have a look', as a sort of service-cum-favour, but from No. 2 onwards, the magazine will be put together in-house. The company has had twelve picture CDs copied by its own advertising agency, and if necessary it can always hire a digital camera. The 48-page magazine will be compiled by two girls from the marketing department for whom the company has splashed out on a desktop publishing course.

You can make magazines that way. No problem. But why bother to bring in designers at all, since nowadays there's a huge selection of dirt-cheap model layouts and graphics available by the cartload?

2. MADE TO MEASURE

Don't hold a competition. A competition is just another way of saying that there's nobody in the company who knows the market well enough to make a decision. Instead, this is what you do: a competent member of staff has a close look at all the top names in the world of corporate publishing. In order to remain anonymous, they order one magazine or another through the firm's advertising agency, study the yearbooks and ads contained in Forum Corporate Publishing's factbook, and make notes while studying the imprints of the magazines chosen. After much humming, hawing profound thought and mature reflection, they then make the decision. Alone and unaided. An appointment is made for a getting-to-know-you session. The more cautious-minded will opt for a team that's already been active in the field, or has even specialized in this particular section of it, while the more enterprising will take on someone who's totally new to it. In this way you can hope for fresh ideas and new approaches, although of course it's essential that the designer should have had adequate experience. Let someone else pay for the learning process and its sometimes nasty consequences. After all, nobody is infallible. Provided you get on, and agreement can be reached on the size of the salary, work can begin. Generally, there's already an overall concept defining the aims of the company and the new magazine. The next step is for the designers to become familiar with the character, philosophy and ambiance of the company that's taken them on. Their perception will never again be as objective as it is during this first phase, because later they'll become just as entangled in the business as everyone else, and so it's important that the first impression should also be a lasting one. Once the aims are clear, you can make some tentative initial designs – tentative because you can never expect to get it right first time. As with the perfect made-to-measure suit, there always has to be tiny adjustments here and corrections there. When the first few pages are ready, it's time to consider the technical details: what format, what paper, what texture, and maybe refinements, embellishments, distinguishing features. As soon as matters of colour and typeface come under discussion, corporate design must also play a role, and an inexperienced newcomer will give the game away by insisting on designing the magazine quite independently of what's already to hand. Of course, magazine design follows very different rules from those governing business reports, shop-fittings, prospectuses, the sides of trucks and the stands at trade fairs. That's only right and proper. The whole point of magazines is that they should give a more objective slant to information, and there shouldn't be even a whiff of self-promotion. Despite this, though, the overall impression created by the company's various public outlets should not be diffuse. Very few companies ever make their mark with just one single message, but the clearer and simpler the messages, the more distinct the impression will be, while too great a diversity will blur the image. It's vital for colour, pictures and text to be integrated in a single unifying concept. Even if the rules that govern business prospectuses and so on cannot be applied to magazines, which go by a more flexible, variable code, it's still essential for the magazine to be recognizable. The balance between recognizable sameness and attractive difference is an extremely fine one. One major problem is maintaining consistency in a company's colours. As there are far more firms than colours that can reasonably be registered as trademarks, you have to make sure that the chosen shade is always reproduced with absolute precision. Many financial institutions, for example, favour blue, and so the particular shade must be the same on everything that appears in public – whether in print, on the screen, on signs, on visiting cards, or at trade fairs. A further complication here is that of reproducing special colours through four-colour printing. This is a daunting prospect, as will be confirmed by anyone who has seen the Pantone range of four-colour comparative values, but for this problem too there are new solutions. There have been many recent developments with pigments, adhesives, and the software for scanners and printing-presses. The Aniva process, for instance, which is especially suitable for company publications, has greatly improved the accuracy of four-colour printing in reproducing special colours.

Anyone who's not happy with standard solutions to these problems – knowing full well that sooner or later things are bound to go radically wrong – but who sets out to find new and better ways, will certainly need time. The same applies to the choice of typeface. Generally, when a typeface is selected for corporate design, people don't think of magazine design. Countless tests are necessary in the quest for the right type, regardless of such details as the way the company's name is to be written in the text as opposed to the logo. Harmonization of fonts can only be achieved by practical experimentation, for such problems can never be solved theoretically. As far as pictorial language is concerned, it's extremely difficult to find anything new, and your old stock material is certainly not going to do the trick. We grasp pictures in a different way from the way we do texts, and they can very rarely convey the message intended by the company. When the pictures are of people, even the man in the street, hardened as he is by the ubiquitousness of posters, ads and TV commercials, can distinguish what is staged or posed from what is genuine.

Since there are virtually no monopolies, no company can afford to ignore competition. It often happens that rival firms will quite unscrupulously take over a good design or an original idea. Perhaps once in a blue moon a designing equivalent of Mozart may burst upon the scene, effortlessly creating the most complex and harmonious themes. But they're the exceptions that prove the rule. It generally requires vast amounts of time and effort to produce anything even approaching the perfect composition. Balance and coordination, and concealment of the time and effort involved, in practice mean a process of endless reshuffling, streamlining, adjusting and adapting. The design comes to life through variety and contrast – round alternating with square, hard with soft, rough with smooth, big with small, colour with black and white, elaborate with simple. Without wishing to labour the musical analogy, you could say that only someone who can conduct the full orchestra of typography, colour, line and surface, photography and illustration will be able to give full dynamism to the complex score that constitutes a magazine.

Magazines are individuals that can mature into strong personalities, and in whose presence you feel at home. The more original and surprising they are, the more time you want to spend with them. Featureless display dummies, waxwork dolls, faceless non-entities that radiate blandness and dullness – these can never create the bonds of friendship. A dull magazine is a paper scarecrow that can serve only to drive its readers away.

TYPOGRAPHY. Headline and Standfirst Combinations

The dual strategy of free and compulsory content, and its typographical variations

Although there's a huge range of headline/standfirst combinations that any article can be opened with, in practice virtually every variation has the same underlying pattern and structure. In its classic form, the headline is the freestyle exercise, open to the creativity of its author. It should stimulate associations in the reader and arouse their curiosity. Sometimes it may allude to well-known titles of books, films or songs, though all too often this can seem clumsy and laboured. A trio of examples which successfully play on the double meanings of words springs to mind:

1) 'Der Brandenburger Tor'. The brainchild of Ferdinand Simoneit, former editor of *Spiegel*, this headline refers to Axel Caesar Springer's *Bildzeitung,* which raged against the student movement of the late 1960s. The apparent reference to the famous gate in Berlin is deceiving: 'das Tor' means 'gate', but 'der Tor' means 'fool'.

2) 'Ohne Waters alles Roger'. When Pink Floyd parted company with their creative genius Roger Waters, everyone thought they would fold – but they didn't. The headline reads 'Without Waters Everything's Roger' – that is, OK.

3) 'Waiting for Bordeaux'. This article on the length of time it takes for a good red wine to mature employed the image of a stage set with spotlights shining on empty glasses – reinforcing the allusion to Samuel Beckett's play *Waiting for Godot*.

Such headlines don't convey any precise information, but they create a certain tension. The counterpart to this freestyle is the compulsory exercise – in this case, the standfirst. Here the subject matter is pinpointed, but without destroying the tension or giving away too much of the content. Now the reader can decide whether to go on or not. In special interest magazines, though, this technique is used far less frequently. The standfirst functions as a summary, and the article that follows springs no surprises but merely goes into detail.

The variety and sophistication of typographical forms that can be applied to this combination of headline and standfirst are astonishing when you remind yourself that they all have the same basic structure. The most common deviation from this basic structure is to combine both parts in a single text, or to make one flow into the other. Evidently there has been little effort to devise any radical alternatives.

1/4 nach 5, No. 5, 2002, Germany

Harper's Bazaar, September 1992, USA

Vogue, February 2000, Italy

City Magazine, July 2000, China (Hong Kong)

Spex, No. 7, 2002, Germany

Adrenalin, No. 7, 2001, Germany

Details, No. 2, 2002, USA

Details, No. 3, 2002, USA

Fast Company, May 2000, USA

Style, December 2000/January 2001, Germany

Mode Max, No. 7, 2002, France

Substance, January/February 2001, Singapore

Esquire, Autumn 2001, USA

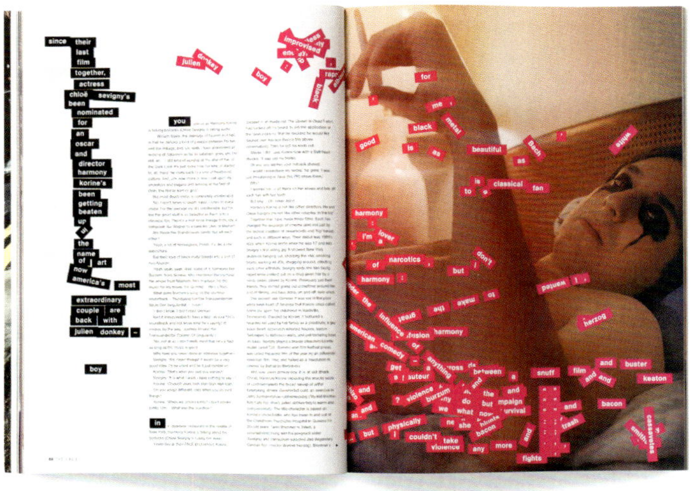

The Face, No. 7, 2000, Great Britain

Man, January/February 2000, Netherlands

Style, March 2002, Germany

Cine Chart, July 2000, Germany

Vogue, August 2000, Italy

Esquire, No. 5, 2001, USA

Harper's Bazaar, August 1994, USA

Harper's Bazaar, August 1994, USA

Esquire, No. 2, 2000, USA

Style, April 2002, Germany

Fast Company, No. 53, 2001, USA

Fast Company, July 2001, USA

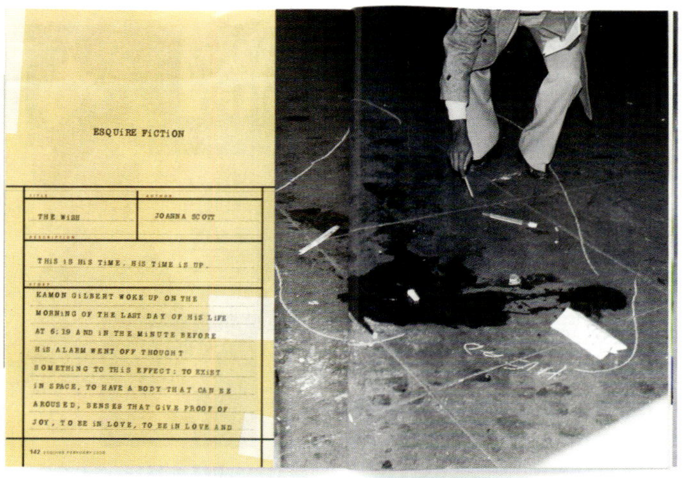

Esquire, No. 2, 2000, USA

Esquire, No. 2, 2000, USA

Fast Company, November 2002, USA

Rolling Stone, April 2000, USA

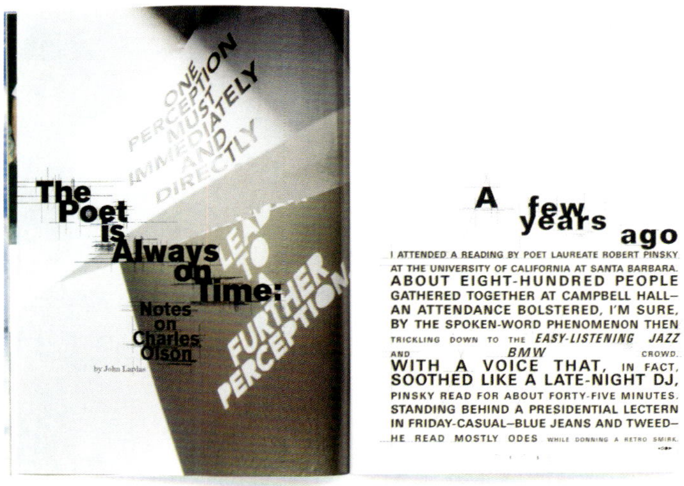

Speak, Winter 1999, USA

TYPOGRAPHY. Section Headings

A useful navigational device

As Henri Nannen, founder of *Stern*, once remarked, magazines can be constructed like surprise packages. When they are, you don't need section divisions. The reader doesn't look for anything in particular, but simply allows themself to be surprised by the discovery of something interesting. Such a method would be totally unsuitable for a specialist magazine, and indeed the more informative a magazine sets out to be, the more essential it is to give it a clear and easily accessible structure. Section headings are extremely helpful in guiding the reader around. Normally, the area at the top of the page is the best place for these headings. Whether it's useful to combine them with a special colour code will depend on the size of the magazine; for instance, if there are 36 pages with six sections, different colours would be pointless, since some of the sections would probably only contain one article. One important decision is whether to use single terms or to give a double reference – you might, for instance, put a whole section under the heading of 'Culture' and supplement this heading with the particular theme dealt with on each page. It doesn't matter a great deal whether the two terms are positioned next to each other, one above the other, or separated by lines; what matters is that the main heading and subheading are easy to recognize. There's a broad repertoire of forms for these headings, including coloured areas, bars and lines, to name but a few, and these are sometimes also used in combination with icons. If there are colours, the question arises whether they should also be taken up in the articles themselves, and if so, in what form. If such patterns are overdone, they can quickly become uninteresting, and so as always, the art lies in finding a discreet balance between consistency and variety.

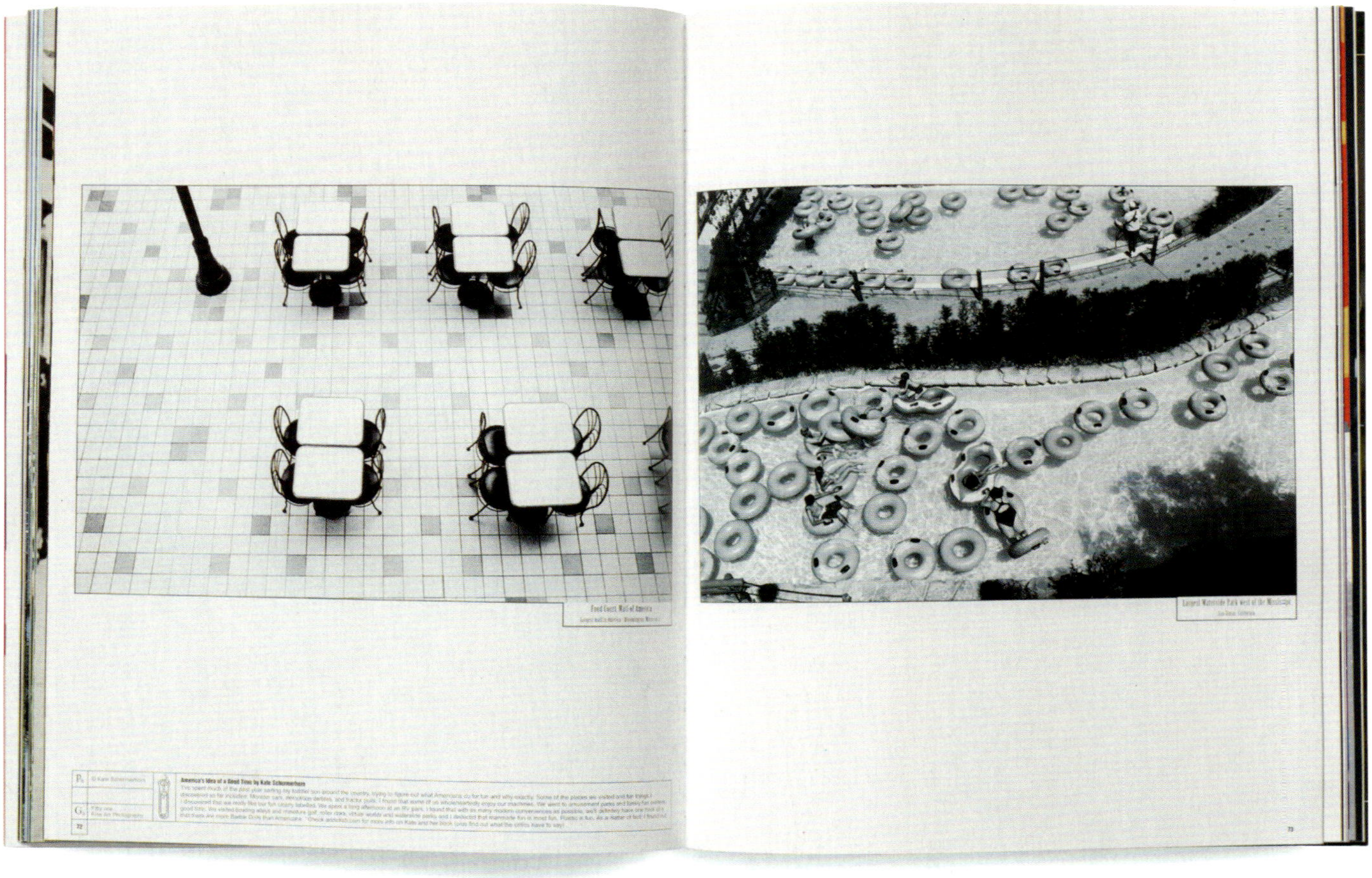

Ad!dict, Spring 2001, Belgium

Wired, February '3000', USA

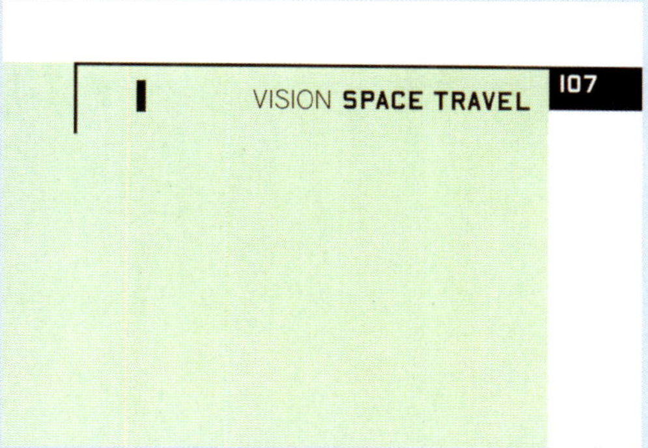

Premium, No. 3, 2001, Germany

Vogue, November 2001, Italy

Details, March 2002, USA

Wired, June 2000, USA

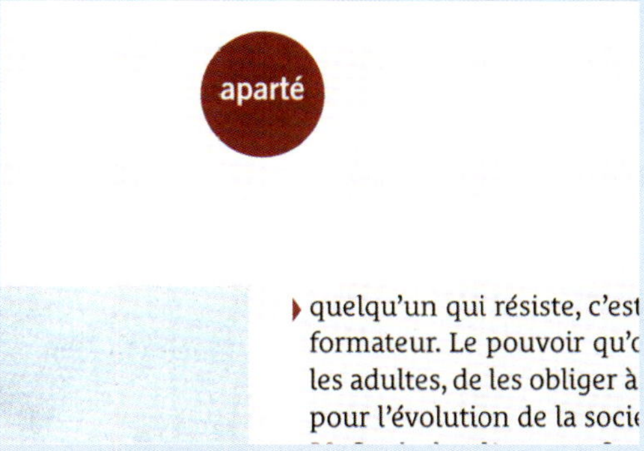

DS, October 2001, France

Squeeze, April/May 2001, Netherlands

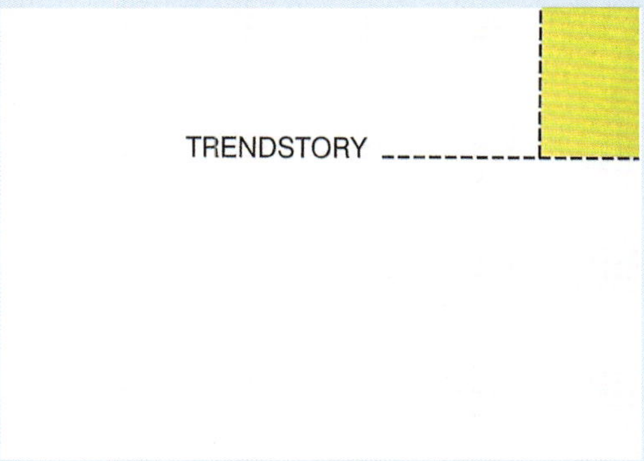

IQ Style, September 2001, Germany

Trace, No. 34, 2001, USA

Mac Magazin, March 2000, Germany

Pur, Autumn 2000, Germany

Junge Karriere (trade paper), March 2002, Germany

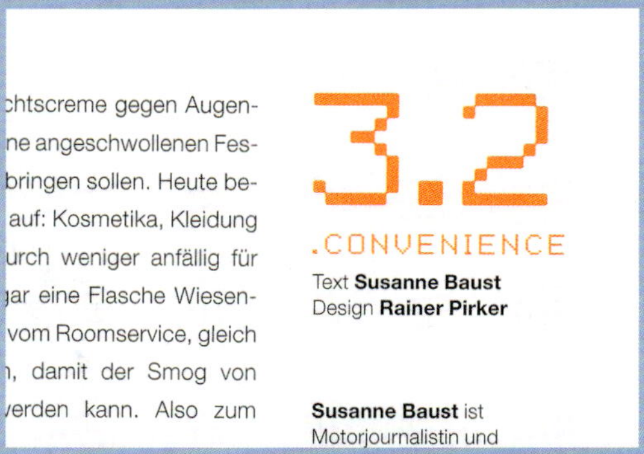

Copy, November 2001, Austria

Spruce, Spring/Summer 2002, USA

Martha Stewart Living, December 2000, USA

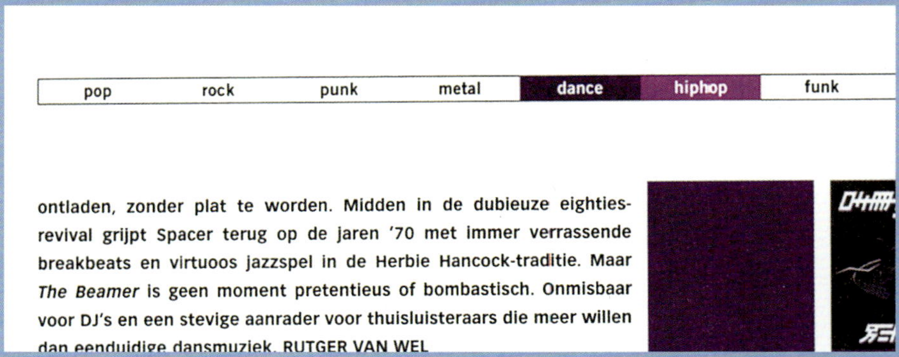

Oor, April 2001, Netherlands

Wired, February '3000', USA

Martha Stewart Living, December 2000, USA

CineChart, November 2001, Germany

Wallpaper, May 2001, Great Britain

Details, March 2002, USA

Vogue Paris, February 2001, France

Mutabor, No. 10, 2002, Germany

Buch Journal, Autumn 2001, Germany

The basis of orientation in magazines

Page numbers are the most basic functional component of any magazine. With their help readers should be able to find their way round the content, but first they need to actually see the numbers – and that's not always easy. The bigger the magazine, the more difficult it is, because generally the thickness is due to a preponderance of unnumbered ads and supplements. Or alternatively, the designer's creative talents have been focused on an element that really should not be the object of their love of experimentation. If you want to spare your reader the pangs of frustration, put your numbers at the bottom of each page, either on the outside or in the middle. In newspaper design it's the top that's favoured, and if your magazine is divided into different sections, the top is also a possibility. In fact nowadays both positions – top and bottom – are equally common. What's really confusing is when both numbers for a double-page spread are put together on just one page. Let's face it, the wheel cannot be reinvented or improved, and similarly any deviation from normal pagination can seem artificial. Even experimental magazines sometimes have to make use of the basics.

IdN, No. 8, 2001, China (Hong Kong)

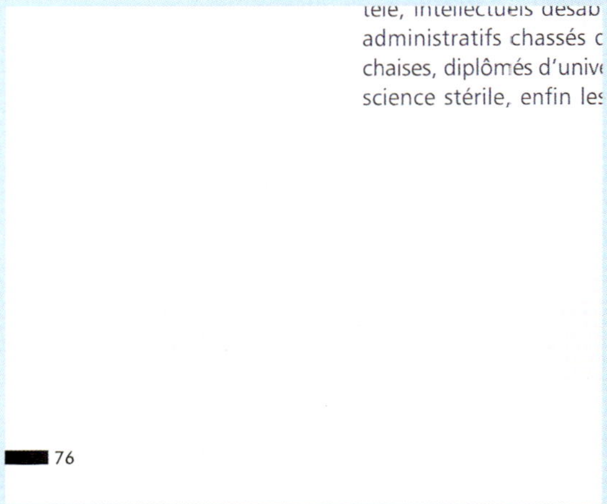

Mixt(e), No. 9, 2000, France

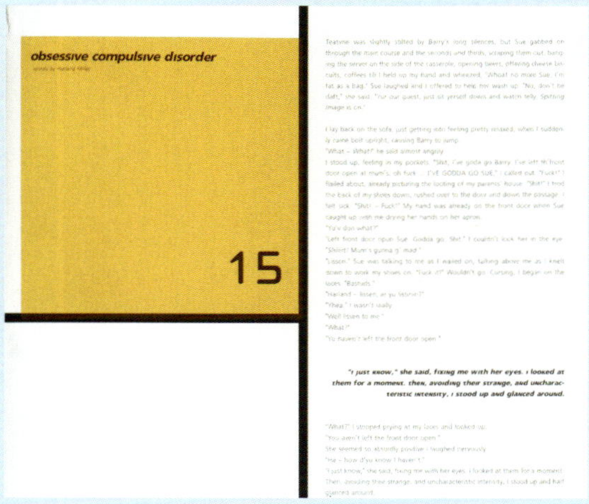

Tank, No. 3, 2001, Great Britain

Pop (The Face), Spring/Summer 2002, Great Britain

Greenpeace Magazin, No. 1, 2000, Germany

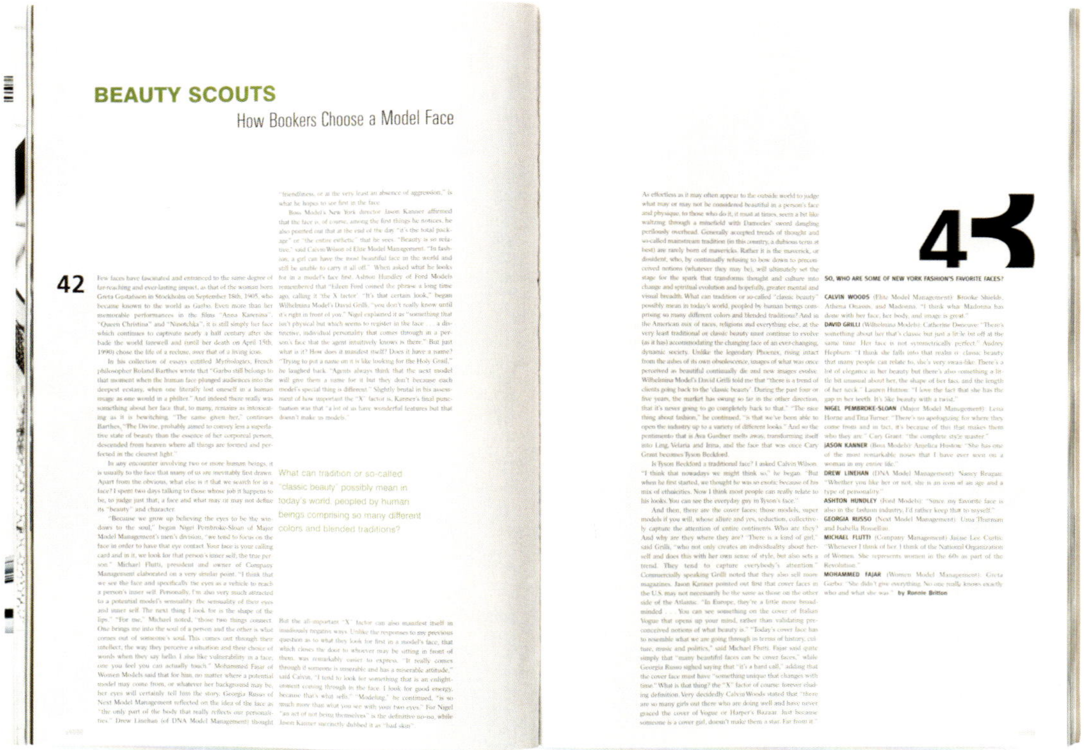

Arude, No. 12, 1999, USA

Surface, No. 32, 2001, USA

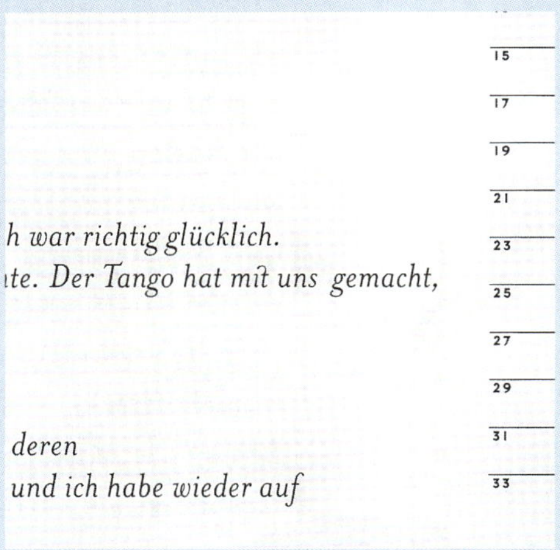

Artur, Summer 1997, Germany

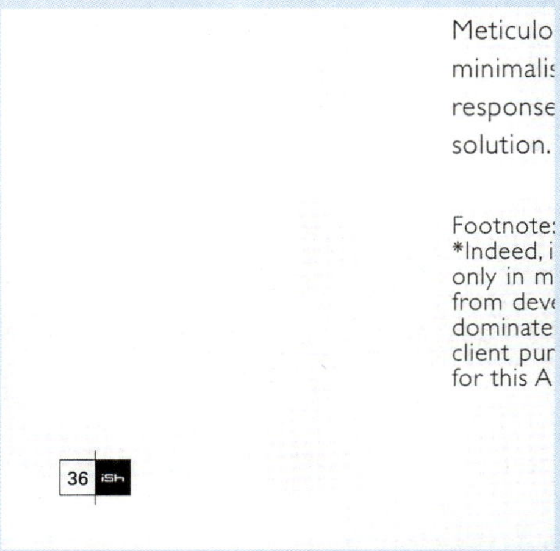

Ish, August 1999, Singapore

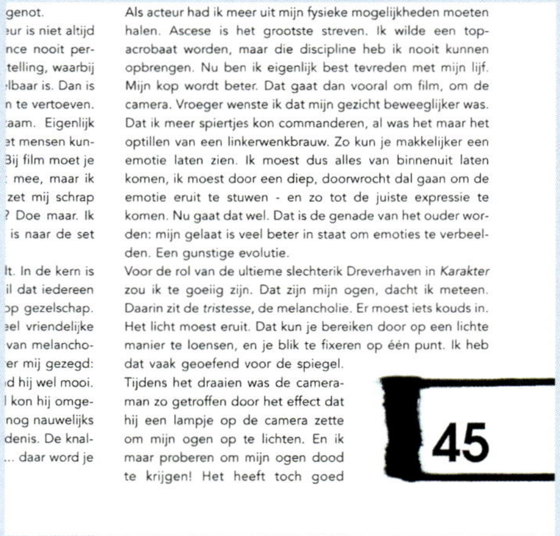
Als acteur had ik meer uit mijn fysieke mogelijkheden moeten halen. Ascese is het grootste streven. Ik wilde een topacrobaat worden, maar die discipline heb ik nooit kunnen opbrengen. Nu ben ik eigenlijk best tevreden met mijn lijf. Mijn kop wordt beter. Dat gaat dan vooral om film, om de camera. Vroeger wenste ik dat mijn gezicht beweeglijker was. Dat ik meer spiertjes kon commanderen, al was het maar het optillen van een linkerwenkbrauw. Zo kun je makkelijker een emotie laten zien. Ik moest dus alles van binnenuit laten komen, ik moest door een diep, doorwrocht dal gaan om de emotie eruit te stuwen - en zo tot de juiste expressie te komen. Nu gaat dat wel. Dat is de genade van het ouder worden: mijn gelaat is veel beter in staat om emoties te verbeelden. Een gunstige evolutie.

Voor de rol van de ultieme slechterik Dreverhaven in *Karakter* zou ik te goeiig zijn. Dat zijn mijn ogen, dacht ik meteen. Daarin zit de *tristesse*, de melancholie. Er moest iets kouds in. Het licht moest eruit. Dat kun je bereiken door op een lichte manier te loensen, en je blik te fixeren op één punt. Ik heb dat vaak geoefend voor de spiegel.

Tijdens het draaien was de cameraman zo getroffen door het effect dat hij een lampje op de camera zette om mijn ogen op te lichten. En ik maar proberen om mijn ogen dood te krijgen! Het heeft toch goed

45

Rails, November 2001, Netherlands

RE, Spring 2001, Netherlands

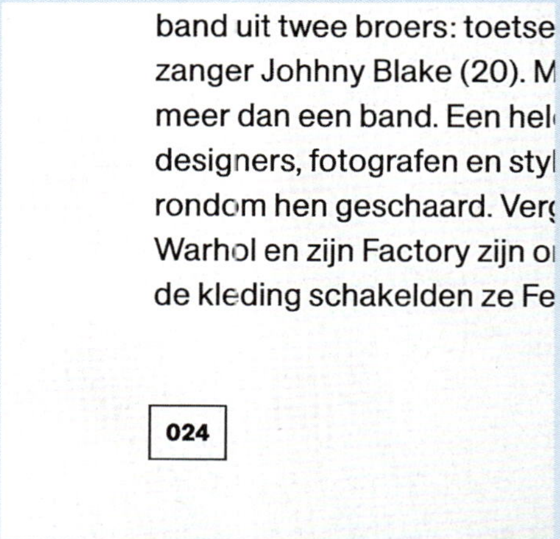

Squeeze, April/May 2001, Netherlands

Artur No19
noch 10 Seiten

Artur, Spring 1999, Germany

Style, February 2001, Germany

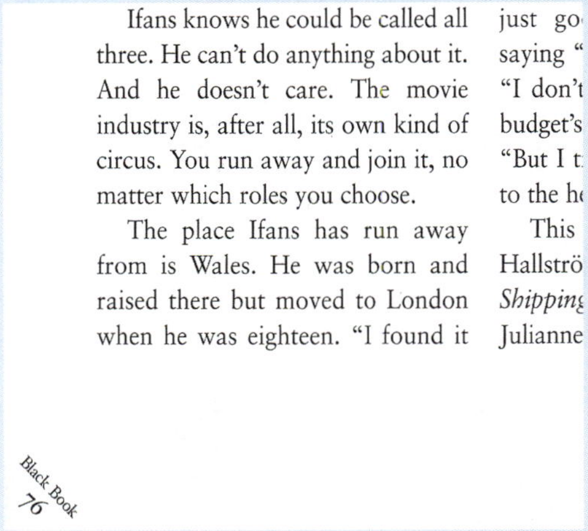

Ifans knows he could be called all three. He can't do anything about it. And he doesn't care. The movie industry is, after all, its own kind of circus. You run away and join it, no matter which roles you choose.

The place Ifans has run away from is Wales. He was born and raised there but moved to London when he was eighteen. "I found it

just go
saying "
"I don't
budget's
"But I t
to the h
This
Hallströ
Shipping
Julianne

Black Book
76

Black Book, Spring 2002, USA

Jeunes Créateurs, No. 6, 2001, France

Different methods of indicating the start of a text

In formal terms, the initial letter (or letters) naturally signifies the beginning of the text. The art of illuminated lettering reached perfection especially in religious books between 800 and 1450. The first letter would be large and impressive, richly embellished, painted in glowing colours and partly gilded. The direct opposite of this is the Bauhaus technique of the 1920s and 1930s, which radically reduced the importance of the initial letter, not only out of antipathy towards the decorative, but also out of hierarchical considerations. Jan Tschichold, however, who was an enthusiastic missionary for Bauhaus ideas, actually reverted in his old age to classical typography, which included the special first letter.

It's possible to distinguish, for example, between the following forms:

- The initial that covers two to five lines.
- The initial that starts on the first line but juts out high above it.
- The initial that stands outside the column.

In the US a different form has become very popular: printing the first three words in block capitals. The repertoire has also been extended by the use of arrows and other symbols. At the beginning of the twenty-first century, special initials are no longer in vogue, but the chances are that this trend will change again, and giant letters like those of Willy Fleckhaus will eventually make a comeback. Their effectiveness depends not only on size, but also on the choice of script. Should you use the same font as in the rest of the text, or deliberately draw attention to the initial by using a different font? And should you only use this at the beginning of the text or repeat it at the start of every paragraph? These are decisions that must be taken in the context of the overall typographical design. From a technical point of view, you need to bear in mind that QuarkXpress does not allow for a great deal of sophistication when it comes to the layout of initials within columns. It's therefore a good idea to give the initial a text box of its own. The size of the first letter should fit in nicely with the headline and the text itself; if there's not much difference between them, the effect can be ugly, especially if they're very close to one another. It's become common practice now to have headline and initial the same size and in the same font, but this isn't very attractive aesthetically. The combination of different fonts demands a high degree of typographical self-confidence. In an unpublished literary supplement for the Swiss magazine *Weltwoche*, the initial letters were set as individual notes – a bit like the cadenza of a violin concerto – together with an otherwise pure, classical typography. They were the only form in which emotion and interpretation were given expression.

MOVIE-STAR NEWLYWEDS
ANGELINA JOLIE AND BILLY BOB
THORNTON'S DELIGHTFUL NEW HOME
{ PART ONE • THE BEDROOM }

HARRY – who is sometimes known as Fat Harry, and who is actually female (though this fact is routinely and systematically ignored by Angelina Jolie because she really wishes Harry was male), and who is partial to pumpkin pie, and who is a rat – lives a few feet from Jolie and Thornton's bed. Harry, who was a gift from husband to wife, spends his days and nights in a cage on their bedroom floor. Sometimes he is invited out to play.

"Billy found me one day sitting in the bathtub in my pajamas, the rat on my lap, feeding it pumpkin pie," Jolie reminisces. "See, that's one of those things that only somebody that really loves

hanced that much bigger?' " Others were a consequ
Lara Croft: "I don't like seeing her in that position
The marketing people joked to her that maybe s
stores. Jolie shakes her head. "I haven't adjusted m
swears that she doesn't want the kind of fame that
out with normal people in a normal way. "It cou
says. "It could be the thing that sends me . . ." – sl
mental institution. That's what I'm really saying.
a flamboyant metaphor. I will learn.
Billy Bob Thornton arrives home.
"I missed you," he says.
"I missed you too, honey."
They kiss, and as they talk, discussing the day's
traces her index finger up and down the zipper of
She has a question for him.
"Weren't we supposed to get married tonight?"
Thornton turns to me and says, by way of exp
married every now and then," and then adds, by
"We're already married – we're so married." (Th
united Jolie, 26, to Thornton, 45, took place in Las
However, Thornton tells his bride that this lates
pening tonight – they didn't get around to bookin
"You want to do it Thursday?" he asks.
"Yeah," she says.

{ PART TWO • *The Livi*

THE LIVING ROOM, WHERE WE WILL DO MOST
ly empty – apart from the leather sofas and the tab
chair which hangs from the ceiling, the shrine to
and the two framed drawings and poems about Joli
ten by her father, Jon Voight. On the table are so
skateboard, another gift from Thornton. "He thoug
"Which I do." There is also, to one side of the roor
to get five of them so that everyone can saddle up
"We were upstairs the other day just laughing
married and this is our home," Jolie says. "We're
dishwasher. We do the simplest things, like he lig
and I'm floored, I'm so proud." She beams. "We'r
Later, Jolie will tell me about the first time she b

Rolling Stone, July 2001, USA

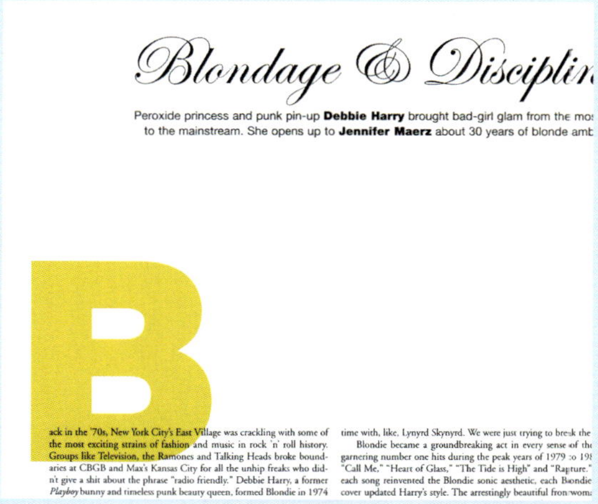

Blondage & Disciplin

Peroxide princess and punk pin-up **Debbie Harry** brought bad-girl glam from the mo
to the mainstream. She opens up to **Jennifer Maerz** about 30 years of blonde amb

Back in the '70s, New York City's East Village was crackling with some of the most exciting strains of fashion and music in rock 'n' roll history. Groups like Television, the Ramones and Talking Heads broke boundaries at CBGB and Max's Kansas City for all the unhip freaks who didn't give a shit about the phrase "radio friendly." Debbie Harry, a former *Playboy* bunny and timeless punk beauty queen, formed Blondie in 1974

time with, like, Lynyrd Skynyrd. We were just trying to break the
Blondie became a groundbreaking act in every sense of th
garnering number one hits during the peak years of 1979 to 19
"Call Me," "Heart of Glass," "The Tide is High" and "Rapture."
each song reinvented the Blondie sonic aesthetic, each Blondie
cover updated Harry's style. The arrestingly beautiful front woma

Detour, Autumn 2001, USA

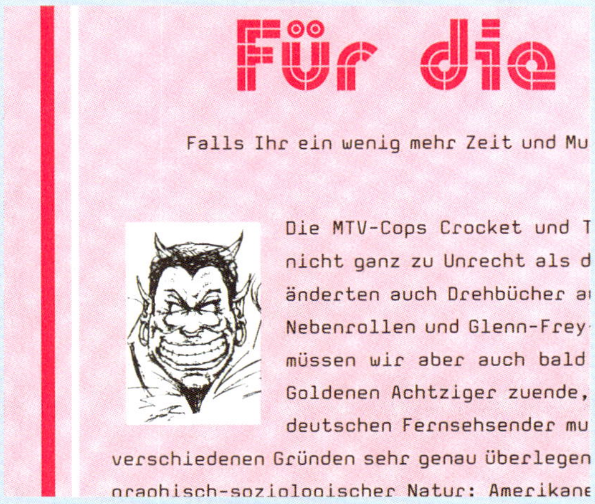

Für die

Falls Ihr ein wenig mehr Zeit und Mu

Die MTV-Cops Crocket und T
nicht ganz zu Unrecht als d
änderten auch Drehbücher a
Nebenrollen und Glenn-Frey
müssen wir aber auch bald
Goldenen Achtziger zuende,
deutschen Fernsehsender mu
verschiedenen Gründen sehr genau überlegen
graphisch-soziologischer Natur: Amerikane

Brett, No. 9, 2000, Germany

as the

arrival of new, fashion and pop
magazines on the media scene reaches fever pitch, it is time for an eva
This large group of small publications has profoundly affected the
mainstream media and advertising, serving as the latest ground for visu

It started as a curiosity in the 1970s and '80s: the creation of pop culture magazines by a handful of visionaries prepared to offer an innovative, avant-garde take on fashion in contrast to the oligarchy of the mainstream press. Their view of the world, often inspired by the look of the street and the culture of the night, was a defiant and radical departure from the reigning spectrum of fashion publications in its refusal to stay between the lines of Hollywood glamour and catalogue chic. But from a counter-culture manifestation aimed at the few and disenfranchised, the niche press has matured into a full-bodied medium of its own. Its pioneers, titles like, Interview

houses and advertisers? Most profoundly, what purpose is it all serving? And most critically, can it last?

To be sure, the attention focused on independent magazines recently, has done its part to swell their ranks. Widespread technology has completely revolutionized publishing—quite obviously online, but in print as well—to the point that anybody with a computer, a contact-laden PR pal, and a dream can start a magazine. A visit to 0fr, the leading Paris-based distributor for style-conscious, cutting-edge publications, reveals mountains of these books; some that regularly and consistently present their evolving

million individuals and total annual
nue estimated roughly at $10 million
to a single issue of American Vogue.

Regardless: though individually sm
ther these publications are a major
hing the limits of creativity and f
Typically built on the intuition of a c
tors, art directors, photographers
magazines are strong, highly pers
and visions of the world as shared b
Their liberation from the pressures
tability to a higher corporate rule e
take risks and often controversial a

Selfservice, No. 14, 2001, France

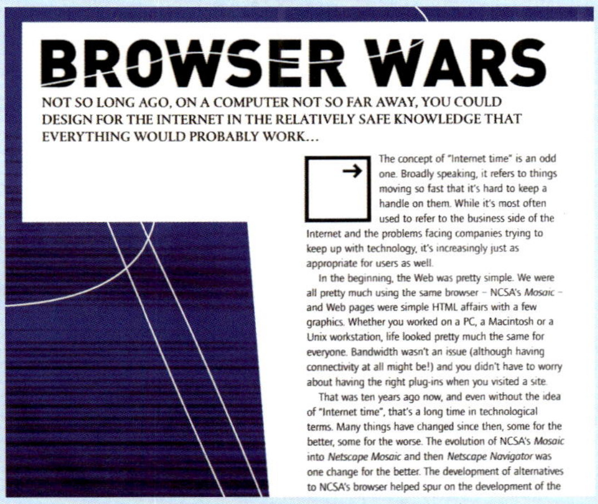

BROWSER WARS

NOT SO LONG AGO, ON A COMPUTER NOT SO FAR AWAY, YOU COULD DESIGN FOR THE INTERNET IN THE RELATIVELY SAFE KNOWLEDGE THAT EVERYTHING WOULD PROBABLY WORK…

The concept of "Internet time" is an odd one. Broadly speaking, it refers to things moving so fast that it's hard to keep a handle on them. While it's most often used to refer to the business side of the Internet and the problems facing companies trying to keep up with technology, it's increasingly just as appropriate for users as well.

In the beginning, the Web was pretty simple. We were all pretty much using the same browser – NCSA's *Mosaic* – and Web pages were simple HTML affairs with a few graphics. Whether you worked on a PC, a Macintosh or a Unix workstation, life looked pretty much the same for everyone. Bandwidth wasn't an issue (although having connectivity at all might be!) and you didn't have to worry about having the right plug-ins when you visited a site.

That was ten years ago now, and even without the idea of "Internet time", that's a long time in technological terms. Many things have changed since then, some for the better, some for the worse. The evolution of NCSA's *Mosaic* into *Netscape Mosaic* and then *Netscape Navigator* was one change for the better. The development of alternatives to NCSA's browser helped spur on the development of the

Cre@te online, April 2001, Great Britain

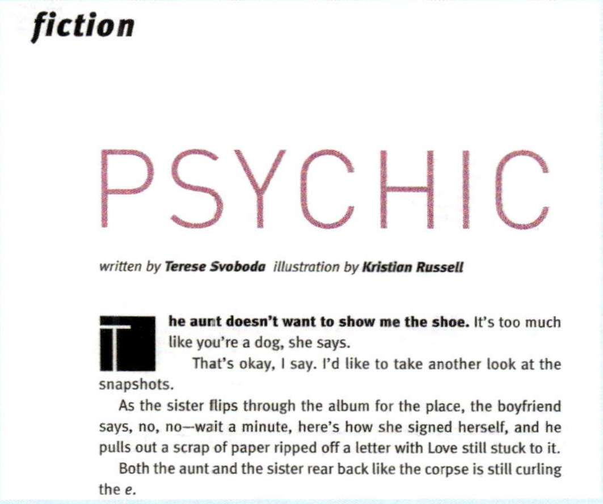

fiction

PSYCHIC

written by ***Terese Svoboda*** *illustration by* ***Kristian Russell***

The aunt doesn't want to show me the shoe. It's too much like you're a dog, she says.

That's okay, I say. I'd like to take another look at the snapshots.

As the sister flips through the album for the place, the boyfriend says, no, no—wait a minute, here's how she signed herself, and he pulls out a scrap of paper ripped off a letter with Love still stuck to it.

Both the aunt and the sister rear back like the corpse is still curling the *e*.

Flaunt, Spring 2001, USA

NATÜRLICH zu einer Zeit, als - möchte man den Veterane
ben - in Brasilien noch Milch und Honig floss
ganz normaler Alltag für den betuchten Mittelstand war, den d
mit Marcos teilten. Für Joao Gilberto, Vinicius de Moraes, Ba
Regina und viele andere Bossa-Nova-Künstler, die Ende der
musikalischen Zirkel bildeten, war das Leben nicht schwer.
Clubs, Bars und Theatern, musizierte gemeinsam und tauscht
Musiker aus wohlhabenden Familien kamen, hatten sie eine
genossen, gehörten zur intellektuellen Oberschicht Rio de Jane
mit profanem Geldverdienen zu beschäftigen. Valle: "Der Bos
Sommer, Strand und dem Rio-de-Janeiro-Gefühl." So konnte m
ren, in Musikschulen Unterricht nehmen oder geben. Doch t
waren die Bossa Nova-Musiker auch der Musik der Armenvierte
Sambatrommeln auf klassischen Instrumenten nach zu empfin
ter auch Funkelemente zu erweitern, war zwar nicht klar formu
aber bald als stilübergreifendes Merkmal des Bossa Nova hera
traditionellen Samba verändert, erweiterte ihn um reichere H
und eine andere Rhythmik", weiß Veteran Valle zu berichte
Gesangsbetonung lehnten sich an die perkussive Musik mi
Wurzeln an. Weil es für Derartiges keinen eigenen Namen gab
Beschreibung eines Journalisten, der über dieses "neue Ding"
Marcos Valle betrat die Bossa-Bühne ein wenig später als Jo

Style, June 2001, Germany

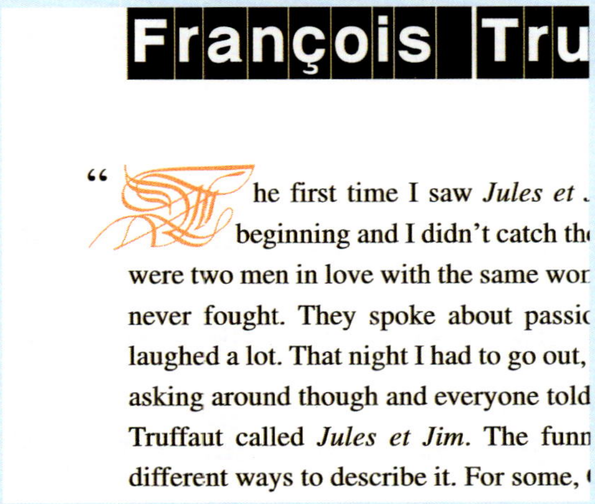

François Tru

"The first time I saw *Jules et J*
beginning and I didn't catch th
were two men in love with the same wo
never fought. They spoke about passi
laughed a lot. That night I had to go out,
asking around though and everyone told
Truffaut called *Jules et Jim*. The funn
different ways to describe it. For some,

Another Magazine, Spring/Summer 2002, Great Britain

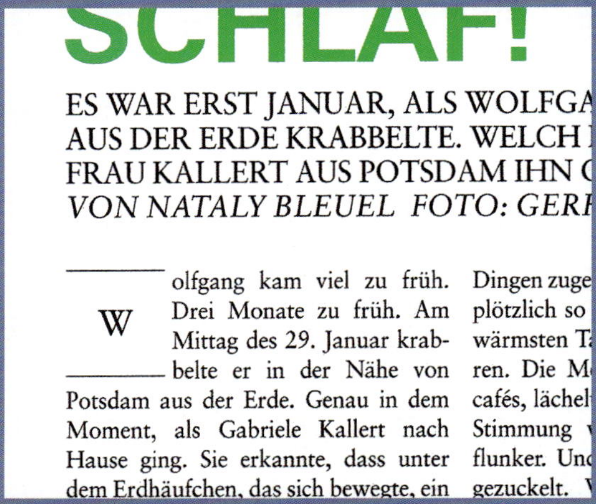

SCHLAF!

ES WAR ERST JANUAR, ALS WOLFGA
AUS DER ERDE KRABBELTE. WELCH
FRAU KALLERT AUS POTSDAM IHN
VON NATALY BLEUEL FOTO: GERI

Wolfgang kam viel zu früh. Drei Monate zu früh. Am Mittag des 29. Januar krabbelte er in der Nähe von Potsdam aus der Erde. Genau in dem Moment, als Gabriele Kallert nach Hause ging. Sie erkannte, dass unter dem Erdhäufchen, das sich bewegte, ein

Süddeutsche Zeitung Magazin, March 2002, Germany

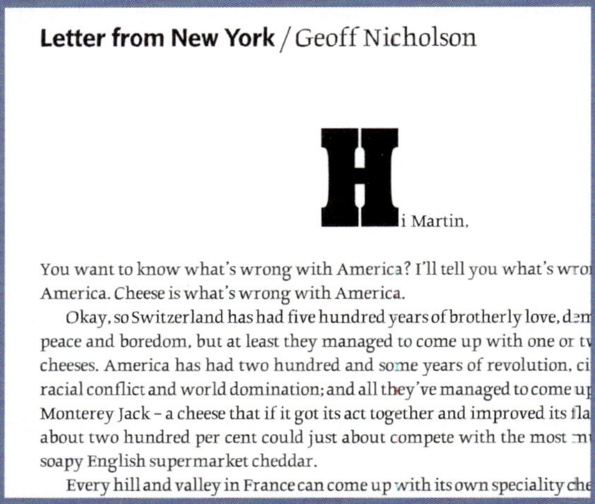

Letter from New York / Geoff Nicholson

Hi Martin,

You want to know what's wrong with America? I'll tell you what's wro
America. Cheese is what's wrong with America.

Okay, so Switzerland has had five hundred years of brotherly love, de
peace and boredom, but at least they managed to come up with one or t
cheeses. America has had two hundred and some years of revolution, ci
racial conflict and world domination; and all they've managed to come u
Monterey Jack – a cheese that if it got its act together and improved its fla
about two hundred per cent could just about compete with the most
soapy English supermarket cheddar.

Every hill and valley in France can come up with its own speciality che

Ambit, No. 161, 2000, Great Britain

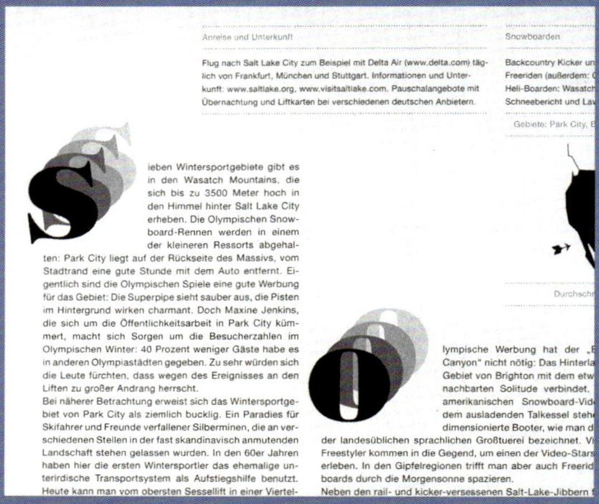

Anreise und Unterkunft

Flug nach Salt Lake City zum Beispiel mit Delta Air (www.delta.com) täglich von Frankfurt, München und Stuttgart. Informationen und Unterkunft: www.saltlake.org, www.visitsaltlake.com. Pauschalangebote mit Übernachtung und Liftkarten bei verschiedenen deutschen Anbietern.

Sieben Wintersportgebiete gibt es in den Wasatch Mountains, die sich bis zu 3500 Meter hoch in den Himmel hinter Salt Lake City erheben. Die Olympischen Snowboard-Rennen werden in einem der kleineren Ressorts abgehalten: Park City liegt auf der Rückseite des Massivs, vom Stadtrand eine gute Stunde mit dem Auto entfernt. Eigentlich sind die Olympischen Spiele eine gute Werbung für das Gebiet: Die Superpipe sieht sauber aus, die Pisten im Hintergrund wirken charmant. Doch Maxine Jenkins, die sich um die Öffentlichkeitsarbeit in Park City kümmert, macht sich Sorgen um die Besucherzahlen im Olympischen Winter: 40 Prozent weniger Gäste habe es in anderen Olympiastädten gegeben. Zu sehr würden sich die Leute fürchten, dass wegen des Ereignisses an den Liften zu großer Andrang herrscht.

Bei näherer Betrachtung erweist sich das Wintersportgebiet von Park City als ziemlich bucklig. Ein Paradies für Skifahrer und Freunde verfallener Silberminen, die an verschiedenen Stellen in der fast skandinavisch anmutenden Landschaft stehen gelassen wurden. In den 60er Jahren haben hier die ersten Wintersportler das ehemalige unterirdische Transportsystem als Aufstiegshilfe benutzt. Heute kann man vom obersten Sessellift in einer Viertel-

Snow, No. 2, 2002, Germany

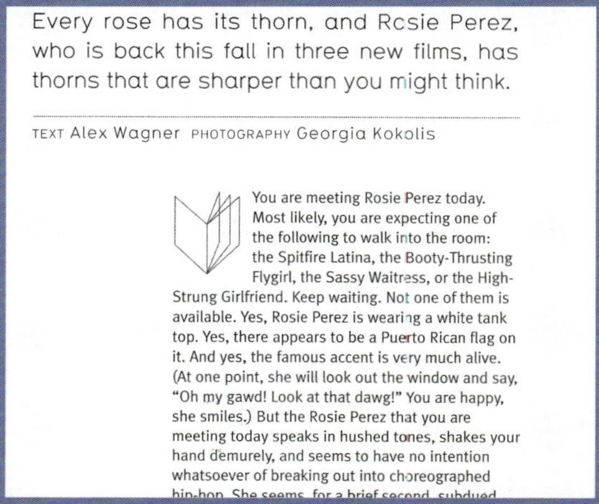

Every rose has its thorn, and Rosie Perez, who is back this fall in three new films, has thorns that are sharper than you might think.

TEXT Alex Wagner PHOTOGRAPHY Georgia Kokolis

You are meeting Rosie Perez today. Most likely, you are expecting one of the following to walk into the room: the Spitfire Latina, the Booty-Thrusting Flygirl, the Sassy Waitress, or the High-Strung Girlfriend. Keep waiting. Not one of them is available. Yes, Rosie Perez is wearing a white tank top. Yes, there appears to be a Puerto Rican flag on it. And yes, the famous accent is very much alive. (At one point, she will look out the window and say, "Oh my gawd! Look at that dawg!" You are happy, she smiles.) But the Rosie Perez that you are meeting today speaks in hushed tones, shakes your hand demurely, and seems to have no intention whatsoever of breaking out into choreographed

Black Book, Autumn 2001, USA

a

MARC NEWSON

Is er één designer is waarvan we in de toekomst veel mogen verwachten, dan is het wel deze van oorsprong Australische Engelsman. Op z'n zesendertigste heeft hij al zo ongeveer alles ontworpen wat je kunt bedenken: van horloges, afdruiprekjes en flessenopeners tot en met meubels, fietsen, auto's en vliegtuigen. Hij bedient zich van een aanstekelijke en inmiddels invloedrijke stijl, een actueel soort futurisme, dat naadloos aansluit bij alle jonge hippe stromingen van dit moment. Marc Newson is onlangs ontdekt als dè nieuwe design-ster van nu, terwijl hij toch al een dikke tien jaar hard bezig is.

Vooral een futuristische auto voor Ford en de private jet waarvoor hij het interieur en het grafisch design van de buitenkant verzorgde, bezorgden Newson de nodige sterrenstatus. En hij heeft ook alles in huis om zich als een echte ster te presenteren.

Man, March 2000, Netherlands

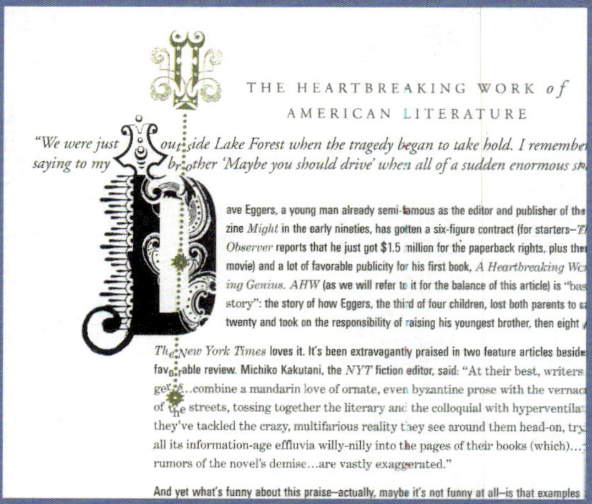

THE HEARTBREAKING WORK *of* AMERICAN LITERATURE

"We were just outside Lake Forest when the tragedy began to take hold. I remember saying to my brother 'Maybe you should drive' when all of a sudden enormous s

Dave Eggers, a young man already semi-famous as the editor and publisher of the zine *Might* in the early nineties, has gotten a six-figure contract (for starters–*The Observer* reports that he just got $1.5 million for the paperback rights, plus the movie) and a lot of favorable publicity for his first book, *A Heartbreaking Wo ing Genius*. *AHW* (as we will refer to it for the balance of this article) is "bas story": the story of how Eggers, the third of four children, lost both parents to c twenty and took on the responsibility of raising his youngest brother, then eight

The New York Times loves it. It's been extravagantly praised in two feature articles beside favorable review. Michiko Kakutani, the *NYT* fiction editor, said: "At their best, writers ge ...combine a mandarin love of ornate, even byzantine prose with the vernac of the streets, tossing together the literary and the colloquial with hyperventila they've tackled the crazy, multifarious reality they see around them head-on, try all its information-age effluvia willy-nilly into the pages of their books (which)... rumors of the novel's demise...are vastly exaggerated."

And yet what's funny about this praise–actually, maybe it's not funny at all–is that examples

Speak, Summer 2000, USA

Artur, Summer 1998, Germany

Rolling Stone, June 2000, USA

A way of dividing up long texts

Longer texts can be structured through the use of subheadings, of which there are two basic types. The first is determined by the content of the article and denotes the start of a new segment. From a design point of view, this type of subheading cannot be shifted. The second type is movable, and can be inserted wherever the designer feels it should go. Its function is to create an optical break in the mass of text, and so its content must be less precise because the text will, so to speak, flow round it.

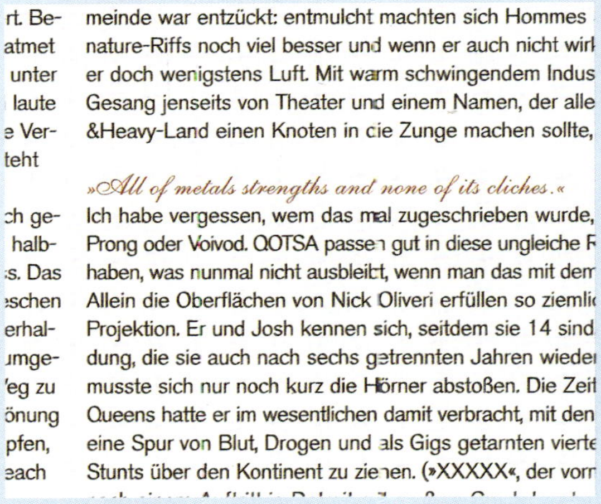
rt. Be- atmet unter laute e Ver- teht meinde war entzückt: entmulcht machten sich Hommes nature-Riffs noch viel besser und wenn er auch nicht wir er doch wenigstens Luft. Mit warm schwingendem Indus Gesang jenseits von Theater und einem Namen, der alle &Heavy-Land einen Knoten in die Zunge machen sollte,

»All of metals strengths and none of its cliches.«

ch ge- halb- s. Das eschen erhal- umge- Weg zu önung pfen, each Ich habe vergessen, wem das mal zugeschrieben wurde, Prong oder Voivod. QOTSA passen gut in diese ungleiche F haben, was nunmal nicht ausbleibt, wenn man das mit dem Allein die Oberflächen von Nick Oliveri erfüllen so ziemli Projektion. Er und Josh kennen sich, seitdem sie 14 sind dung, die sie auch nach sechs getrennten Jahren wieder musste sich nur noch kurz die Hörner abstoßen. Die Zeit Queens hatte er im wesentlichen damit verbracht, mit den eine Spur von Blut, Drogen und als Gigs getarnten vierte Stunts über den Kontinent zu ziehen. (»XXXXX«, der vorr

Spex, No. 8, 2002, Germany

Die Medien haben ihn in den letzten Jahren grausam behandelt

Es gab auch einen George, der extrem zynisch sein konnte

54 · Rolling Stone, Februar, 2002

Rolling Stone, February 2002, Germany

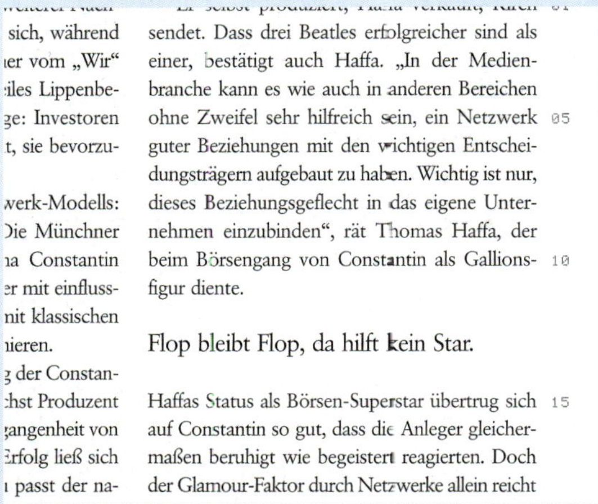
sich, während er vom „Wir" iles Lippenbe- ge: Investoren t, sie bevorzu- werk-Modells: Die Münchner a Constantin er mit einfluss- mit klassischen ieren. sendet. Dass drei Beatles erfolgreicher sind als einer, bestätigt auch Haffa. „In der Medienbranche kann es wie auch in anderen Bereichen ohne Zweifel sehr hilfreich sein, ein Netzwerk guter Beziehungen mit den wichtigen Entscheidungsträgern aufgebaut zu haben. Wichtig ist nur, dieses Beziehungsgeflecht in das eigene Unternehmen einzubinden", rät Thomas Haffa, der beim Börsengang von Constantin als Gallionsfigur diente.

Flop bleibt Flop, da hilft kein Star.

g der Constan- chst Produzent gangenheit von Erfolg ließ sich passt der na- Haffas Status als Börsen-Superstar übertrug sich auf Constantin so gut, dass die Anleger gleichermaßen beruhigt wie begeistert reagierten. Doch der Glamour-Faktor durch Netzwerke allein reicht

Brand eins, February 2000, Germany

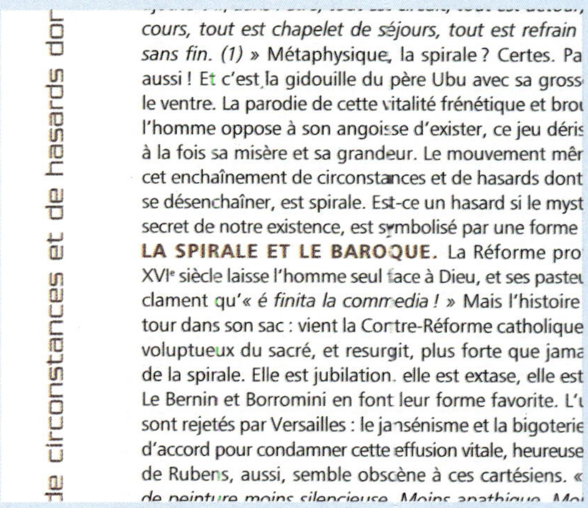

cours, tout est chapelet de séjours, tout est refrain sans fin. (1) » Métaphysique, la spirale ? Certes. Pa aussi ! Et c'est la gidouille du père Ubu avec sa gross le ventre. La parodie de cette vitalité frénétique et brou l'homme oppose à son angoisse d'exister, ce jeu déris à la fois sa misère et sa grandeur. Le mouvement mêr cet enchaînement de circonstances et de hasards dont se désenchaîner, est spirale. Est-ce un hasard si le myst secret de notre existence, est symbolisé par une forme **LA SPIRALE ET LE BAROQUE.** La Réforme pro XVIe siècle laisse l'homme seul face à Dieu, et ses pasteu clament qu'« *é finita la commedia !* » Mais l'histoire tour dans son sac : vient la Contre-Réforme catholique voluptueux du sacré, et resurgit, plus forte que jama de la spirale. Elle est jubilation. elle est extase, elle est Le Bernin et Borromini en font leur forme favorite. L'u sont rejetés par Versailles : le jansénisme et la bigoterie d'accord pour condamner cette effusion vitale, heureuse de Rubens, aussi, semble obscène à ces cartésiens. «

Mixt(e), No. 9, 2000, France

d

Uno

De Degas contó John Berger que después de decir que hay amor y una vida de trabajo y un solo corazón él eligió y puso su corazón en su vida de trabajo. Boris Pasternak escribió: "Si el lector continúa con esta frase, empezará una tormenta de nieve". William Blake dio antes otro salto mortal: "Quien desea y no actúa engendra la peste", que no sé hasta qué punto cortó la hierba para que Albert Camus hablara del "divorcio entre la mente que desea y el mundo que decepciona". Degas y Blake eligieron, Pasternak convocó su tormenta entre los abedules y Camus se estrelló antes de que hubiera consumado la decepción de su deseo. Hay santos de tu devoción y santos de tu desdén. Las frases hechas son campos minados. Vienen a la lengua impulsadas por halcones tan peregrinos como el de la pereza, el desdén, la necesidad, la desesperación e incluso la melancolía, un agente no consolidado entre los enemigos del capitalismo. Demasiado laxo para ser considerado como un terrorista de confianza, demasiado sutil para que se sacuda el barro de los zapatos cuando los analistas esparcen sobre el damero maldito las condiciones objetivas y las otras. Roald Dahl no es santo de mi devoción, pero dice: "Sólo los hombres jóvenes estallan con violencia, creo que por estar aburridos. Pero en general el ser humano no es muy agradable. No es un animal bueno". Descifrar a Isaac Albéniz no es lo mismo que descifrar a Roald Dahl. Para descifrar a Albéniz no basta con saber tocar el piano. Para descifrar a Dahl basta con tener algún sentido. Cinco dedos no son cinco sentidos. Las frases fuera de contexto son más fáciles de descifrar que los discursos íntegros, igual que no es lo mismo descifrar la *Suite Iberia* que *Rondeña*, ni recordar lo que sabemos mientras escuchamos que comprobar lo que sentimos mientras vemos el mar desde el hotelito azul de la Isleta del Moro, acabamos de casarnos, nos hemos dado cuenta de nuestro soberano error y nos aferramos a *El sentido de la vista* para descifrar el tiempo que hace fuera y el tiempo que hace en nuestro interior. También Rafael Sánchez-Ferlosio, este sí santo de mi devoción, tal vez porque tiene poco de santo y aborrece las devociones, sobre todo las que le suben a él a la peana, aunque sea una peana cívica y de palosanto, o incluso de palo de limonero, blanco luminoso y flexible, dijo una vez que "ojalá" tuviera él dentro un "buen animal". Damos palos de ciego y parece como si diéramos luz a cuartos cerrados. Tragaluces donde el cerebro lleva siglos estibado, envuelto en fardos negros de hule y duelas. Damos de comer a nuestra melancolía y desciframos dos palabras, como si la palabra animal dividiera el mundo en dos, en diez, en doce, en dividendos que dieran trigo como a veces dan los sueños.

Dos

Dice Roald Dahl que el niño ve a los adultos como "unos gigantes. Todos los adultos que rodean a un niño, desde padres a profesores, les dicen continuamente lo que deben hacer. Los niños siempre verán a los adultos como enemigos porque al nacer uno está incivilizado y el proceso para hacernos personas civilizadas es doloroso, difícil y hostil. Si tú tienes que escribir libros que gusten a los niños debes estar de su parte, contra los mayores. Este es el secreto para escribir libros para niños".

(La primera recapitulación de dados y des dice: devoción, desdén y desesperación, tras pasar por la estación del deseo que destila decepción. Y sigue así, pero saliendo del espejo hasta este lado de la nada: debes, difícil, doloroso, dicen y dan dividendos, es decir: doce, diez y dos. El columpio colgaba del nogal no del dondiego ni del dátil, y con el rumor del mundo y del invierno, mientras mi abuela deambulaba entre los espantapájaros de la higuera y del maíz, y cantaba: dividiera, desciframos, damos. Las galletas de coco como una forma de alquilar el hórreo vacío y frío del mundo. Si aquí das un salto mortal puede que dudes y en esa duda te pierdas y te rompas la crisma. Pero sin duda no hay circo y menos teatro. Eso es la escritura o ese es el juego de las divisiones, de uno en uno, de dos en dos, de tres en tres, hasta darte cuenta de que esta no era la dirección que habías pensado tomar cuando pensaste en Dresde, Dios, dinero, duro, diezmo, Danubio, dalia, dedicatoria, decimal, durante, día, después, domesticar, Dublín, dulce, diario, dinosaurio, delfín, Duero.

Dos otra vez: por un lado Dallas/Texas, por el otro Guy Debord. Pero veamos cómo se barajan estas cartas que nunca dan dos ni tres ni todo lo contrario, mientras jugamos a vernos en el espejo, es por la mañana, es por la tarde, nos damos una vuelta por nuestras devociones, nos casamos, nos descasamos, nos masturbamos, nos amamos, nos desamamos, partimos el pan como lo hacía Dios vestido de Jesucristo jugando a los dados del destino, partimos en tren como partía Miguel de Unamuno, con una mano en el corazón y la otra en el junquillo de los sueños. Es el turno del discurso de Michel Baier, que dejó escrito: "La moral de *Dallas* representa la justificación de las reglas de intercambio: todo don debe tener un contra don". Su argumento sigue después de un punto y aparte, que en este caso es como uno de aquellos pasos a nivel de Kiev bajo el disfraz del comunismo, bajo la nieve sucia que pisó Walter Benjamin en Moscú mientras dudaba acerca de cómo escribir acerca de Goethe y Asja Lacis le decía que sí y que no al mismo tiempo, y todas las ventanas encendidas en los edificios hablaban de una melancolía proletaria tan temprano, tan temprano. Hace catorce años que Michel Baier dejó escrito en un diario que ya no es el que era (aunque me temo que ninguno fuimos jamás los que creímos ser, los que fuimos aunque lo dijéramos y halláramos fotos que parecen corroborar con nuestro aspecto lo que pensábamos pese a lo que decíamos): "Una moral semejante" (la moral de *Dallas*, conviene recordar después de tanta agua dura y panzuda bajo los puentes) "se adapta perfectamente a la idea que todos tenemos de Texas. Dallas es la ciudad donde se ha cometido el parricidio por excelencia: el asesinato de un presidente. Todos se toman la justicia por su mano, en contra de las leyes más fundamentales. Texas concentra en un sólo lugar el pasado y el presente de Estados Unidos: el pasado, con la conquista del Oeste y los ranchos; el presente, con el mundo de los negocios y el petróleo. Así, viendo el folletín, los estadounidenses vuelven a vivir la formación de su sociedad: todavía no se ha consolidado la moral; tiene que vérselas seriamente con la inmoralidad. Pero una moral semejante también es universal". ¿Qué pinta aquí *Dallas*, con tan poquitas des para paliar la duda de si dorar la píldora con dudosas maniobras para que la página sea duradera?

Ahora que los medios de comunicación de masas se han convertido en agentes de festejos del pensamiento único sacamos a un suicida del armario de su propio olvido y leemos sus palabras como si el mar no borrara una y otra vez la antigua pizarra de arena y Guy Debord no se hubiera arrancado de cuajo de este lado de la pista de patinaje. "El espectáculo es la ideología por excelencia, porque expone y manifiesta en toda su plenitud la esencia de todo sistema ideológico: el empobrecimiento, la sumisión y la negación de la vida real". Qué mejor ejemplo que el de la devoración de África, convertida por los medios en una constelación de volcanes en erupción, que deslumbra primero y abruma después, pero que no explica el contenido de la historia ni el reparto de las culpas, no sólo grabadas en los hombros de los colonizadores, sino también a prorratear entre muchos africanos que se convirtieron en los más entusiastas practicantes de una nueva colonización de sus pueblos. África como líquido de revelado. El dramaturgo de Congo-Brazzaville Sony Labou Tansi fustiga a los africanos a través de su personaje de Mallot en *Je soussigné cardiaque*: "Nos hemos vuelto los mayores productores mundiales de vacío. Nos hemos equivocado de lucha. Nos hemos equivocado de independencia. Brutalmente equivocado". Pero desde nuestro lado en el bastión de fabricantes de realidad vendemos cada vez más entradas para el partido incomprensible del mundo. Como el mundo es oscuro e incomprensible jugamos al fútbol y a hacernos ricos para olvidar que hace tiempo nos arrebataron el lugar en la historia. Ya que no queda nada que hacer, dividamos el tiempo entre trabajo y diversión. No volverá Carlos Gurméndez a aguarnos la fiesta con palabras como alienación.

(La segunda recapitulación habrá que hacerla bien entrada la noche, cuando los niños estén profundamente dormidos y tú te resistas, te resistas pensando en un juego para cuando llegue la mañana y se despierten. Esta misma página servirá, como una receta, cocina del mundo. Que cuenten todas las palabras que empiecen por la letra d. Acostarlas en la playa de papel y así construir un tejado de pizarra para las próximas intemperies. Mientras ellos pintan des tú puedes preparar unas natillas o leche frita, y mientras el postre se hace aprovechar para leer unos fragmentos de la *Guía espiritual de Castilla*, de José Jiménez Lozano, o del *Robinson Crusoe*, de Daniel Defoe (Marcel Proust siempre supo que era mejor la Venecia del ensueño que la Venecia real).

El mercado de las palabras no es el de los fabricantes de máscaras, sobre todo si no empleamos los términos en su sentido literal. La d es la cuarta letra del abecedario de la luz y de la oscuridad. Guy Debord alumbra desde la muerte como John Berger alumbra desde este lado de la oscuridad. Hubiera querido escribir desde cinco dedos sentidos, pero lo que digo no es todo lo que pienso. Decir forma parte de las estratagemas del damero maldito, de los dioses fieramente humanos, de la duración de un texto como si fuera una sintonía para las noches de conducción nocturna, cuando hemos perdido el destino y la razón del viaje, acaso llueva, acaso soñemos otro texto, otra vida, otra dirección. Ese deseo que descifra signos en la noche y que pese a la decepción sigue buscando en la negrura, con faros que van al faro. Dar es la contraseña para la próxima frontera.

Matador, D, 1999, Spain

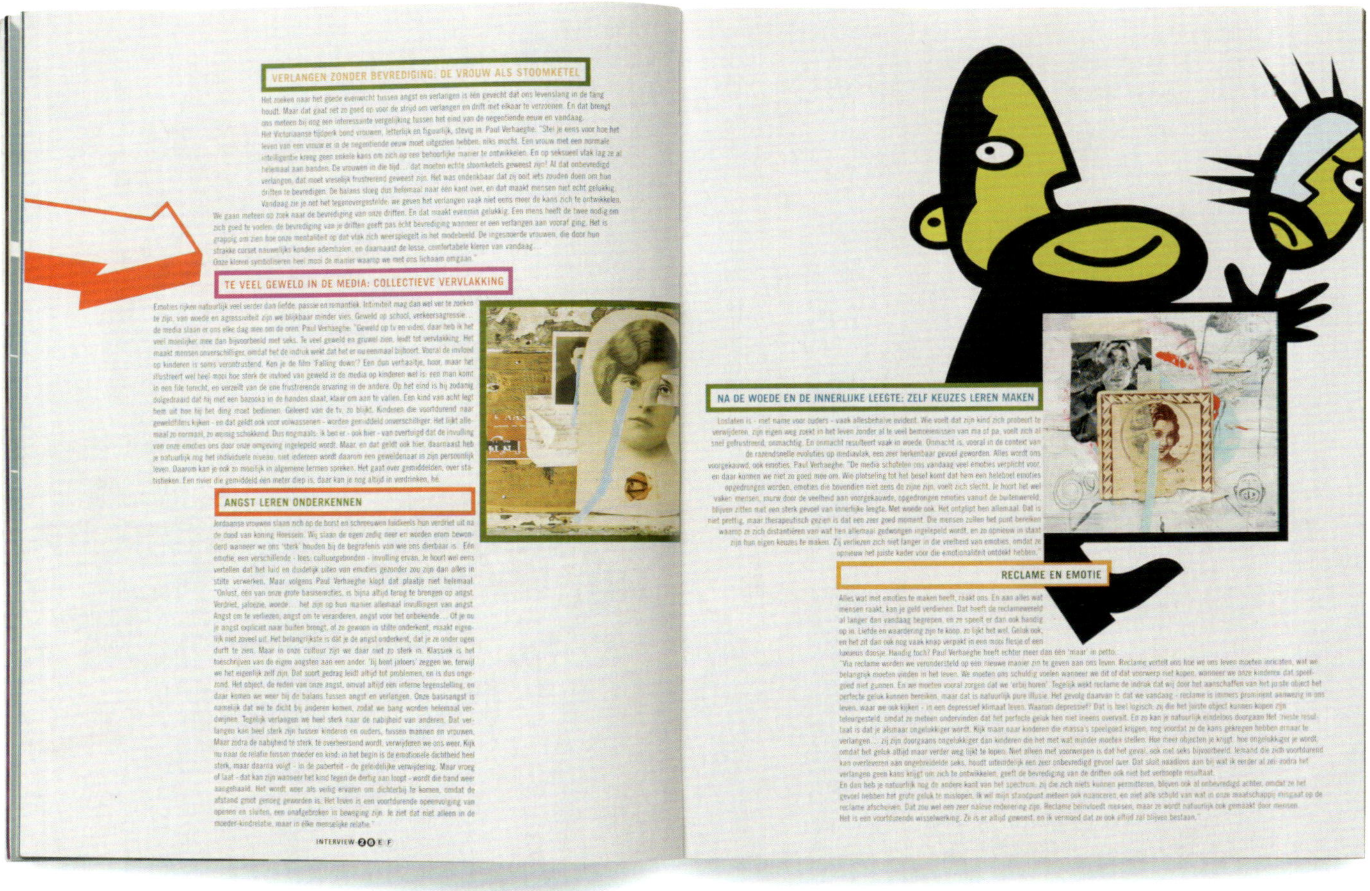

VERLANGEN ZONDER BEVREDIGING: DE VROUW ALS STOOMKETEL

TE VEEL GEWELD IN DE MEDIA: COLLECTIEVE VERVLAKKING

ANGST LEREN ONDERKENNEN

NA DE WOEDE EN DE INNERLIJKE LEEGTE: ZELF KEUZES LEREN MAKEN

RECLAME EN EMOTIE

INTERVIEW

Artur, Summer 1998, Germany

marked with a black permanent marker. "Venison 1-1/2 pounds tied roast," the label might say, or "1 pound Venison steak," and then the year. I was happy for two reasons: the deer would no longer haunt my walk to the car, and dinner would be magnificent.

SOMEWHERE along the way, though, I started to question that dinner so proudly served. I still wonder exactly what it was that started to draw me away from meat, but as much as the violence of hunting, it must have been the fact that when one is around hunting, it's impossible to disassociate meat from its origin. Meat isn't something prepackaged at the grocery store; it comes from an animal—one that, probably, we kept pictures of on our living room walls, next to pictures of loved ones.

Speak, Summer 2000, USA

SIX

o Zustand_.

)TOS **CHRISTOPHE MARGOT**

Geburt und Tod (Bardo des gewöhnlichen Lebens), zwischen Einschlafen und Aufwachen (Bardo der Träume) und zwischen Tod und nächstem Leben (Bardo des Werdens). Zu jedem Zeitpunkt befindet sich der Mensch in einer oder mehreren Bardo-Situationen, Vorangetrieben durch die Kraft vergangener, eigener Handlungen (Karma).Einzigartig an den sechs Yoga-Traditionen ist, dass sie eine Anzahl von meditativen Techniken anbieten, um diese drei Zustände zu erreichen .Eine besonders effektive Übung ist demnach, auch wenn das für den Laien unverständlich klingt, das Yoga des Sterbens.

~~Entsprechend der Schriften beginnt der Tod mit einem Prozess der teilweisen Auflösung, in der Sinne und Energien, die an das Bewusstsein gekoppelt sind, stufenweise zerfallen.~~ Die Auflösungen beruhen zum Teil auf Erfahrungen aus unserem täglichen Leben, vor allen auf denen, die wir beim Einschlafen machen. Sie können von fortgeschrittenen Yoga-Schülern durch Meditation bewusst herbeigeführt werden. Aber nur im Moment des Todes erfährt man sie ganz und unausweichlich. Wenn Übende ihre Fähigkeiten in dieser Hinsicht verfeinern, lernen sie auch, diese Techniken im Schlaf herbeizuführen. Das soll den Vorteil haben, dass der Tod für derart Ausgebildete jeden Schrecken verliert. Für sie ist der Tod, als „würde ein Säugling in den Mutterleib zurückkehren", wie es in Tibet heißt.

Um es also einmal ganz profan auf den Punkt zu bringen: Die Ausbildung in Yoga ist so etwas wie eine Führerscheinprüfung für den post-mortalen Raum. Denn nur der Yogafan ist im Moment des Todes in der Lage, sich überhaupt aus dem Kreislauf aus Geburt und Tod zu befreien. Und nur er ist dank seiner Meditationen mit der Situation vertraut.

Adrenalin, No. 6, 2001, Germany

too. He likes well-turned wood like these columns with their raked angles and soft edges, so beautifully mitered and dovetailed and especially pleasing because of the way they butt up against metal. It gives you the pleasure of the unexpected, putting familiar things in new contexts.

Pleasure,

Surprise,

Comfort,

Entertain,

these are the important words in the book Rizzoli is putting out about him, the carrots he followed out of nowhere to run an eighty-person firm that designed the new Academy Awards theater (the one with the goofy facade, the five-story theater curtain pulled to one side) and the billion-dollar Mohegan Sun casino and the new headquarters for advertising firm McCann-Erickson and the new children's hospital in the Bronx—the guy the City of New York approached to design the viewing platforms for the site of the former World Trade Center. In a field deeply rooted in

Esquire, March 2002, USA

Once upon a time, women didn't swear. Women didn't soil their dainty mouths with expletives. There was no need. They used gentle words to get their womanly point across. Women weren't women back then – they were ladies. They wore hats. And in place of swearing, they would cry, 'Oh sugar!' Even while giving birth. Those days are long gone, of course. Madonna scandalised America by saying 'fuck' during an appearance on David Letterman's late-night chat show in 1994. Not only did she say 'fuck', she said it 14 times. Someone actually bothered to count. If Madonna had been a man, no one would have even cared.

'A GIRL WHO SAYS, "PASS ME THE FUCKIN' SALT," "PASS ME THE FUCKIN' SALAD," "PASS ME THE FUCKIN' WINE," AND THEN SAYS, "LET'S GO FUCK" – BY THAT TIME, WHO WANTS TO?' BURT REYNOLDS

When it comes to women and cursing, hypocrisy is alive and well. It's OK for rap artists of both sexes to rhyme obscenity after obscenity. It's expected of professional wrestlers to have mouths so filthy they can't kiss their mothers. Surgeons must swear blue streaks during surgery. Porters can't ask for a cuppa without a few choice words thrown in. As for soldiers, well, we all know what they say about troopers. But let one woman slip up with a tiny, 'Fuck a duck!' and formerly normal people mutate into righteous jerks.

In a recent survey conducted by NOP on foul language, 70 per cent of women said that profanity was more shocking when uttered by a woman. If that woman is a mum, the sin is even worse. Many of us vividly recall the first time we heard our mothers swear. For many of us, this was the first time we realised mum was actually human. 'She was middle-class, *Guardian*-reading and she said, "Oh, fuck," and I was stunned,' says a friend of the time her best friend's mum cursed out loud. 'My mother has never said that word. It was as if her mum had come downstairs naked and reeking of gin and said, "OK, who wants me first?"'

Swearing is a manly thing – so manly that a swearing woman turns the world upside down. Julia Roberts' character in *Erin Brockovich* was considered low-class because of her bulging breasts, but ultimately unstoppable because she swore like a man. Of course, some women think swearing makes us just

Men swear more often, it's true. But after studyi[…] words of British English conversations, Dr Tony M[…] multilingual corpus linguistics at Lancaster Unive[…] that while men swear more than women, women […] slouches. 'Women,' he says, 'actually swear pretty[…] And they don't shy away from particular types of […] such as "Fuck you" or general imprecations such […]

Women will catch up with men in the swearing […] that's for sure. Swearing is too natural, fun and se[…] Besides, the reasons for us not to swear are slowl[…] world isn't 'ladylike' these days. If women aren't '[…] with a stream of expletives, we'll have to take the […] and demand fucking verbal equality. Men, like the[…] yelp as they please. They can also pee outside, bo[…] As we can't do one, we'll do the other.

Anyway, it turns out that swearing is good for you[…] normal way to express emotions,' says Dr Timothy […] psychology at Massachusetts College of Liberal Ar[…] don't swear is saying that they don't have any emo[…] your car. It's built into us.' It's so natural, in fact, th[…] they know which side of the brain – the right – is r[…] air blue. Patients with damage to the left side cann[…] but they don't lose the ability to snap eloquently at[…]

Everyone – man, woman and child – is swearing […] today. There is no mystery as to why. As comic P[…] up: 'Things are more irritating than ever.' Women […] not more daily stress than men. That's why, when […] themselves, swearing is such a release. Women c[…] to shock, to vent, to warn interlopers that they are[…]

'THE DOG WHIMPERS IN ITS SLEEP; IT'S HAV[…] SO AM I. IT'S CALLED LIVING IN FUCKING BR[…]

Mostly though, women swear because swearing […] swearing among friends is the accepted – and ofte[…]

Nova, No. 9, 2000, Great Britain

Integen-
n ik me

ngewoon
Gouden
ox kreeg
zodat-ie
uit naam
Ook dat
de jonge
nde vra-
gebrek?
o ja, wie
rpeinzin-
le uitver-
.
======

======
pdracht-
leb jij die

o leuk is,

than-life. Dat is voorbij. De kijkers hebben wel door hoe reclame […] mand kijkt meer naar een Martini-reclame en denkt: "Als ik Martini[…] waan ik me op een paradijselijk strand." Het is gewoon maar een […] Mooie vrouwen, lekker rennen, een kokosnoot die breekt, het is lac[…] geworden.'

==

2. Humor in een postmoderne wereld

==

Want in een postmoderne wereld kijken we door de signalen heen […] willen laten kopen. We weten dat men op ons geld uit is, laat die […] op z'n minst leuk zijn.

'Ja, reclame ontwikkelt zich steeds meer in de richting van entertai[…] je *Shots* [Engels videomagazine met commercials, red.] bekijkt, […] allemaal geestig.'

Daar win je prijzen mee.

'Of met schoonheid. Ik ken een Braziliaanse commercial van een[…] een meisje die samen zitten te eten. Het meisje ziet er goed uit: […] ten, alles. De jongen is breed en heeft een volle haardos. Die twee[…] discussie in de trant van: zou je nog van me houden als ik niet zo'n[…] dervlekje had? Ja, zegt die jongen. Haalt het meisje die moedervle[…] gezicht. En zou je nog van me houden als... Die borsten blijken […] zijn pruik af, verwijdert z'n schoudervullingen. Heel mooi gearmd lo[…] eindelijk weg. De pay-off is dan zoiets als: dit drankje is puur ook

Credits, No. 1, 2000, Netherlands

us paragon of
than with
nic super-
e album
cent experi-
track: "Race
multi-tracked
ecay, disease,
the edge of
acy and the
Lots and lots

omp comes
erspective
stances:
ssist Michael
d drummer
poisonous
e creepy
tion of the
he new
s like "A
Light," and

only the performers—at the same time, we're also the technicians. That really is our identity now, to be the technicians of this emotion, instead of there being guys who cry into the microphone and the guys in the white coats make it all work. We're occupying both roles at the same time. The idea of being an explorer, of being a curious guy, I want that to be part of it, because we're always complaining about how things are, and how we could change the world."

"STILL THE LAST VOLUNTEER BATTLES ON. . ."

The Flaming Lips saga, and their journey from the transgressive to the transcendent, goes back to 1983, when Coyne, brother Mark, Ivins, and the forgotten first in a long line of drummers gigged at an Oklahoma City transvestite bar called the Blue Note. What made the Lips stand out from the hardcore pack was that their Oklahoma punk rock was filtered through classic icons like Zep, Floyd and the Who, resulting in such brain-bursting albums as 1987's sophomore outing, *Oh*

Raygun, August 1999, USA

A second level of information within the text

Like the free-standing subheading, quotes function as a means of breaking up the text in order to make it more accessible. They can be direct quotations, or they can be in the form of short summaries. In both cases, they create a second level of information which should be designed in such a manner that it stands out from the rest of the text and gives the reader a new impetus. There are lots of formal variations possible – a different font from that of the main text, other typographical distinctions, and even the possibility of combining the quote with photos and coloured areas.

Harper's Bazaar, September 1993, USA

Fast Company, No. 11, 2000, Great Britain

His cell phone rings. *Doodle-loodle-leet. Doodle-loodle-leet.* It's his dad on the cell phone. His dad is saying, How about I make liver and onions on the stove for when you come home to Warren, Ohio, tomorrow? Korey feels a glow of happiness inside him. It's this whole situation, is what it is. Here in his roomy house in the fine Hillcrest Lakeview Farms development in suburban Minneapolis, with Kelci upstairs cooking chicken in the oven and their three-year-old boy, Kodie, watching Dipsy and Tinky Winky on the kitchen TV. And him, Korey Stringer, down here on the supersized black leather couch in front of the big-screen with the PlayStation on, and now with his dad calling about cooking liver and onions on the stove for when he comes home. Has there ever been a more perfect and comfortable intersection of time and space? This, he thinks, is what people long for. People don't really long to be rich or famous. Most people long to be comfortable. Comfortable with their families and comfortable with their houses and comfortable in themselves.

He realizes, okay, comfort differs from man to man. Because for him, comfort is also the feeling of being in like thirty car wrecks every Sunday afternoon. Yeah. Comfort is trying to knock the living shit out of some enormous, angry, bile-spewing brute snarling at you from across the line, over and over again, every play, like eighty times, banging your head into a wall of viciousness and barbarity. It really is. You know, football is a *violent* game. That's why you use words like *destroy* and *crush* and *dominate* and *kill* and all like that. Most people, like the average person, if you were an offensive lineman and you ached in the places that he aches after the game, after three hours of just heaving your entire body into men the size of side-by-side refrigerators, you would go to the hospital probably. You would go to the hospital and get yourself checked out.

"When I was going to college, I was like, I'm gonna have a good career in college and come back and be a teacher, you know, live a good life, put some pictures on the wall. But it worked out differently. I'm going to have to wait a few years before I go home and teach."

But it makes him comfortable, so that's his gig. It makes him comfortable because he's an expert in controlled rage. He's twenty-seven years old, he's started all but three games at right tackle for the Minnesota Vikings since he entered the NFL seven years ago, he's been doing this since junior high school, so trust him, he's an expert. Football gets in your muscle memory, is where it gets. It gets to where the hard part is *not* doing it. That's where in the past he has always messed up. That's where, more or less, you could see his life falling apart. During the off-season. Never during the season, when he had the sweet, dependable rhythm of getting in thirty car wrecks every Sunday to count on.

How nimble is big Korey Stringer? So nimble that he took the test for his driver's license wedged behind the wheel of his friend's wee Dodge Neon. And passed.

This brings to mind his second tattoo. He pulls his sleeve up to provide the view. Yeah, they make belts for women that would be too small to fit around this upper arm. Yeah. But here on this upper arm, we have the initials "FTW" forming an arc over the planet earth, which is being cupped by a human hand supposedly intent on crushing it. This piece, inscribed on Korey's right arm when he was twenty-two years old, bears full and exact witness to the sum of his belief system at the time of its inscription: "Fuck the World." Yeah. That pretty much said it. He calls this period of time his FTW stage. It was his second year in the NFL. It was ugly. It was the culmination of everything. It was the dark cave into which the pilgrim retreats and, if it shall come to pass that he truly is to become the mythic hero, finds the way.

Which is damn convenient. Because now in his sizable square head, he has converted FTW from "Fuck the World" to "Find the Way." And when you really examine the tattoo, you have to note that the hand isn't really going to crush the earth at all; matter of fact, that hand is *holding up* the earth and all its people with all their problems and all their badness and all their goodness, whatever their gig may be.

His gig. Is he wandering too far off his original point? He's sorry, but this is the way his head works. He spends a lot of time alone with his head. That's like his most comfortable place probably in the world. He'll just sit there and talk to himself in his head, and of course when you're talking to yourself in your head, it doesn't matter how much you wander off your original point. It's funny. People don't automatically associate the word *pensive* with a giant football player such as him. Matter of fact, people don't expect anything they first get from Korey. Like, he's a clown. He's an entertainer. He can do impressions of anybody; he'll keep the crowd happy no matter what it takes. His perspective on it is, he has a duty to give you every opportunity to have the chance to like him. But people have no idea, like maybe only a couple people have an idea, that in his head he isn't funny, he's serious, he's thinking stuff through constantly.

He's sweating. He brings up a towel to wipe off the sweat. He almost always has a towel with him to wipe off the sweat. His position on it is, you've been blessed with an automatic sprinkler system, you should always bring a towel. He changes the big-screen from PlayStation over to ESPN. He holds the remote gently, like it's a gerbil or a hamster maybe. His fingers are long and thin and still and tender, his forearm as thick as a car door.

His gig. Don't get him wrong, there are frustrations during the season. There are the ones you've probably heard of. Like a defensive lineman, that guy could be on the field for fifty plays in a game, but he gets two sacks, and, you know, he had a great game. He's player of the week. Then you take an offensive lineman who doesn't really get a break, doesn't get to rotate and stay fresh like the defensive linemen do, has to continually stand there and bash himself into guys, and he might be on the field for eighty plays in the game, but he gives up two sacks and he's a bum. He's trade bait. Regardless of whether the other seventy-eight plays were excellent. It's those two sacks that everybody is going to talk about. It's not a good position to play if your intent is glory.

But there is another frustration. There is this whole business of being cut off from where you just came from. From the

152 ESQUIRE SEPTEMBER 2001

Esquire, September 2001, USA

Dazed & Confused, March 2002, USA

Harper's Bazaar, October 1993, USA

Mixt(e), No. 8, 2000, France

This house was first owned by the Barlow family, in the 1840s," says John "Jellybean" Benitez, standing at one of the waxy front windows of his five-story brownstone on New York's Gramercy Park. "Barlow was an eccentric. That means he was rich. If he were poor, he'd just have been crazy."

One of those celebrities on a nickname basis with many in pop culture's pantheon, Benitez is scuffing across the marble floors of his new home with his wife, Carolyn, a former Wilhelmina model, now co-owner of the successful Coffee Shop on Union Square in downtown Manhattan. Their daughters, Reya, 3, and Layia, 2, are asleep upstairs.

"I want a comfortable place filled with things we love," explains Carolyn of her plans for their landmarked 12,000-square-foot work-in-progress filled with Louis XIV paneling, spiraling stone stairways, a dumbwaiter, and 13 fireplaces. "Jellybean's only requirements are a couch, a TV, and a phone in every room." (She's working with architect Vatche Simonian, who designed Whitney Houston's New Jersey home.)

"We're going to build a DJ booth," Benitez adds, joking, dressed down in jeans and a sweatshirt, his brown hair tied in a ponytail, a single gold earring glinting. "She's giving me one room for me, all my friends, and 6000 records and 3000 CDs."

It's a bit of a head spin to be looking out at patrician Gramercy Park with this early aficionado of break beats and Afrika Bambaataa, this wild thing who made his (singular) name as a DJ in some of the funkiest sweatboxes in New York City and as a producer (and for two years, boyfriend) of the Madonna of "Holiday" and "Borderline." A totem of the late '70s and the '80s, Benitez kept reinventing himself memorably during those roaring years as club DJ; concocter of the famous "Jellybean Mix" danceathon on WKTU radio; remixer of Paul McCartney and Michael Jackson's "Say, Say, Say," Billy Joel's "Tell Her About It," and the title song of *Flashdance*.

Yet his remix of himself during the subtler '90s has been mature and perhaps even more ambitious. At 37, Benitez is now a mogul with a $15 million investment from the Wall Street firm of Wasserstein Perella for his latest venture—a

"I want a comfortable place filled with things we love," explains Carolyn of their landmarked 12,000-square-foot work-in-progress on Gramercy Park.

bilingual Spanish/English music label and publishing company. "All the artists will be of Hispanic descent, probably second or third generation," says Benitez of the scheme he's been pitching as a Latino Motown. "It would be as if you had 'All I Wanna Do' by Sheryl Crow—except her name would be Maria Hernandez and she'd be from Spanish Harlem or the South Bronx, and we'd record her song in Spanish, English, and Spanglish." Offices are planned by the end of the year for Miami, Chicago, San Antonio, and Los Angeles.

All of this activity—winding up in Gramercy Park, which is fast reconfiguring itself as a Place des Vosges for young success stories—would be colorful news from anyone. Yet Benitez's version has special force. As a Puerto Rican kid who grew up in a burned-out neighborhood of the South Bronx with a single mom and younger sister, he's taken the crossing-the-bridge fairy-tale ending of *Saturday Night Fever* to the max. "A lot of my friends were sniffing glue," he recalls of his boyhood, "then they were smoking pot, a month later they were heroin addicts, and six months later they were dead."

A high school dropout, Benitez was first dismissed for truancy from De Witt Clinton High School, a tinderbox of 6000 black and Latino boys and one of the first public schools in New York City to install metal detectors. From there he switched, briefly, to John F. Kennedy High School, which he describes as "a 90 percent upper-middle-class Anglo high school in the North Bronx. I had excuses they'd never even heard of for why I didn't do my homework."

An entire block of his friends wiped out by drugs, Benitez, evidently a survivor, was left to hang out with their older brothers: "They'd sit around trying to figure out how they could collect unemployment, get welfare, and be bouncers in Manhattan." One aspiring bouncer took Benitez to Sanctuary, a dance club in the West 40s. "I was blown away by the DJ, who had two turntables, all these

160

Harper's Bazaar, June 1995, USA

Wolken calls the field of modern dance "a large geography. The map is enormous, and we're expanding it. We're changing the landscape the way moles and worms do. Dance is handmade, it's not virtual."

Motion

Black Book, June/July/August 2000, Great Britain

Rolling Stone, December 2000, USA

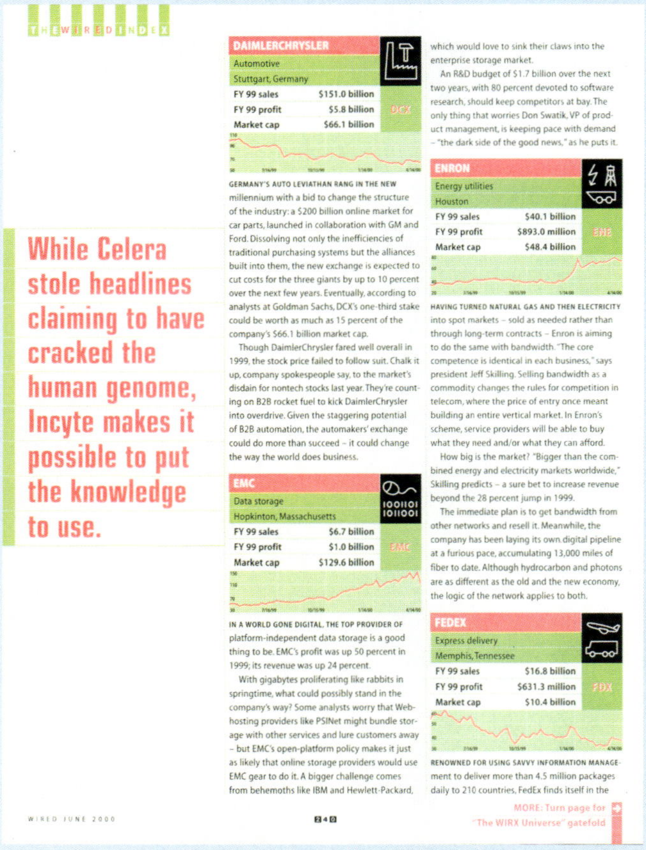

THE WIRED INDEX

While Celera stole headlines claiming to have cracked the human genome, Incyte makes it possible to put the knowledge to use.

DAIMLERCHRYSLER	
Automotive	
Stuttgart, Germany	
FY 99 sales	$151.0 billion
FY 99 profit	$5.8 billion
Market cap	$66.1 billion

DCX

GERMANY'S AUTO LEVIATHAN RANG IN THE NEW millennium with a bid to change the structure of the industry: a $200 billion online market for car parts, launched in collaboration with GM and Ford. Dissolving not only the inefficiencies of traditional purchasing systems but the alliances built into them, the new exchange is expected to cut costs for the three giants by up to 10 percent over the next few years. Eventually, according to analysts at Goldman Sachs, DCX's one-third stake could be worth as much as 15 percent of the company's $66.1 billion market cap.

Though DaimlerChrysler fared well overall in 1999, the stock price failed to follow suit. Chalk it up, company spokespeople say, to the market's disdain for nontech stocks last year. They're counting on B2B rocket fuel to kick DaimlerChrysler into overdrive. Given the staggering potential of B2B automation, the automakers' exchange could do more than succeed – it could change the way the world does business.

EMC	
Data storage	
Hopkinton, Massachusetts	
FY 99 sales	$6.7 billion
FY 99 profit	$1.0 billion
Market cap	$129.6 billion

EMC

IN A WORLD GONE DIGITAL, THE TOP PROVIDER OF platform-independent data storage is a good thing to be. EMC's profit was up 50 percent in 1999; its revenue was up 24 percent.

With gigabytes proliferating like rabbits in springtime, what could possibly stand in the company's way? Some analysts worry that Web-hosting providers like PSINet might bundle storage with other services and lure customers away – but EMC's open-platform policy makes it just as likely that online storage providers would use EMC gear to do it. A bigger challenge comes from behemoths like IBM and Hewlett-Packard, which would love to sink their claws into the enterprise storage market.

An R&D budget of $1.7 billion over the next two years, with 80 percent devoted to software research, should keep competitors at bay. The only thing that worries Don Swatik, VP of product management, is keeping pace with demand – "the dark side of the good news," as he puts it.

ENRON	
Energy utilities	
Houston	
FY 99 sales	$40.1 billion
FY 99 profit	$893.0 million
Market cap	$48.4 billion

ENE

HAVING TURNED NATURAL GAS AND THEN ELECTRICITY into spot markets – sold as needed rather than through long-term contracts – Enron is aiming to do the same with bandwidth. "The core competence is identical in each business," says president Jeff Skilling. Selling bandwidth as a commodity changes the rules for competition in telecom, where the price of entry once meant building an entire vertical market. In Enron's scheme, service providers will be able to buy what they need and/or what they can afford.

How big is the market? "Bigger than the combined energy and electricity markets worldwide," Skilling predicts – a sure bet to increase revenue beyond the 28 percent jump in 1999.

The immediate plan is to get bandwidth from other networks and resell it. Meanwhile, the company has been laying its own digital pipeline at a furious pace, accumulating 13,000 miles of fiber to date. Although hydrocarbon and photons are as different as the old and the new economy, the logic of the network applies to both.

FEDEX	
Express delivery	
Memphis, Tennessee	
FY 99 sales	$16.8 billion
FY 99 profit	$631.3 million
Market cap	$10.4 billion

FDX

RENOWNED FOR USING SAVVY INFORMATION MANAGEMENT to deliver more than 4.5 million packages daily to 210 countries, FedEx finds itself in the

MORE: Turn page for "The WIRX Universe" gatefold

WIRED JUNE 2000 240

Wired, June 2002, USA

Rolling Stone, December 2000, USA

Rolling Stone, June 2000, USA

Harper's Bazaar, December 1993, USA

cluding 408 homicides. About ten percent of all the city's gang crimes were occurring in the Rampart Division, eight square miles of decaying apartment buildings and scabrous storefronts located between Hollywood and downtown. Rampart neighborhoods were the most densely populated in Los Angeles, home to perhaps the highest percentage of illegal immigrants in the state. Vendors who peddled oranges and rock cocaine worked side by side, while nannies and gardeners who sent half their paychecks back home waited for buses along the perimeter of McArthur Park, which had become probably the largest open-air drug market in the U.S.

Most of that drug trade was controlled by the Eighteenth Street Gang, by far the city's biggest, with as many as 20,000 members scattered in subgroups, or "cliques," up and down the West Coast, from Tijuana, Mexico, to Portland, Oregon. The gang wove together layers of criminal enterprise that used a system of "tax" collection to link drug trafficking all the way from the powerful, prison-based Mexican mafia at the top to the small-time independent dealers at the bottom. More than 150 murders were tied to the Eighteenth Street Gang between 1985 and 1995. Residents all across the city, and especially in the neighborhoods most affected, wanted the gang dealt with.

In this context, joining CRASH during the mid-1990s was more like becoming a Special Forces fighter in a wartime army than anything resembling traditional police work. An officer's performance was judged almost entirely by how many gangsters he put behind bars. Rampart's CRASH team not only had its own logo – the aces and eights of Wild Bill Hickock's Dead Man's Hand – but even its own headquarters in a detective substation a mile from the main division station. WE INTIMIDATE THOSE WHO INTIMIDATE OTHERS, read the motto above the front entrance. Officers worked mostly at night and without any real supervision. If an officer made arrests that led to convictions, he was doing a good job; if not, he lacked the "initiative" that anti-gang work required.

Ray Perez had been a top "producer" as an undercover narcotics cop and continued to make a high number of arrests on the Rampart CRASH unit. And perhaps no other detective on the LAPD could match his effectiveness as a witness in court. Public defender Tamar Toister recalls feeling helpless as she watched Perez testify against her client Javier Ovando in early 1997. Toister figured that both judge and jury might feel sympathy for her client. Perez and his partner, Nino Durden, shot Ovando three times in the process of arresting him, and the nineteen-year-old was left paralyzed from the waist down. Ovando had to be wheeled into court on a gurney at his preliminary hearing and would be confined to a wheelchair for the rest of his life.

But after Perez described how Ovando (whose gang name was Sniper) had attempted to ambush him and his partner with an assault rifle, Ovando's fate was sealed. "He was better on the witness stand," Toister says, "than any police officer I've ever cross-examined: smooth, sincere, articulate, with just the right amount of emotion." Duly impressed, Judge Stephen Czuleger sentenced Ovando to twenty-three years in state prison – even more time than the prosecutor had asked for. "That was entirely due to how good Perez had been on the stand," Toister says. "I have to admit, I believed him myself."

Perez's career probably would be thriving still if Poole hadn't started looking into the detective's involvement with Mack at almost exactly the same time a clerk in the LAPD's Property Division discovered that more than six pounds of pure cocaine had been either lost or stolen. Even then, only Perez's bad luck permitted the LAPD to tie him to the missing coke. The dope had been signed out on March 2nd, 1998, to LAPD officer Joel Perez, who was startled by an April notice asking him to return it to the Property Division. He hadn't checked out any three kilos of coke, Joel Perez said. Shown a sign-out sheet bearing his name and badge number, the officer insisted it was a forgery. The property officer who had released the coke, Laura Castellanos, said she didn't remember ever seeing Joel but did recall handing over a carton of narcotics to an Officer Ray Perez.

RAFAEL PEREZ *gave testimony that exposed the Rampart scandal but cut short the bigger case.*

Facing jail time for theft, Perez gave prosecutors a statement that implicated more than seventy of his fellow officers. He said that in one incident, a gang member was used as a human battering ram until his head punched through a wall; in another, a man was hung from a fire escape by his ankles until he talked.

Once detectives put Ray under surveillance, they began to wonder just how large a criminal conspiracy they were dealing with. "Perez and Durden and Sammy Martin were meeting for lunch every day," Poole says. "Then they'd reconnoiter in the middle of the night behind a urinal stall in Griffith Park."

By late spring of 1998, Perez was the target of a specially formed LAPD unit. Today it is called the Rampart Task Force, but back then it was known simply as the Robbery-Homicide Task Force, and its creation was almost entirely a response to the detective work of Poole. "The connections that Russ Poole had made between the David Mack bank robbery and the Biggie Smalls murder, including the possibility that LAPD officers might be involved, were the origin of the task force," says Richard Rosenthal, the first prosecutor assigned to the task force by the district attorney's office. "Then you had the theft of the cocaine, and at that point, Chief Parks says, 'OK, wait. What's going on here?' "

By 1998, task-force detectives realized that Perez had for some time been taking advantage of the LAPD's absurdly loose system for checking out drugs as court evidence. Essentially, all a detective had to do was make a phone call to the Property Division, give his last name and badge number, then ask that the dope be sent to him by courier. The drugs had to be returned, of course, but the Property Division rarely checked to find out whether what they got back was pure cocaine or a bag of Bisquick.

A "close audit" of all narcotics evidence checked out during the previous six months swiftly turned up a second (and earlier) suspicious transfer of cocaine to the Rampart Division, this one involving a pound booked into evidence by Detective Frank Lyga. Poole soon became convinced – and so did several other detectives – that Perez had targeted Lyga's coke as retaliation for the shooting of Kevin Gaines. "We all agreed this was just way too big a coincidence," says Poole.

In July 1998, while still under surveillance, Perez was photographed in a "romantic embrace" with a juicy-looking nightclub singer whom he knew as Bella Rios. Her real name was Veronica Quesada. During one surveillance operation, Poole and another detective knocked at her door at a time when they knew she would answer.

"Veronica Quesada knows English, but she wouldn't speak it to us," Poole says. "She kept saying, '*No comprendo.*' She's no easy mark, I can tell you that." Frustrated, Poole began to look about the woman's living room, where he spotted a photograph of Ray Perez wearing a red sweat suit and flashing a Bloods gang sign. "I remember thinking, 'I knew it,' " Poole recalls. A moment later, Quesada's brother Carlos Romero walked into the apartment carrying a quarter-pound of cocaine. "The brother was so dumbfounded, he just stood there," says Poole. "It might have been the easiest coke bust in history."

Within a couple of weeks, detectives from the task force established numerous links between Perez, Quesada and Carlos Romero. The most significant of these was that in the past year both Quesada and Romero had been convicted of felonies for dealing cocaine, yet each had received a suspended sentence. In both cases, the judges who heard their cases received requests for leniency from Detective Ray Perez.

At the time of her arrest in April 1997, detectives learned that Quesada was in possession of "pay/owe" sheets bearing the initials "RP" and the phone number for the Rampart Division. On the date that the three kilos of cocaine were checked out of the LAPD's Property Division, supposedly by officer Joel Perez, Ray Perez had made a total of eight phone calls to Quesada and Romero. The detective had made more than 160 calls to the same numbers between November 1997 and June 1998.

When questioned, Perez explained both his requests for leniency and the phone calls by claiming that Quesada was a "former informant" with whom he had, unfortunately, become sexually involved. "The guy was cool under questioning," says Poole. "But when I saw him one afternoon at the police academy, you could tell he was scared shitless. He was looking around all the time, over his shoulder and behind his back. He knew we were closing in on him."

98 · ROLLING STONE, JUNE 7, 2001

Rolling Stone, June 2001, USA

Premium, No. 3, 2001, Germany

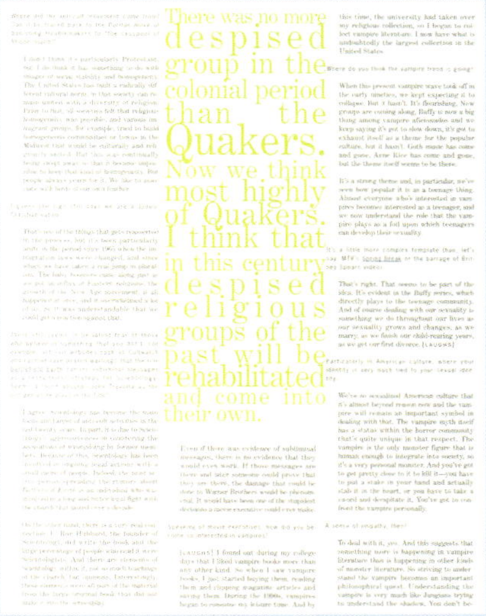

Speak, February 2000, USA

Blvd., No. 3, 2001, Netherlands

TYPOGRAPHY. Captions

A meaningful combination of textual and pictorial information

Captions are not headings, even if some creative spirits prefer to put them above the picture. In terms of content, a caption should provide a meaningful explanation of the picture, rather than merely describing it. A popular form is the division into a factual part and a commentary, sometimes separated by a colon. In the layout, the gap between picture and caption must be clear, and the font must also be easily distinguishable from that of the main text. There's no need for the pictures themselves to conform to the layout grid. Quite often captions are actually positioned within the photo, either by reversing them out or by overprinting. This method cannot be applied indiscriminately, but must fit in with the overall concept of the magazine. The higher the quality and information content of the picture, the more irksome will be the incorporation of a text. A carefully thought out combination of picture and text can have a definite impact on the style of a magazine. As regards the use of purely symbolic pictures, captions are superfluous, since they would actually destroy the whole purpose of the symbol.

Mare, December 2001/January 2002, Germany

A&W, June/July 2001, Germany

Ahead, No. 1, 2001, Austria

DFusion, March 1999, Germany

Greenpeace Magazin, January/February 2001, Germany

Big, No. 28, 2000, USA

Premium, No. 1, 2001, Germany

Blvd., December 2000, Netherlands

Rolling Stone, February 2002, Germany

Style, July/August 2001, Germany

AD, December 2001/January 2002, France

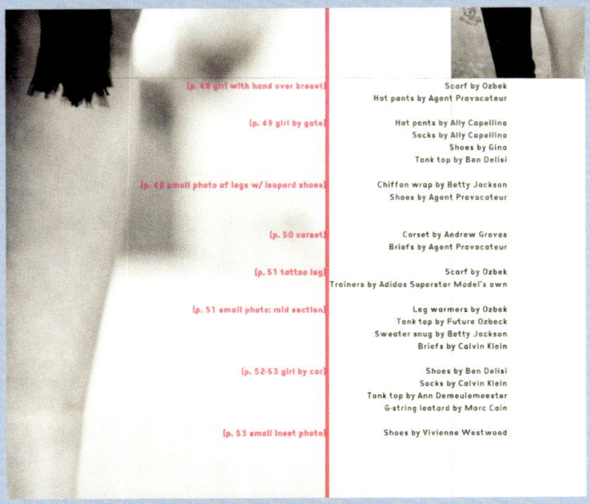

Raygun, March 1999, USA

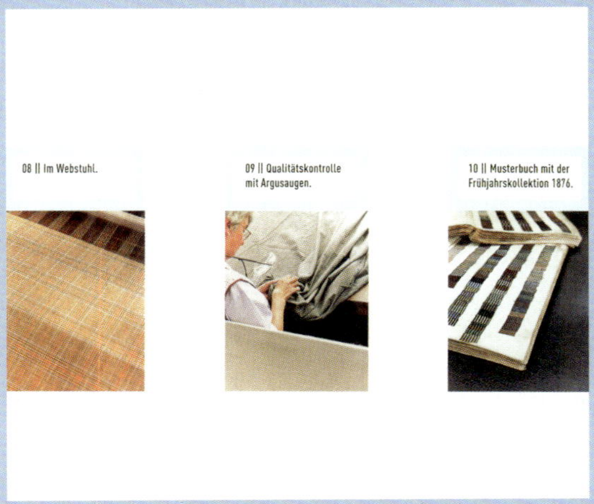

Premium, No. 3, 2001, Germany

A system for the quick grasp of comparable information

The function of tables is to offer the reader a clearly laid out collection of factual information. In most magazines little attention is paid to their design: tables can rarely be enhanced with graphics or illustrations as this would generally detract from their clarity and accessibility. Even so, within these restricted parameters it's still possible to make their design attractive. In addition to purely typographical means, good use can be made of lines and spaces. In choosing the font, it's important to ensure that single-spaced tabular numerals are used, as the different sets of numbers and decimal points must stand directly below one another. Old-style numerals are generally inappropriate for this function, and because of their long ascenders and descenders tend to look very messy.

	ALLEN EDMONDS	ALDEN	BONORA	TANINO CRISCI	BERLUTI	GRENSON	STEFANOBI	SUTOR MANTELLASSI
Modelli	Novanta con quattro linee continuative: Dress Shoes, Dress Casual Shoes, Casual Shoes, Men's Furnishings.	Cinquanta continuativi disponibili a stock.	Circa cinquanta e dieci linee continuative, alcune delle quali mantengono inalterate le loro forme dal 1880.	Quaranta.	Circa quarantacinque, tra cui la famosa 'escarpin à ... a tre lacci, il mocassino 'Andy Warhol'. Da quest'anno anche tre nuove linee sport.	Centoventi di cui trenta continuativi.	Sessanta e tre linee continuative: Essential, Classic, Première.	Circa ottanta della linea Benchmade, interamente realizzata a mano.
Lavorazioni	Goodyear, handsewn. Cento passaggi per tre giorni di lavorazioni.	Esclusivamente Goodyear, con un ciclo produttivo di otto settimane e circa 160-180 passaggi di lavorazione.	Goodyear a mano (a guardolo). Norvegese (a stagno). Dopo la fase di montaggio, nove giorni di riposo sulla forma di legno e successivamente tre fasi di rifinitura e lucidatura a mano.	Blake, Goodyear, Norvegese, Ago, mocassini tubolari o sfoderati. Quattro settimane di lavorazione dal taglio al finissaggio.	Blake, Goodyear, Norvegesi. Un solo pellame utilizzato, 'Venezia', con brevetto esclusivo di Olga Berluti, che possiede una naturalissima colorazione creata ad hoc da un'equipe di coloristi per ogni paio di scarpe.	Goodyear, 200 passaggi effettuati per ogni paio di calzature.	Blake, Goodyear, Norvegese, Ferrarese. Cinque macrofasi per un totale di dieci giorni di lavorazione.	A guardolo (doppia suola) con triple cuciture eseguite a mano. Norvegese con tomaia rigirata all'esterno e doppia cucitura sul guardolo. Circa 150 passaggi.
Target	Professionisti.	Businessmen, 30-45 anni, dal gusto classico-sportivo, amanti della qualità.	Una persona con il culto delle scarpe handmade, eleganti e durature.	Gli amanti di un'eleganza esclusiva e sobria, ricca di accurati dettagli.	Uomini di sofisticata cultura.	Un city-man.	Tra i 30 e i 50 anni, con una posizione sociale medio-alta.	Il manager che vuole unire la tradizione all'innovazione.
Taglie	Dal 5 al 16 con mezzi numeri. Per la larghezza 10 lettere da AAA a EEE.	Dal 5 al 13 e larghezze da AAA a EEE.	Tutti i numeri e i mezzi numeri, tre calzate (E-F-G) e su ordinazione anche D e H.	Dal 5 al 12 compresi i mezzi numeri.	Dal 6 al 13 (dal 38 al 45).	Dal 5 al 13 taglie inglesi.	Numeri e mezzi numeri, dal 5 al 13, due calzate (F e G), più quelle americana e giapponese.	Dal 39 al 46 con mezzi numeri e tre diverse calzate.
Su misura: prove, costi e tempi di consegna	Una sola prova, consegna dopo 4-6 settimane. Costo: 20% in più delle serie normali.		Tre prove (misurazioni, scarpetta di prova, prova definitiva). Costo: 2milioni300mila lire. Tempo: 6-7 mesi.	Una prova, con tempi di consegna di 4-8 settimane. Costo maggiorato del 30% rispetto alla collezione.	Dopo la presa delle misure passano 4 mesi per la prima prova e altri 5 per la consegna. Il prezzo parte da 4milioni800mila lire.	Due o tre prove con una consegna entro tre mesi e un prezzo di 1milione200mila circa.		Due prove o più se necessario. Il prezzo si eleva del 30% rispetto alle calzature 'prêt-à-porter'. 5-6 settimane per la consegna.
Servizi post-vendita	Recrafting.	Total 'restyling'.	Lucidatura, riparazione, risuolatura.	Assistenza e manutenzione.	Tutti.	'Restoration', un accurato processo di rivitalizzazione della scarpa.	Assistenza e riparazione.	Risuolatura, rilucidatura, sostituzione fibbie o accessori logorati.
Prezzo	Fascia alta.	Camoscio e vitello 750-890mila. Shell cordovan 1milione-1milione300mila.	Da 690mila lire a 3milioni500mila (in coccodrillo).	Fascia lusso.	Da 1milione100mila a 1milione e mezzo.	600-700mila lire.	Fascia alta.	Fascia alta.
'Ideal' client	Il Presidente della Repubblica. Tra i clienti dell'azienda: il Vaticano e la Casa Bianca.	Tutti gli uomini con gusto e personalità.	I clienti Amedeo D'Aosta, Marco Tronchetti Provera, Lamberto Dini, Vittorio Sgarbi.		Gli uomini che amano essere più che 'farsi vedere'.	Kevin Spacey e Richard Gere, che già le indossano.		Marcello Mastroianni, che è stato anche testimonial.
Trend A/I 2001-2002	Forme sfilate in vitello o cordovan nei colori nero, merlot e chestnut. Fondi doppi con guardolo.	Forme classiche, nelle gamme brown e nelle tonalità melanzana.	Forme sfilate dei modelli 'Duke of Windsor' con fondi rigorosamente in cuoio bagnato e tirato a mano.	Calzature sottili, in vitello, capretto, rettile, canguro, alce e camoscio.	Un concetto sportivo che sposa i toni della natura: marroni e verdi con qualche divagazione verso i colori spirituali come il viola.		Un classico rivisitato, che segue le lavorazioni della tradizione artigiana. Linee affusolate.	Forme 'a lancia' e English style. Vitelli morbidi, coccodrillo, struzzo e suole in cuoio stagionato.

Vogue Pelle, No. 7, 2001, Italy

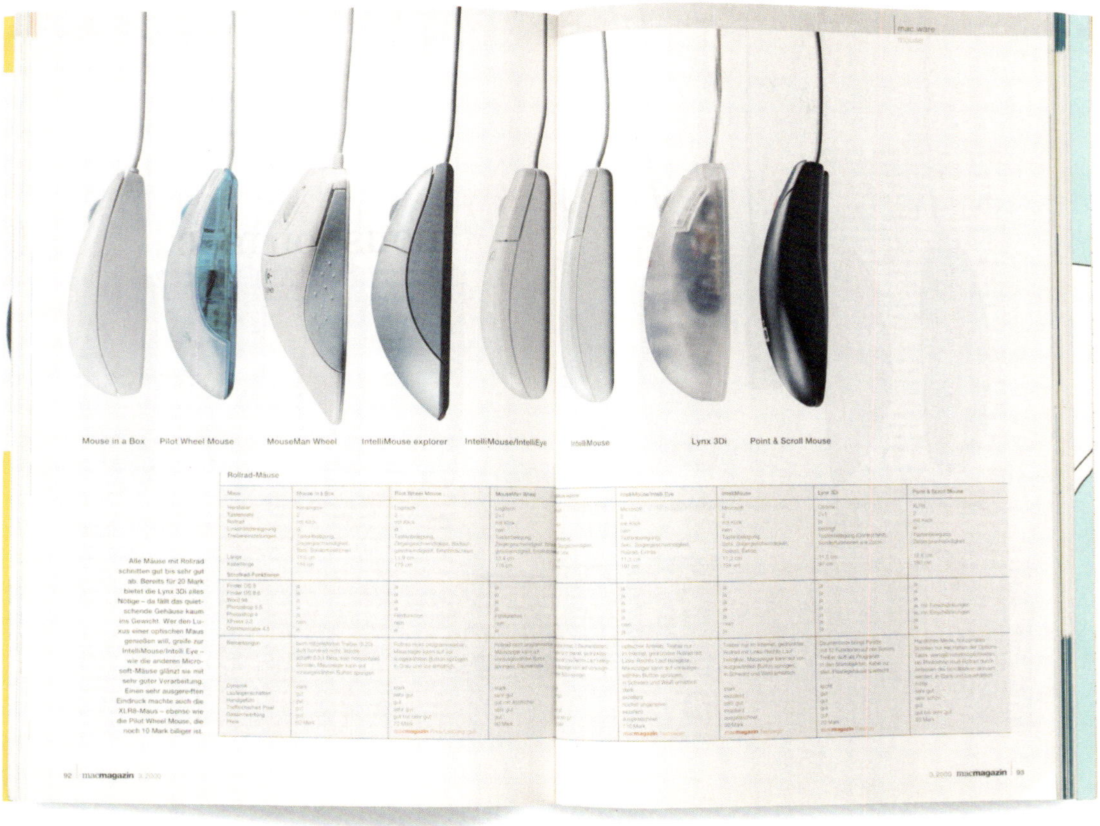

Mac Magazin, No. 3, 2000, Germany

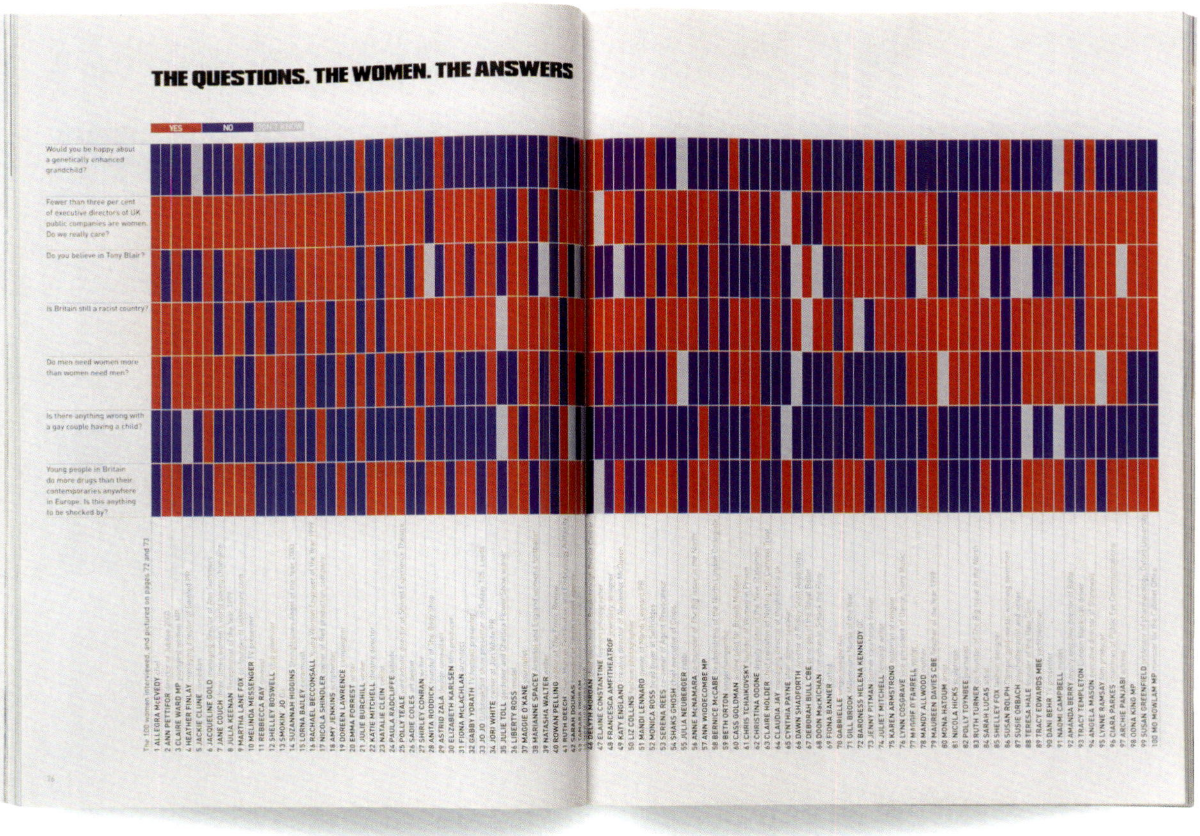

Nova, No. 6, 2000, Great Britain

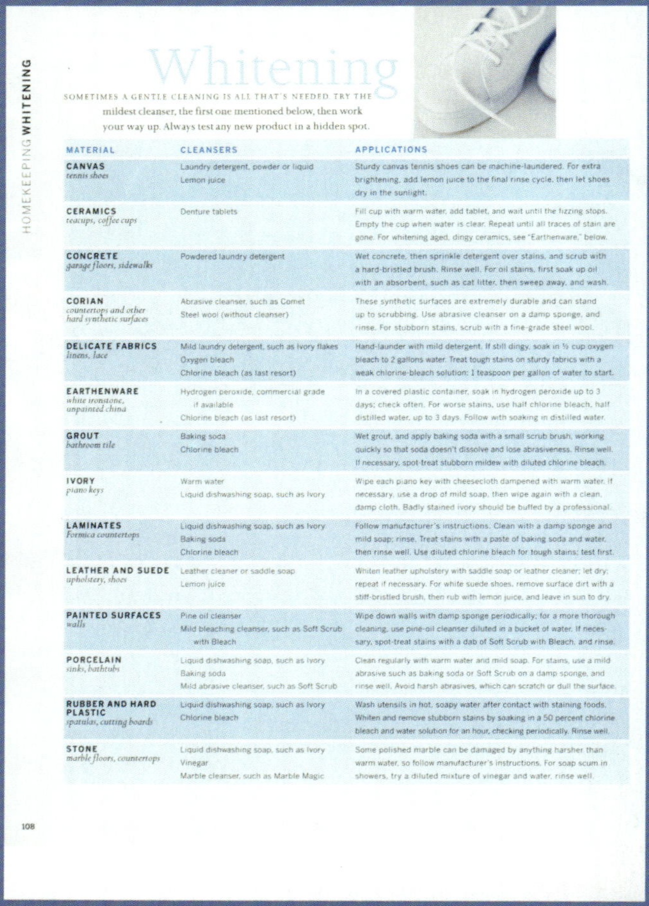

Whitening

SOMETIMES A GENTLE CLEANING IS ALL THAT'S NEEDED. TRY THE mildest cleanser, the first one mentioned below, then work your way up. Always test any new product in a hidden spot.

MATERIAL	CLEANSERS	APPLICATIONS
CANVAS *tennis shoes*	Laundry detergent, powder or liquid Lemon juice	Sturdy canvas tennis shoes can be machine-laundered. For extra brightening, add lemon juice to the final rinse cycle, then let shoes dry in the sunlight.
CERAMICS *teacups, coffee cups*	Denture tablets	Fill cup with warm water, add tablet, and wait until the fizzing stops. Empty the cup when water is clear. Repeat until all traces of stain are gone. For whitening aged, dingy ceramics, see "Earthenware," below.
CONCRETE *garage floors, sidewalks*	Powdered laundry detergent	Wet concrete, then sprinkle detergent over stains, and scrub with a hard-bristled brush. Rinse well. For oil stains, first soak up oil with an absorbent, such as cat litter, then sweep away, and wash.
CORIAN *countertops and other hard synthetic surfaces*	Abrasive cleanser, such as Comet Steel wool (without cleanser)	These synthetic surfaces are extremely durable and can stand up to scrubbing. Use abrasive cleanser on a damp sponge, and rinse. For stubborn stains, scrub with a fine-grade steel wool.
DELICATE FABRICS *linens, lace*	Mild laundry detergent, such as Ivory flakes Oxygen bleach Chlorine bleach (as last resort)	Hand-launder with mild detergent. If still dingy, soak in ½ cup oxygen bleach to 2 gallons water. Treat tough stains on sturdy fabrics with a weak chlorine-bleach solution: 1 teaspoon per gallon of water to start.
EARTHENWARE *white ironstone, unpainted china*	Hydrogen peroxide, commercial grade if available Chlorine bleach (as last resort)	In a covered plastic container, soak in hydrogen peroxide up to 3 days; check often. For worse stains, use half chlorine bleach, half distilled water, up to 3 days. Follow with soaking in distilled water.
GROUT *bathroom tile*	Baking soda Chlorine bleach	Wet grout, and apply baking soda with a small scrub brush, working quickly so that soda doesn't dissolve and lose abrasiveness. Rinse well. If necessary, spot-treat stubborn mildew with diluted chlorine bleach.
IVORY *piano keys*	Warm water Liquid dishwashing soap, such as Ivory	Wipe each piano key with cheesecloth dampened with warm water. If necessary, use a drop of mild soap, then wipe again with a clean, damp cloth. Badly stained ivory should be buffed by a professional.
LAMINATES *Formica countertops*	Liquid dishwashing soap, such as Ivory Baking soda Chlorine bleach	Follow manufacturer's instructions. Clean with a damp sponge and mild soap; rinse. Treat stains with a paste of baking soda and water, then rinse well. Use diluted chlorine bleach for tough stains; test first.
LEATHER AND SUEDE *upholstery, shoes*	Leather cleaner or saddle soap Lemon juice	Whiten leather upholstery with saddle soap or leather cleaner; let dry; repeat if necessary. For white suede shoes, remove surface dirt with a stiff-bristled brush, then rub with lemon juice, and leave in sun to dry.
PAINTED SURFACES *walls*	Pine oil cleanser Mild bleaching cleanser, such as Soft Scrub with Bleach	Wipe down walls with damp sponge periodically; for a more thorough cleaning, use pine-oil cleanser diluted in a bucket of water. If necessary, spot-treat stains with a dab of Soft Scrub with Bleach, and rinse.
PORCELAIN *sinks, bathtubs*	Liquid dishwashing soap, such as Ivory Baking soda Mild abrasive cleanser, such as Soft Scrub	Clean regularly with warm water and mild soap. For stains, use a mild abrasive such as baking soda or Soft Scrub on a damp sponge, and rinse well. Avoid harsh abrasives, which can scratch or dull the surface.
RUBBER AND HARD PLASTIC *spatulas, cutting boards*	Liquid dishwashing soap, such as Ivory Chlorine bleach	Wash utensils in hot, soapy water after contact with staining foods. Whiten and remove stubborn stains by soaking in a 50 percent chlorine bleach and water solution for an hour, checking periodically. Rinse well.
STONE *marble floors, countertops*	Liquid dishwashing soap, such as Ivory Vinegar Marble cleanser, such as Marble Magic	Some polished marble can be damaged by anything harsher than warm water, so follow manufacturer's instructions. For soap scum in showers, try a diluted mixture of vinegar and water, rinse well.

Living, No. 5, 2000, Great Britain

Wachstumsfirmen enttäuschen

Die 20 besten Geschäftsberichte der Nemax-50-Unternehmer (Maximale Punktzahl: 100)

Rang	Unternehmen	Inhalt	Finanz-kommunikation	Optik	Sprache	Gesamt*	Urteil**
1	EM.TV	56,90	60,00	64,57	78,33	65,56	gut
2	Brokat	54,38	51,00	66,89	59,16	59,91	befriedigend
3	Intershop	50,30	52,00	51,98	82,91	59,76	befriedigend
4	Heyde	48,38	55,00	50,82	85,00	55,23	befriedigend
5	SER Systeme	54,38	57,00	38,63	69,58	54,69	befriedigend
6	Mobilcom	50,36	46,00	50,05	79,58	54,04	befriedigend
7	Pfeiffer Vacuum	46,13	55,50	48,89	82,50	53,40	befriedigend
8	Kinowelt	50,35	45,50	36,50	65,83	49,87	ausreichend
9	SCM Microsystems	39,51	41,00	59,15	85,41	49,56	ausreichend
10	Edel Music	39,45	46,00	53,34	81,66	48,85	ausreichend
11	1&1	46,82	47,00	34,17	71,25	48,62	ausreichend
12	mb Software	40,72	40,50	50,44	83,33	48,54	ausreichend
13	ce Consumer Electronic	43,37	41,00	50,82	71,66	48,38	ausreichend
14	Infomatec	42,84	48,50	43,85	69,16	47,79	ausreichend
15	Qiagen	44,86	41,00	26,43	77,08	46,35	ausreichend
16	Aixtron	42,08	43,50	27,01	75,41	45,03	ausreichend
17	Micrologica	39,52	36,50	52,57	65,83	44,97	ausreichend
18	Singulus	39,98	43,50	40,37	64,13	44,19	ausreichend
19	Ixos	36,46	42,00	43,85	73,38	43,93	ausreichend
20	Teldafax	37,49	41,00	37,85	67,91	42,64	ausreichend

*Setzt sich zusammen aus den Ergebnissen in den vier Beurteilungskategorien sowie dem abschließenden Urteil der Jury. **Schulnotensytem: Ab 75 Punkte: sehr gut, von 74,99 bis 62,50: gut, von 62,49 bis 50,00: befriedigend, von 49,99 bis 37,50: ausreichend, weniger als 37,50: mangelhaft.

Newcomer bieten viel Durchschnitt

Die 20 besten Geschäftsberichte der Börsenneulinge (Maximale Punktzahl: 100)

Rang	Unternehmen	Inhalt	Finanz-kommunikation	Optik	Sprache	Gesamt*	Urteil**
1	Celanese	55,50	67,00	57,02	79,58	65,77	gut
2	Stinnes	55,79	60,50	54,50	82,08	64,10	gut
3	Edscha	54,80	54,00	59,54	87,08	63,79	gut
4	Vivanco	55,74	56,00	57,02	77,50	59,24	befriedigend
5	Epcos	56,15	62,00	50,05	74,16	58,81	befriedigend
6	Elexis	55,69	55,50	48,50	76,25	57,67	befriedigend
7	Schuler	51,32	57,50	48,69	75,58	55,49	befriedigend
8	BinTec Communications	51,37	47,00	56,44	75,83	55,14	befriedigend
9	Adcon Telemetry	55,56	50,00	37,85	73,75	54,80	befriedigend
10	Adva Optical	52,47	49,50	45,98	72,91	54,12	befriedigend
11	MVV Energie	52,56	54,00	44,43	69,58	54,11	befriedigend
12	CyBio	52,09	47,00	38,04	82,50	53,78	befriedigend
13	Agfa-Gevaert	51,96	43,50	46,95	69,16	53,27	befriedigend
14	ADS	53,51	50,00	31,46	74,58	52,84	befriedigend
15	CPU Softwarehouse	52,45	46,00	40,76	71,25	52,55	befriedigend
16	AT&S Austria Technologies	51,56	53,00	31,66	75,00	52,31	befriedigend
17	Zapf Creation	48,96	46,50	46,95	73,75	52,01	befriedigend
18	Beate Uhse	50,57	51,50	37,66	69,16	51,56	befriedigend
19	PC-Spezialist	53,51	55,50	27,20	63,33	51,33	befriedigend
20	Easy Software	49,00	50,00	40,56	67,08	50,60	befriedigend

*Setzt sich zusammen aus den Ergebnissen in den vier Beurteilungskategorien sowie dem abschließenden Urteil der Jury. **Schulnotensystem: Ab 75 Punkte: sehr gut, von 74,99 bis 62,50: gut, von 62,49 bis 50,00: befriedigend, von 49,99 bis 37,50: ausreichend, weniger als 37,50: mangelhaft.

Manager Magazin, No. 10, 2000, Ge-many

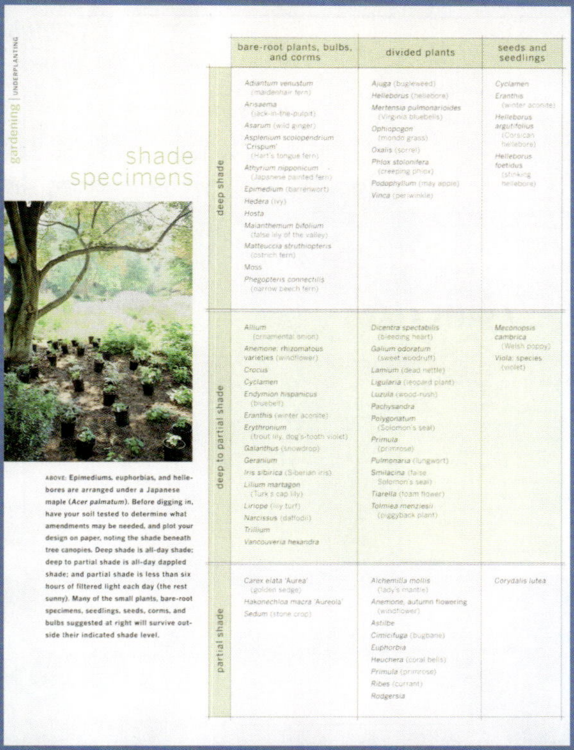

Martha Stewart Living, March 2002, USA

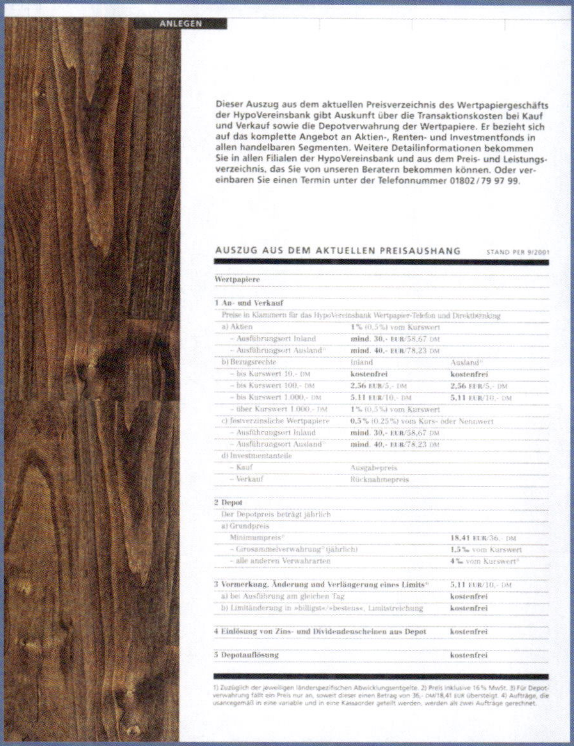

Anleger, No. 3, 2001, Germany

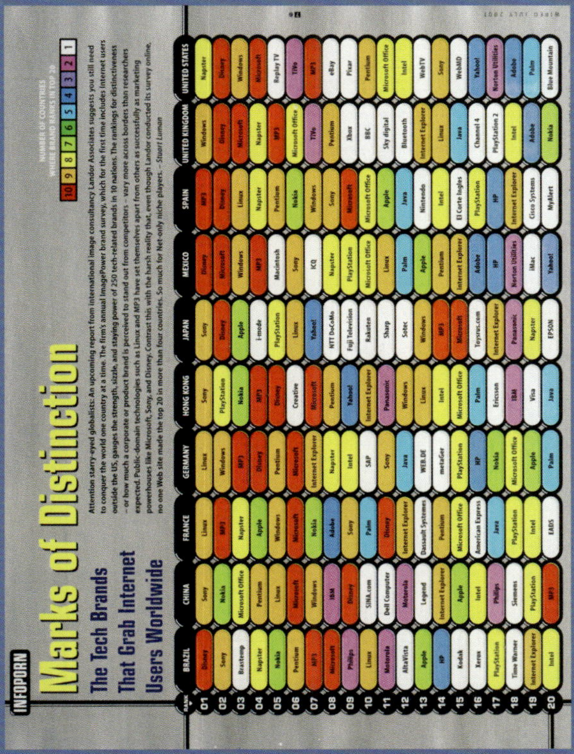

Wired, July 2001, USA

Wired, June 2000, USA

Three basic forms and their illustrative permutations

Charts are mainly used in business and financial magazines, and can basically be divided into three types. First, the pie chart, which starts out whole (i.e. 100%) and is then cut up into larger or smaller pieces. Dynamic developments cannot be traced with this form, only the status quo. The second form is the bar chart, which compares sizes and quantities in precise figures, but cannot effectively display percentages. Graphically, the representation can range from two-dimensional figures to round or rectangular columns, sometimes combined with different structures or shades. The third type is the graph, with systems of coordinates that can show developments over time. This is most commonly used to show the progress of items like shares. Since one chart may often contain several graphs, sometimes intersecting, the use of structures or shades can be a hindrance. As always, the main consideration has to be clarity, precision of layout, and instant grasp of the facts.

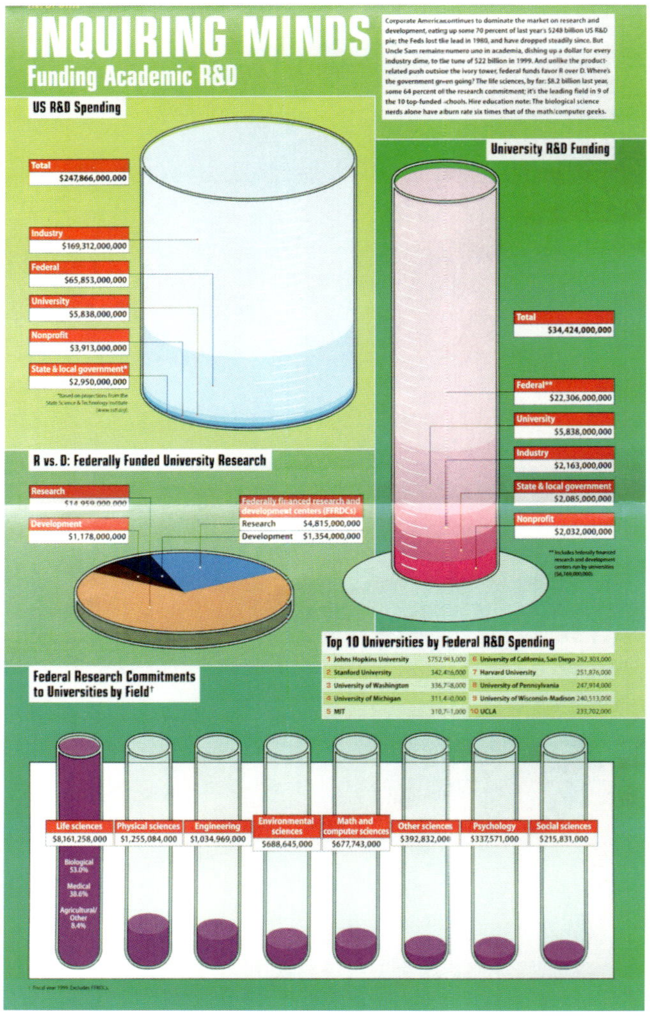

Wired, April 2002, USA

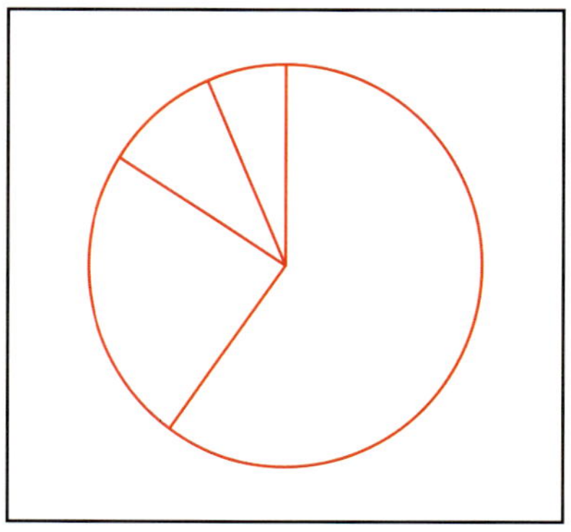

Pie chart

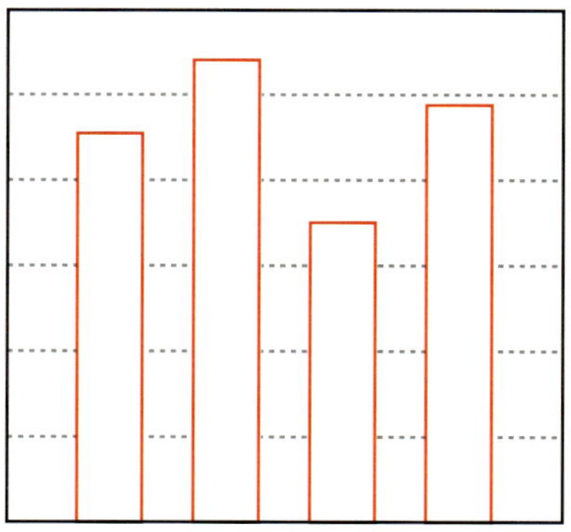

Bar chart

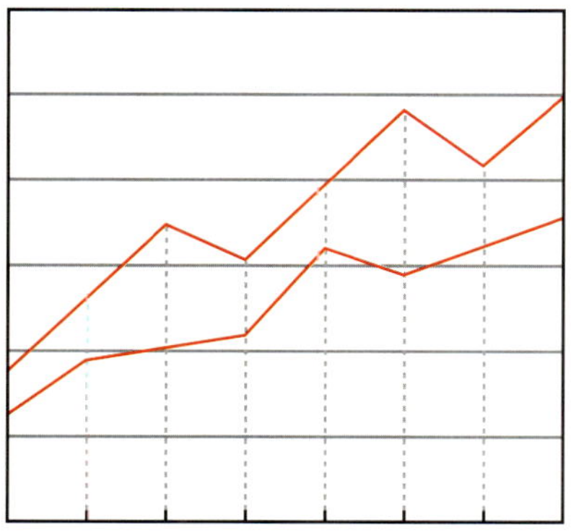

Graph

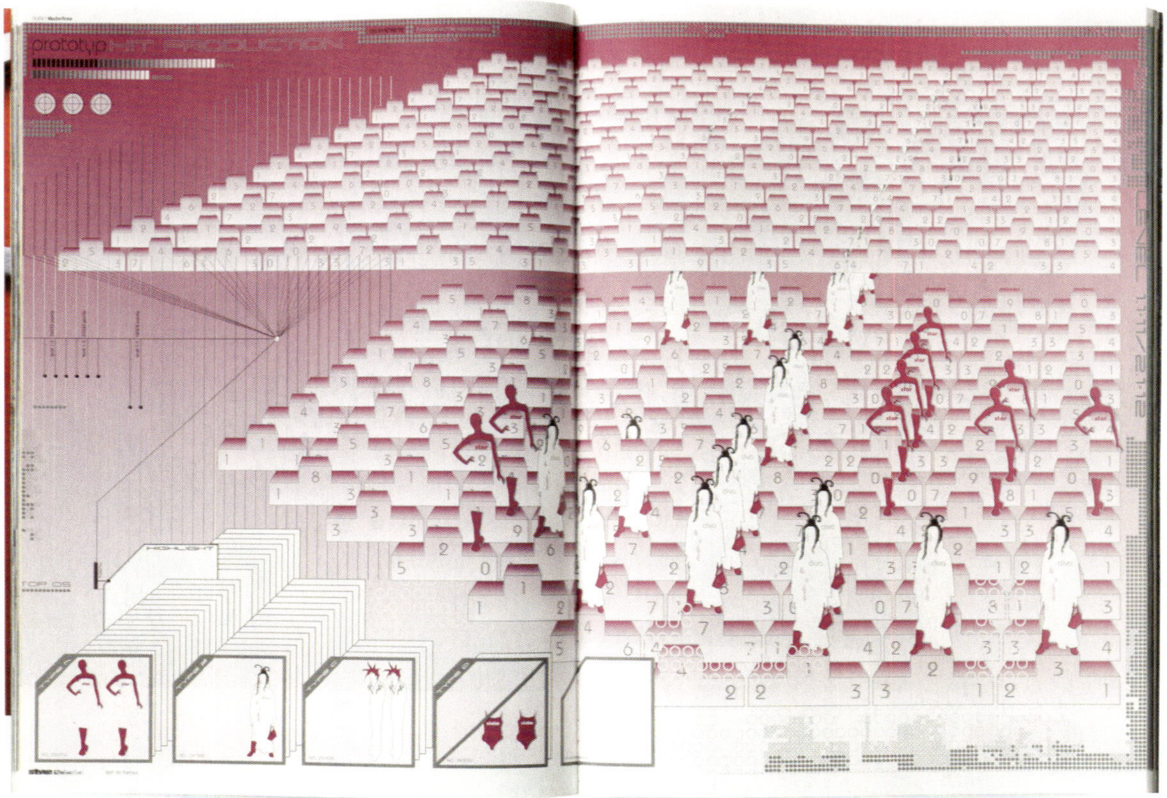

Style, November 2001, Germany

Fast Company, March 2000, USA

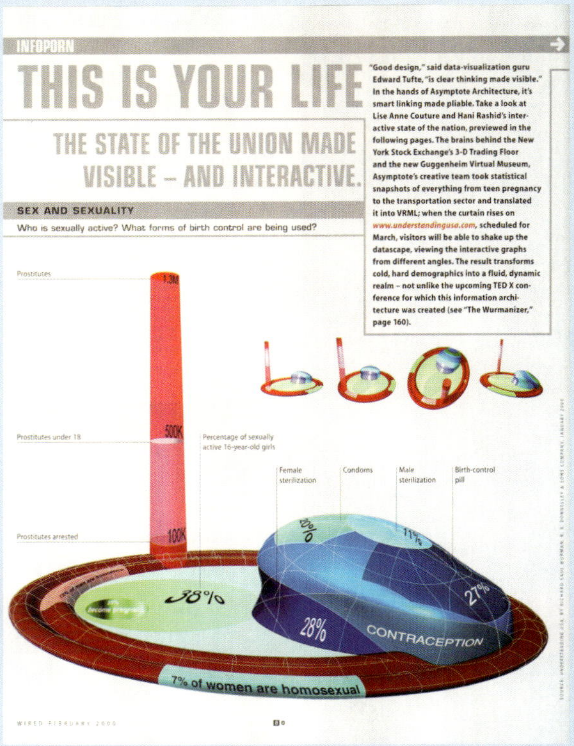

Wired, February 2000, USA

Wired, November 2000, USA

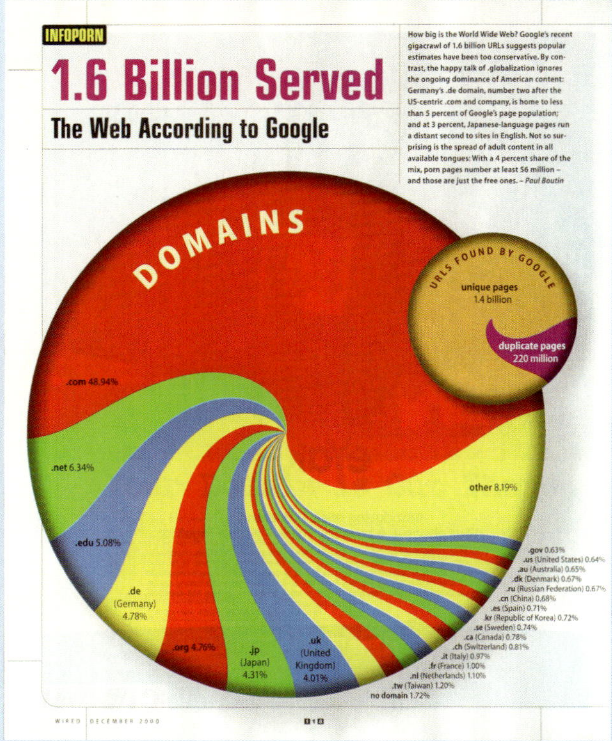

Wired, December 2000, USA

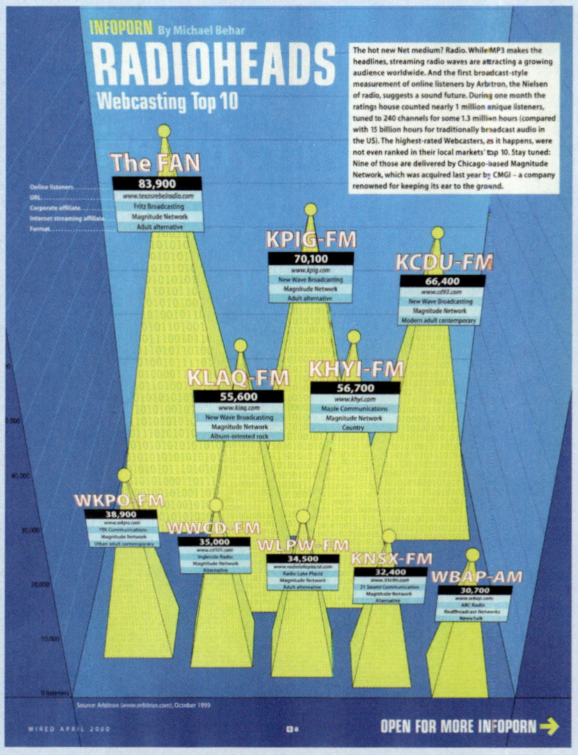

Wired, April 2000, USA

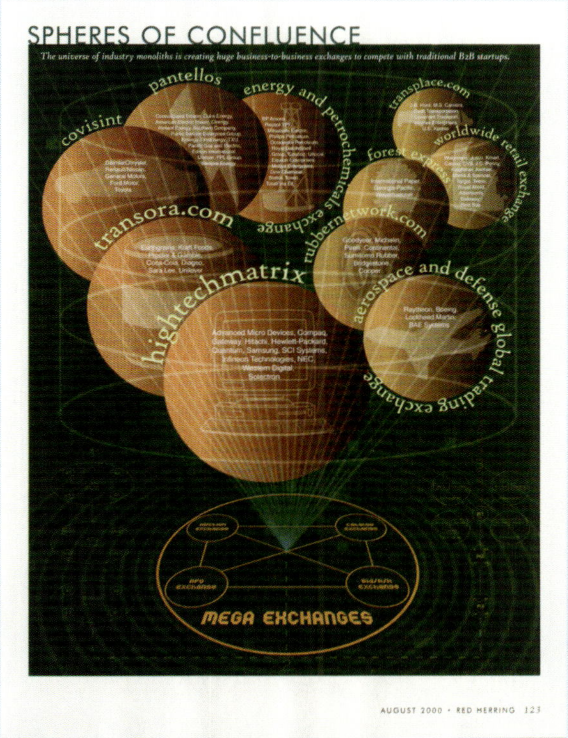

Red Herring, August 2000, USA

Wired, June 2000, USA

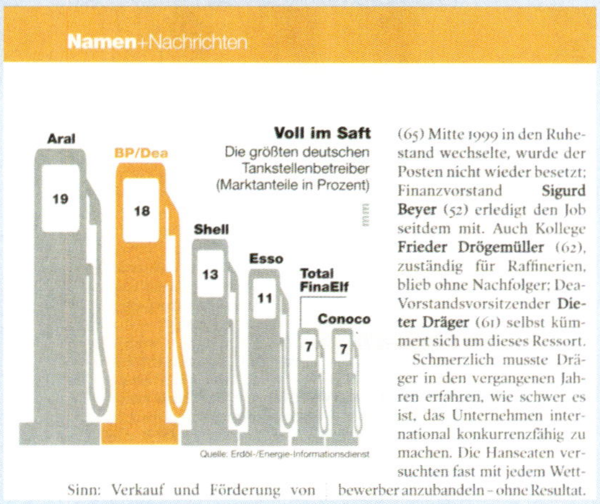

Manager Magazin, October 2000, Germany

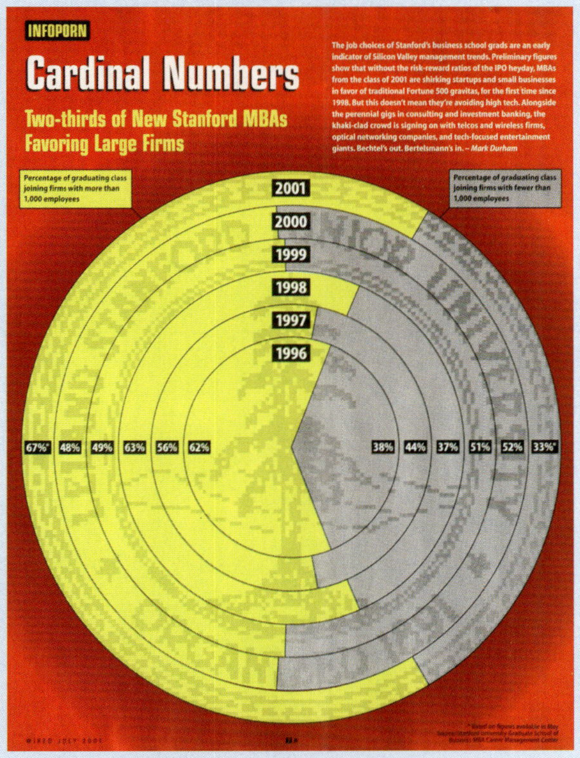

Wired, July 2001, USA

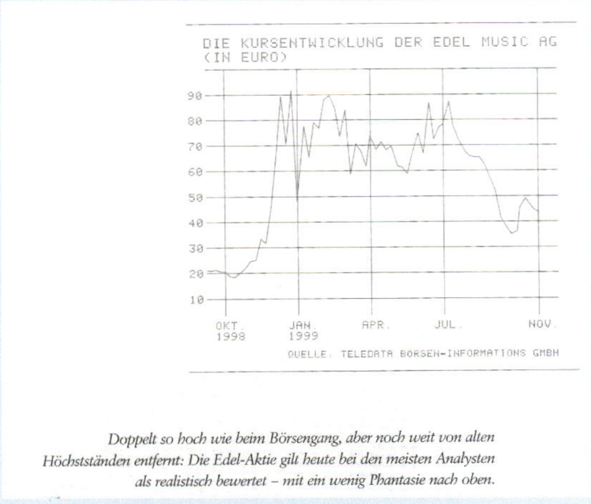

Brand eins, December 1999/January 2000, Germany

Displaying information to supplement the main text

Texts which enrich an article with additional information (appendages, extracts, summaries, and so on) are often laid out in separate boxes. Even interviews that accompany the main article can be separated in the same way, creating an additional textual level.

It's important that the article itself is long enough to accommodate the extra information, and there's sometimes the danger in specialist magazines of overloading articles with boxes. In such situations, it's sensible to provide a summary of all the additions within the layout system.

There are no formal restrictions for boxes – they can be combined with photos, illustrations, lines and coloured areas. The font should be clearly distinguishable from the one used in the main text, and generally a sans serif type is preferable. If the box is narrow, it's best to use unjustified type rather than justified.

SPECIAL FOCUS | JAPAN

CAPITAL STEPS

Four Japanese corporations with venture efforts and a sampling of their portfolios.

NEC* www.convergencepartners.com

Clickability Designs and builds tools that enhance content providers' Web site traffic and that reinforce brand awareness. Total capital raised: $6.5 million.

OneMediaPlace Provides an online exchange for advertising services. The site allows buyers to submit requests for print, broadcast, and online advertising media. Buyers and sellers can also negotiate and adjust pricing, as well as close and invoice the deals online. Total capital raised: $96 million.

Tropian Develops and manufactures integrated circuits for mobile devices. Total capital raised: $44.3 million.

Panasonic www.vcpanasonic.com

InterActual Technologies Develops software to provide DVD technologies and services for integrating video with direct links to Web sites. Total capital raised: $4.5 million.

Ivast Develops streaming-media technologies for consumer appliances. Total capital raised: $12 million.

Tensilica Allows chip designers to optimize semiconductors to the specific power, speed, and feature requirements of hardware devices like digital cameras, communications gear, and mobile devices. Total capital raised: $33 million.

Sony www.sonyvc.com

Ntru Cryptosystems Develops public-key cryptography systems designed for consumer devices. Total capital raised: $12 million.

Reflectivity Develops light-valve microdisplay technology for digital display devices. Total capital raised: $16.5 million.

Tao Building a media-content software platform for digital appliances connected to home and mobile networks. Total capital raised: $12.5 million.

Toshiba www.tvc.toshiba.co.jp

NewsWatch Delivers selected news tailored to users' specifications and interests directly to their computers every morning. Total capital raised: would not disclose funding.

NuVisio Develops Internet-based sales, marketing, and advertising technologies. Raised $4 million in a second round of funding.

*Investments made through Convergence Partners, a U.S. venture firm in which NEC holds a majority stake.

Web-based content to mobile devices; and AgentArts International, a service that delivers personalized entertainment to users based on their individual preferences. To ensure that at least some of these technologies are brought back to the homeland, a handful of Panasonic executives from Japan will come to America and work directly with many of the

up a research lab somewhere in Santa Clara County. They quickly realized that most top engineers in the Valley had no desire to work for a corporate behemoth that didn't offer competitive stock options or salaries.

NEC, for its part, chose to enter the venture world somewhat covertly. Instead of setting up its own fund, it decided

Red Herring, January 2001, Great Britain

Jones has one mantra in his life now: Security, stability, success. Going to Vancouver is the path toward achieving all of those things. He knows what it's like to live on the margin, and he doesn't want to go there again. He dropped out of high school in the 10th grade. He worked at Wherehouse Music. He worked at Mail Boxes Etc. He knows the tune to the minimum-wage blues. He once lived homeless for a month on the streets of Hollywood, sleeping on a secluded roof until a 33-year-old woman took him in. He doesn't want to climb a fire escape to go to bed ever again. He doesn't have to anymore. But, in exchange for that security, he knows the tune to the explosive-

ON THE VERGE OF GREATNESS

KNOW HOW TO GROW

AT THQ, 10 RULES OF GROWTH HAVE EMERGED FROM THE VIDEO-GAME OUTFIT'S RAPID RISE INTO THE ranks of America's fastest-growing companies

1. **Break the silence.** Create as many channels of communication as possible and use them as often as possible. Praise others often; don't boast of your own triumphs.
2. **Be humble, be tough.** Don't let success go to your head. And never get discouraged by mistakes or by failures. THQ's CEO Brian Farrell's motto: "Failure isn't fatal. Success isn't final."
3. **Avoid the Midas touch.** Don't be lulled by your company's rapid growth into thinking that anything you touch will turn into gold. It won't.
4. **Avoid the Goethe syndrome.** Goethe, the great 18th-century German poet, supposedly knew everything there was to know in his age. Nobody in a growing corporation can know everything. Define jobs clearly. Narrow spans of control.
5. **Think cheap.** Spend only when you need to. Find ways to get the most return on the least investment.
6. **Fire people.** Separate the wheat from the chaff. If you can't, hire someone who can.
7. **Stick to your knitting.** Do only what you do best. Don't expand to a new level or take major risks unless you have no other choice.
8. **Do paperwork, do meetings.** Create professional systems for project management, and stick to them religiously.
9. **Walk around.** The silence that creeps into large organizations can be broken by executives who wander throughout the company and who talk to workers directly.
10. **Underpromise, overdeliver.** Alison Locke, senior VP of sales and marketing at THQ, believes that rapidly growing companies must avoid discouragement. "Constantly beating our own expectations over the past four years has been our story," she says.

Fast Company, October 2000, USA

JARGON WATCH

For decades, the guardians of the French language have fought a losing battle against Americanisms such as le week-end, le blue-jean, *and* le drugstore. *As their country is invaded by a fresh horde of new economy buzzwords, the ministries of culture and finance have responded with the inevitable list of purely Gallic equivalents. A few have caught on – you do hear the Web referred to as* la Toile *– but others don't exactly roll off the tongue:*

startups = *jeunes pousses d'entreprises* (young sprouts of companies)
one-stop shopping = *tout à la fois* (all at once)
mergermania = *fusionite* (fusionitis)
trend = *tendance structurelle* (structural tendency)
fulfillment = *gestion optimale des commandes* (optimal management of orders)
webcasting = *diffusion réticulaire systématique* (systematic reticular broadcasting)

Wired, June 2000, USA

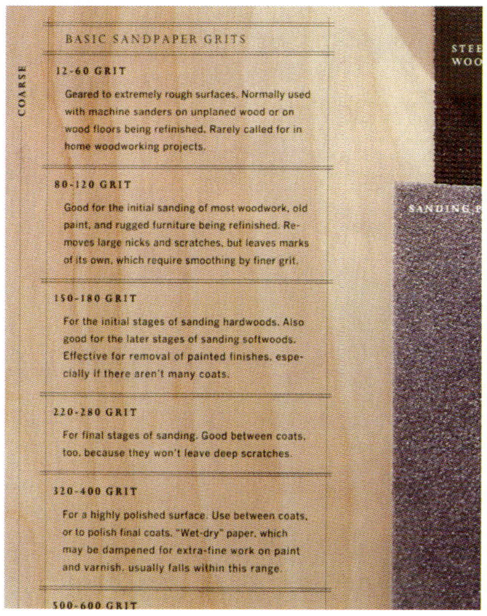

BASIC SANDPAPER GRITS

COARSE

12-60 GRIT

Geared to extremely rough surfaces. Normally used with machine sanders on unplaned wood or on wood floors being refinished. Rarely called for in home woodworking projects.

80-120 GRIT

Good for the initial sanding of most woodwork, old paint, and rugged furniture being refinished. Removes large nicks and scratches, but leaves marks of its own, which require smoothing by finer grit.

150-180 GRIT

For the initial stages of sanding hardwoods. Also good for the later stages of sanding softwoods. Effective for removal of painted finishes, especially if there aren't many coats.

220-280 GRIT

For final stages of sanding. Good between coats, too, because they won't leave deep scratches.

320-400 GRIT

For a highly polished surface. Use between coats, or to polish final coats. "Wet-dry" paper, which may be dampened for extra-fine work on paint and varnish, usually falls within this range.

500-600 GRIT

Martha Stewart Living, April 2000, USA

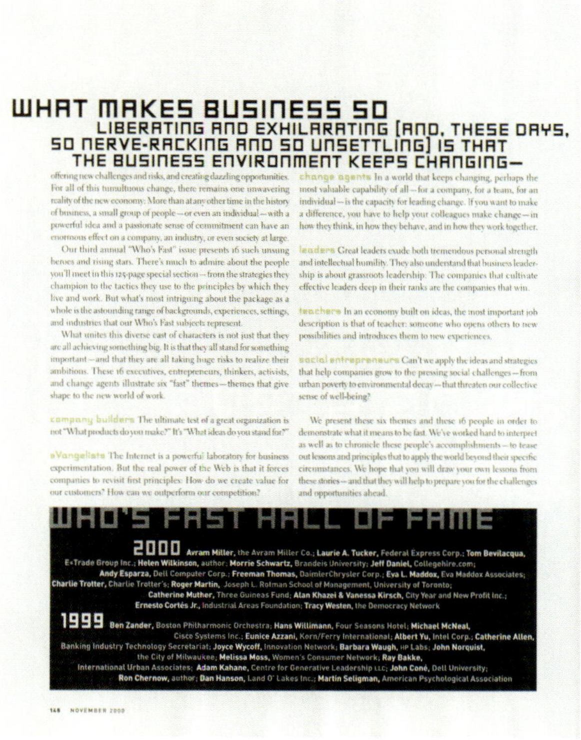
WHAT MAKES BUSINESS SO LIBERATING AND EXHILARATING [AND, THESE DAYS, SO NERVE-RACKING AND SO UNSETTLING] IS THAT THE BUSINESS ENVIRONMENT KEEPS CHANGING—

WHO'S FAST HALL OF FAME

Fast Company, No. 11, 2000, Great Britain

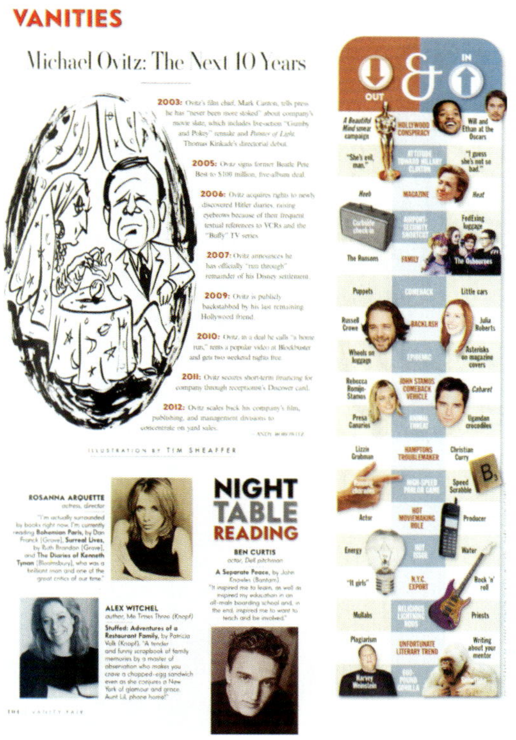

Vanity Fair, No. 6, 2002, Great Britain

The Face, No. 5, 2002, Great Britain

Maps, cross-sections and three-dimensional representations

Explanatory illustrations are needed to present complicated factual information or situations that are normally hidden from us, perhaps because they're microscopically small, somewhere out there in the infinite universe, or down at the centre of the earth. They're also used to explain complex structures that can only be visualized if the roof is taken off, so to speak, offering an inside view of what's normally closed off.

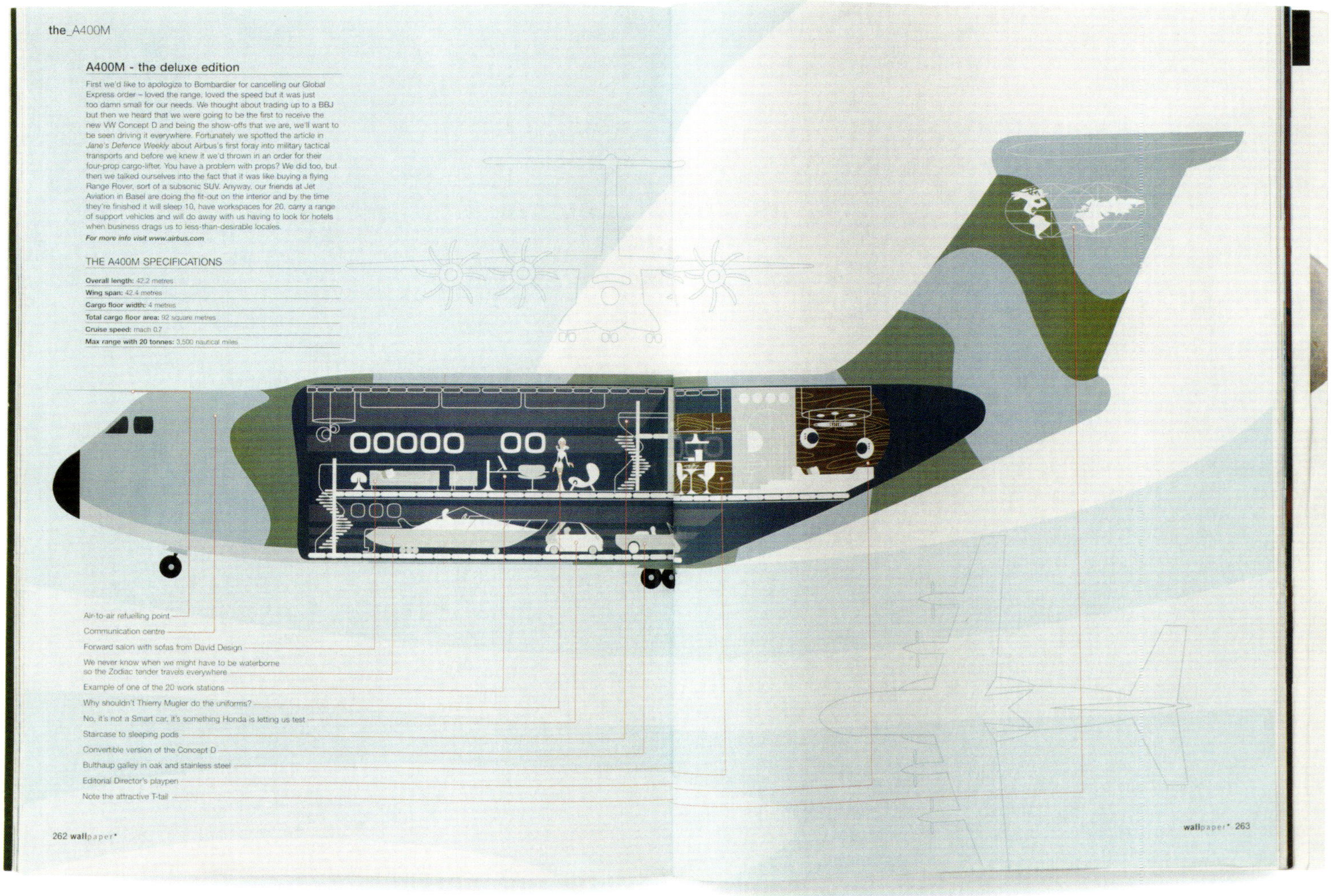

the_A400M

A400M - the deluxe edition

First we'd like to apologize to Bombardier for cancelling our Global Express order – loved the range, loved the speed but it was just too damn small for our needs. We thought about trading up to a BBJ but then we heard that we were going to be the first to receive the new VW Concept D and being the show-offs that we are, we'll want to be seen driving it everywhere. Fortunately we spotted the article in *Jane's Defence Weekly* about Airbus's first foray into military tactical transports and before we knew it we'd thrown in an order for their four-prop cargo-lifter. You have a problem with props? We did too, but then we talked ourselves into the fact that it was like buying a flying Range Rover, sort of a subsonic SUV. Anyway, our friends at Jet Aviation in Basel are doing the fit-out on the interior and by the time they're finished it will sleep 10, have workspaces for 20, carry a range of support vehicles and will do away with us having to look for hotels when business drags us to less-than-desirable locales.

For more info visit www.airbus.com

THE A400M SPECIFICATIONS

Overall length: 42.2 metres
Wing span: 42.4 metres
Cargo floor width: 4 metres
Total cargo floor area: 92 square metres
Cruise speed: mach 0.7
Max range with 20 tonnes: 3,500 nautical miles

Wallpaper, No. 12, 2000, Great Britain

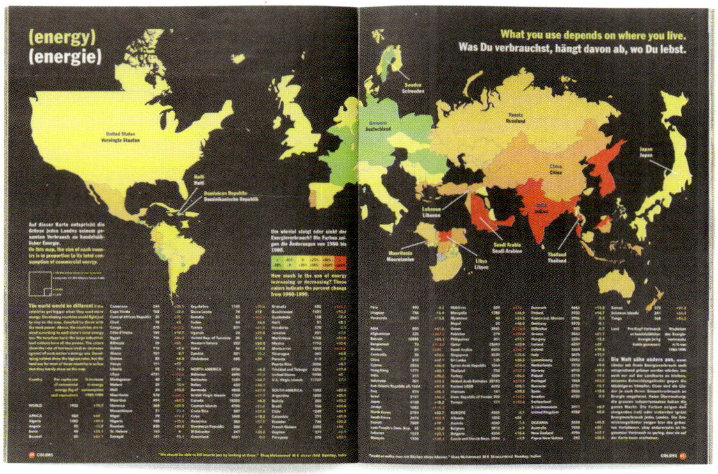

Colors, No. 6, 1994, Italy

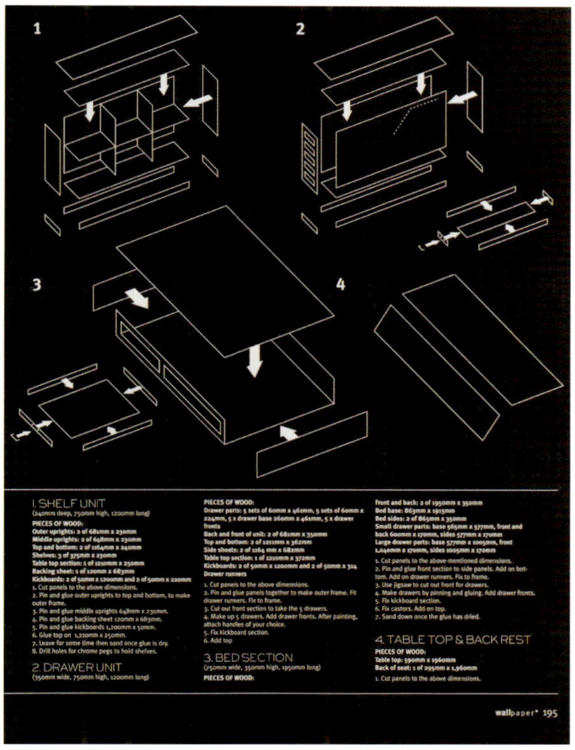

Wallpaper, July/August 2000, Great Britain

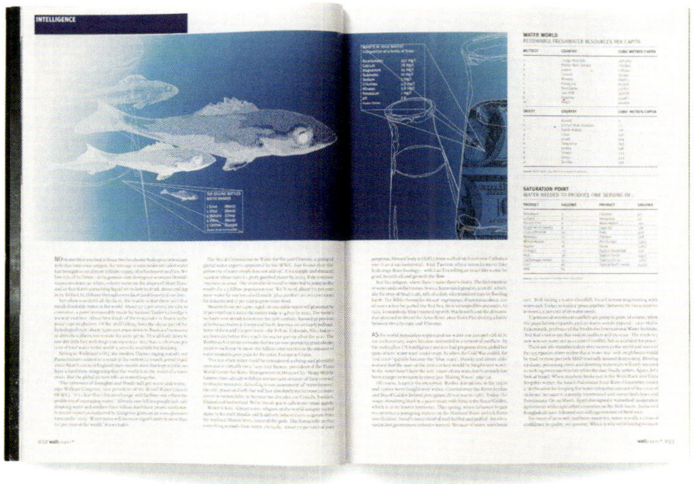

Wallpaper, No. 6, 2001, Great Britain

Geo, No. 6, 2002, Germany

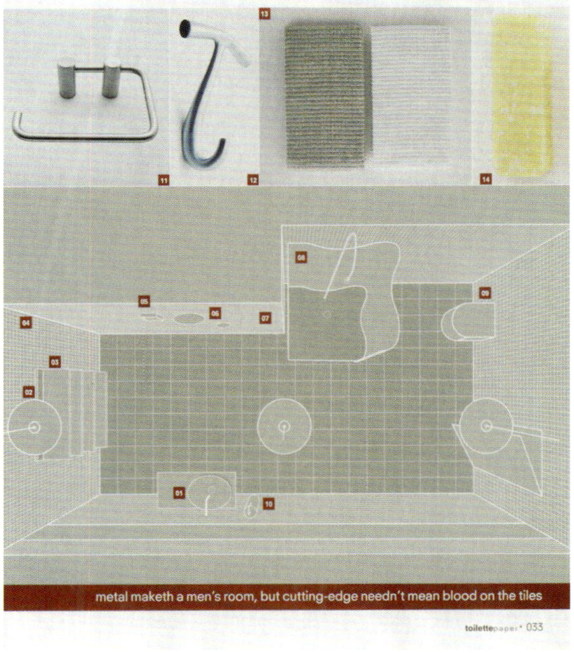

Wallpaper, No. 3, 2000, Great Britain

TYPES OF PAGE. Editorial

Where the editor meets the reader

The editorial is the editor's means of greeting the reader. It's usually situated on page three, but in magazines that start off with a collection of ads, it will be on the first page of text. There are some cases where the editorial is on the same page as the list of contents, and others where it's combined with a half-page ad. A common component is a picture of the editor plus his or her signature, but there are also purely typographical presentations without a picture. That usually depends on the nature of the editorial itself.

Here are a few different forms:

- The leader: the personal opinion of the editor
- The presentation: a survey of the contents, introducing important topics, sometimes even accompanied by pictures.
- The behind-the-scenes: background information on how individual contributions came to be written.
- The diary.

The editorial is generally the last item to be written, and it's often only finished just before the deadline.

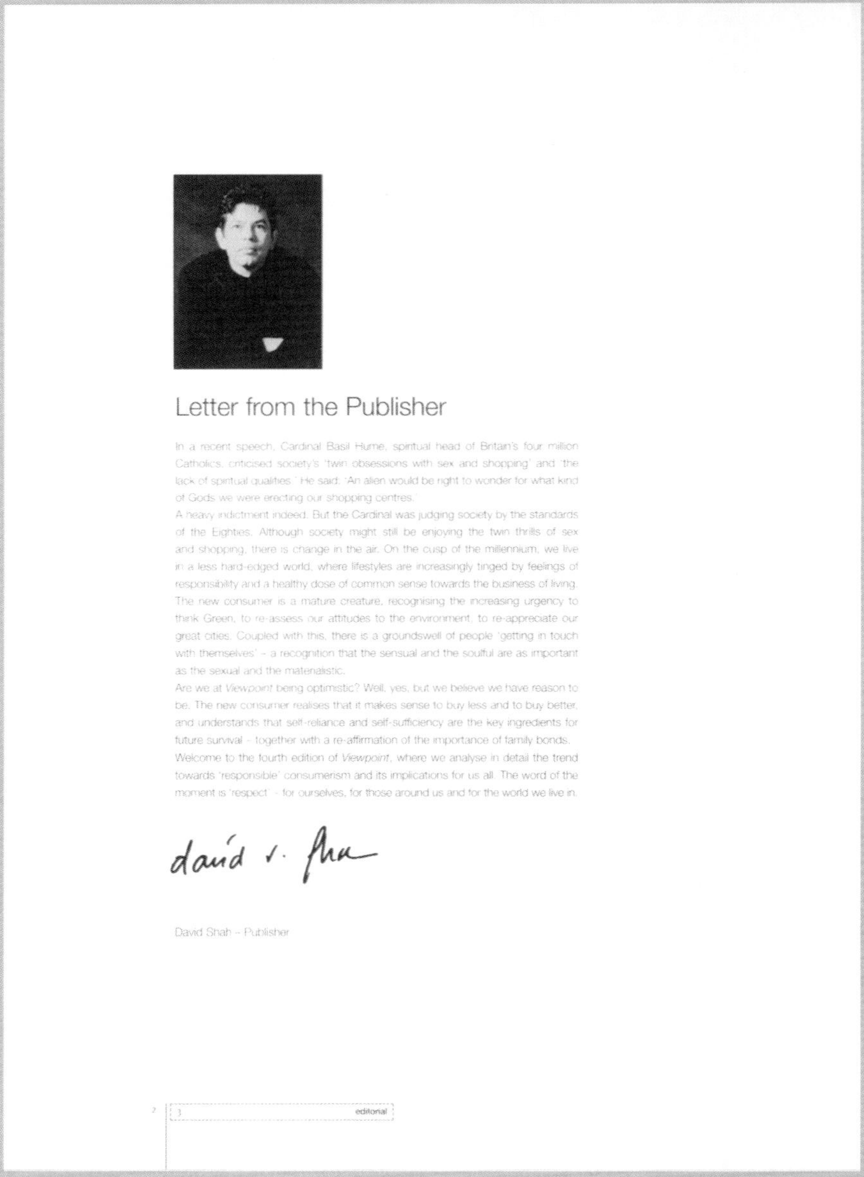

Letter from the Publisher

In a recent speech, Cardinal Basil Hume, spiritual head of Britain's four million Catholics, criticised society's 'twin obsessions with sex and shopping' and 'the lack of spiritual qualities.' He said: 'An alien would be right to wonder for what kind of Gods we were erecting our shopping centres.'

A heavy indictment indeed. But the Cardinal was judging society by the standards of the Eighties. Although society might still be enjoying the twin thrills of sex and shopping, there is change in the air. On the cusp of the millennium, we live in a less hard-edged world, where lifestyles are increasingly tinged by feelings of responsibility and a healthy dose of common sense towards the business of living. The new consumer is a mature creature, recognising the increasing urgency to think Green, to re-assess our attitudes to the environment, to re-appreciate our great cities. Coupled with this, there is a groundswell of people 'getting in touch with themselves' – a recognition that the sensual and the soulful are as important as the sexual and the materialistic.

Are we at *Viewpoint* being optimistic? Well, yes, but we believe we have reason to be. The new consumer realises that it makes sense to buy less and to buy better, and understands that self-reliance and self-sufficiency are the key ingredients for future survival – together with a re-affirmation of the importance of family bonds.

Welcome to the fourth edition of *Viewpoint*, where we analyse in detail the trend towards 'responsible' consumerism and its implications for us all. The word of the moment is 'respect' – for ourselves, for those around us and for the world we live in.

David Shah – Publisher

3 editorial

Viewpoint, September 1998, Netherlands

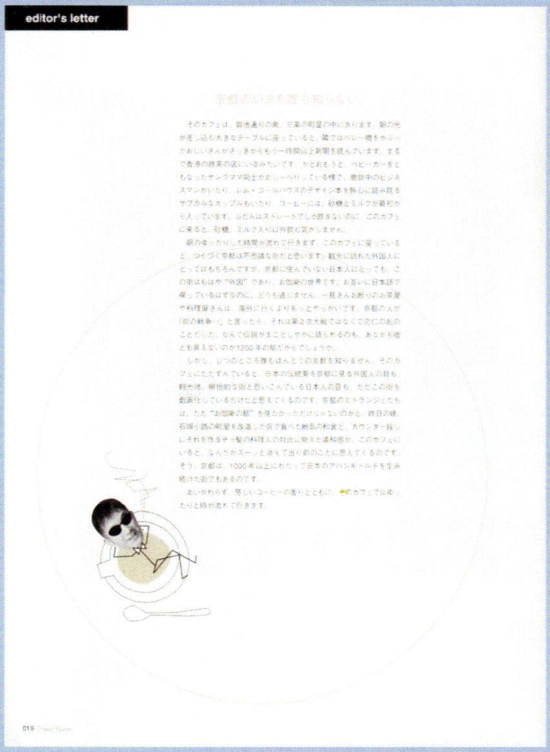
editor's letter

Vogue Nippon, No. 2, 2002, Japan

editorial 編者的話

The last quarter of 2000 saw The Substation making the news with two fund-raising events: a gala dinner featuring Charlotte Church, and Art Power 2000, an exhibition of 28 Singapore artists' works including Tang Da Wu's "Don't Give Money to the Arts" – a jacket with those words embroidered across the back, which was up for silent auction.

Da Wu first wore this jacket in an act at the gala openings of two major Singapore art exhibitions in 1995. That year saw the withdrawal of public funding for performance art. Da Wu left the interpretation of "Don't Give Money to the Arts" to those who viewed his act.

The reappearance of Da Wu's jacket in 2000 reignites questions regarding arts funding and sponsorship, in the wake of the national commitment towards a "Renaissance City". The auctioning of the jacket explicitly foregrounded the act of "giving money to the arts". Perhaps the irony of this act moved some to question the rationale for funding the arts. A very Singaporean question would be: Why should money be given to something that carries no guaranteed financial returns?

Returns from art cannot be calculated in dollars and cents for they are usually intangible. The value we place on art is not calculated according to fixed objective criteria. This brings me to the Charlotte Church phenomenon. The donors who paid thousands of dollars to listen to a 14-year-old sing obviously felt that her talent and the pleasure she could give them through her music were worth that outlay. Would they part with the same amount for a local or Asian artist? While there is no denying Charlotte Church's talent, one wonders about the role of marketing in determining the prices we are willing to pay. The same goes for the commercial art market. So how do we measure the worth of art?

Sponsors often measure the amount they give against "audience reach". Small artistic events inevitably suffer in this sort of marketplace, yet sometimes the most fulfilling work (for both artist and audience) is small-scale work. Ultimately, arts sponsorship is not the same as advertising: investing in an arts project isn't only about buying ad space or airtime. The benefits are not always immediate. Arts sponsorship can also be an investment into an artist, the development of the his/her skill, and the impact of the artist's work in society.

So why give money to the arts? Just imagine a world without art. Some of us in the arts community are trying to do just that, by observing a "no arts day". We invite you to share your thoughts with us on this.

On a slightly different note, a man who knows about the value of art is Mr Lam Pin Foo, who has just retired after many years serving on The Substation's Board of Directors. We thank him for his constant support and wish him all the best.

Audrey Wong
Artistic Co-Director

Audrey Wong
艺术总监

02 ALL-ANIMATION NITES
08 REVIEW: MAKING IT DIGITAL WORKSHOP
10 CHARLOTTE CHURCH CHARITY GALA DINNER
11 THE SUBSTATION'S ARTPOWER 2000
12 CALENDAR
16 計劃

Substance, January/February 2001, Singapore

LEADER

Don't criminalize cloning research.

THE CRUSADE to criminalize human cloning, motivated by the desire not to start down the slippery slope to eugenics, will inflict substantial collateral damage to potentially life-saving therapeutic cloning of stem cells for use in cell regeneration. Numerous proposed federal and state bills in the United States would "stop the cloning process at the beginning" (in the words of one such bill) by banning even the most rudimentary experimentation, like transferring DNA into an egg cell without a nucleus, that could potentially lead to cloned individuals. The federal bills, which carry penalties of up to ten years in prison, enjoy bipartisan and presidential support. They should not.

Proponents of the bills argue that permitting the cloning of human cells would make it impossible to prevent full reproductive cloning. Maybe so, but it's worth the risk. Cloning technologies might one day produce insulin-secreting islet cells that effectively treat diabetes, or nerve cells that can repair a damaged spinal cord. Who knows what other great medical advances could emerge from this promising line of scientific inquiry? Politicians think they do know, however, and have decided these advances aren't worth risking an "affront to human dignity." Patients wasting away with Parkinson's disease or congestive heart failure may disagree.

The panic over cloning feeds off of the popular fear of a brave new world, threats by the Raelian cult to clone humans, and warnings by talking heads like William Kristol, editor and publisher of the *Weekly Standard*, about the "eugenic manipulation of human nature." But brave new worlds are more often created by authoritarian rule, not by individuals making personal medical choices. You don't spare human dignity by jailing those trying to ease human suffering.■

Write to editorialpage@redherring.com.

AUGUST 15, 2001 · RED HERRING 21

Red Herring, August 2001, USA

Brett, No. 8, 2000, Germany

Ausdruck, Spring 1997, Germany

Passionate, No. 1, 2001, Netherlands

Numéro, No. 31, 2002, France

éd
ito
rial

Ce serait comme une envie de vacances, de soleil en avance, de jours déjà longs. Cette saison, la mode oublie d'être histoire pour devenir géographie, et métamorphose votre dressing en malle de voyage aux accents ethniques. Ce septième numéro de *Max Mode* est une invitation au voyage, mais pas n'importe lequel : direction les Suds, du désert américain au souk, des barrios aux ragazzi.

Les Suds, comme un mode de vie qui invite à enfiler une chemise-djellabah pour partir au travail en rêvant de Méditerranée, un pantalon moulant de toréador pour transformer un dance-floor en arène, une paire de tongs pour enfin faire surgir la plage sur le bitume, le temps d'une séance de bronzage d'orteils en terrasse.

Les Suds, comme une attitude, propices à la nonchalance d'une nuit au palace ou d'une balade en mobylette aux portes de Marrakech. Ou encore, comme un rêve, une pause en maillot de bain sous l'objectif de Jack Pierson, quelque part vers Paris, Texas.

Les Suds, comme l'Italie. Nous avons convié de jeunes Romains bien informés à nous faire visiter leur ville et ses trésors. Nous n'avons pas fait ce choix au hasard : il fallait donner la parole à ceux qui refusent les sirènes du populisme au pouvoir. Tous témoignent que Rome, heureusement, ne cède pas, et résiste par l'art, la fête, la séduction, quand elle ne verse pas dans la contestation pure et simple. Pasolini et Hervé Guibert viennent en fantômes guider vos pas dans une autre Rome mythique, celle des mauvais garçons. Le photographe Max Vadukul y saisit la dolce vita 2002. Vous n'avez plus qu'à piocher dans les cinquante meilleures adresses romaines sélectionnées par *Max Mode* pour aller y voir vous-même, le temps d'un week-end ou davantage. Les Suds, comme ceux que vous inventerez.

25

Mode Max, No. 7, 2002, France

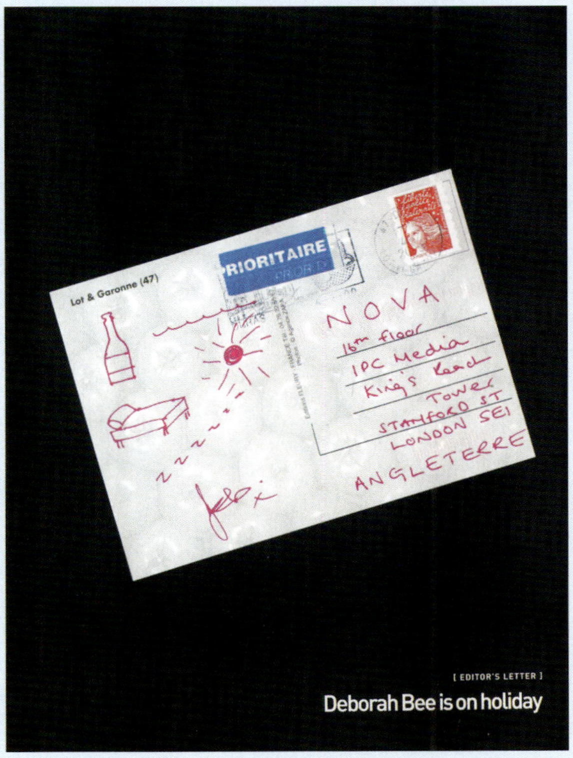

Nova, No. 9, 2000, Great Britain

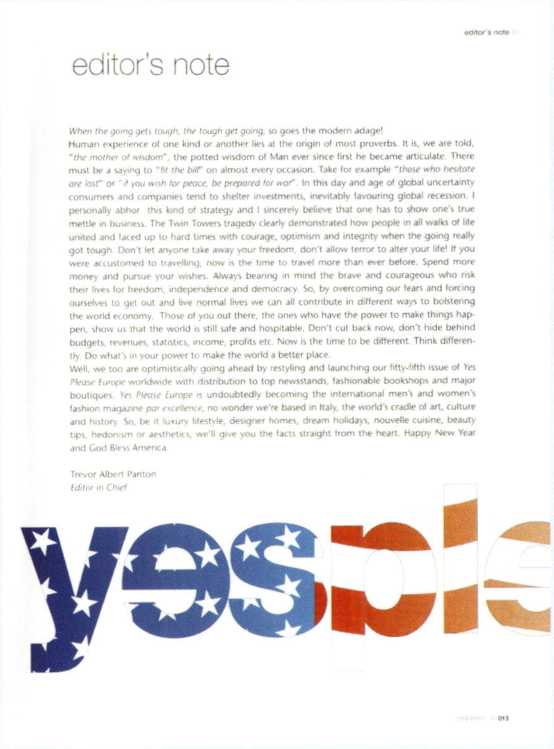
editor's note

editor's note

When the going gets tough, the tough get going, so goes the modern adage!

Human experience of one kind or another lies at the origin of most proverbs. It is, we are told, "*the mother of wisdom*", the potted wisdom of Man ever since first he became articulate. There must be a saying to "*fit the bill*" on almost every occasion. Take for example "*those who hesitate are lost*" or "*if you wish for peace, be prepared for war*". In this day and age of global uncertainty consumers and companies tend to shelter investments, inevitably favouring global recession. I personally abhor this kind of strategy and I sincerely believe that one has to show one's true mettle in business. The Twin Towers tragedy clearly demonstrated how people in all walks of life united and faced up to hard times with courage, optimism and integrity when the going really got tough. Don't let anyone take away your freedom, don't allow terror to alter your life! If you were accustomed to travelling, now is the time to travel more than ever before. Spend more money and pursue your wishes. Always bearing in mind the brave and courageous who risk their lives for freedom, independence and democracy. So, by overcoming our fears and forcing ourselves to get out and live normal lives we can all contribute in different ways to bolstering the world economy. Those of you out there, the ones who have the power to make things happen, show us that the world is still safe and hospitable. Don't cut back now, don't hide behind budgets, revenues, statistics, income, profits etc. Now is the time to be different. Think differently. Do what's in your power to make the world a better place.

Well, we too are optimistically going ahead by restyling and launching our fifty-fifth issue of *Yes Please Europe* worldwide with distribution to top newsstands, fashionable bookshops and major boutiques. *Yes Please Europe* is undoubtedly becoming the international men's and women's fashion magazine *par excellence*, no wonder we're based in Italy, the world's cradle of art, culture and history. So, be it luxury lifestyle, designer homes, dream holidays, nouvelle cuisine, beauty tips, hedonism or aesthetics, we'll give you the facts straight from the heart. Happy New Year and God Bless America.

Trevor Albert Panton
Editor in Chief

Yesplease, December 2001/January 2002, Italy

From a neutral list to a mouth-watering menu

There are various factors that determine the design of a list of contents. The main one is, of course, the character of the magazine itself: special interest and current affairs magazines require a different approach from that of, say, lifestyle. The form is dictated by the function. If people only read the magazine selectively, the list of contents will be different from that of a magazine that people leaf through with no particular item in mind, just waiting for something to catch their eye. In all cases, though, the list should reflect the structure of the magazine, following its sections and the order of its articles. Generally there are two levels, one pictorial and one textual, with the emphasis again depending on the nature of the magazine. Pictures may be used to emphasize certain central themes, but they also help to attract the more visually orientated reader to one particular subject. For this reason, such pictures should be supplemented with captions and page numbers. The contents page is especially attractive to advertisers, as most readers will turn to it, and lengthy lists are often spread out over two separate pages so that they can be split up by two full-page ads. For the reader, though, it's clearly easier to follow if the contents are on one page or, in really thick magazines, put together on a double-page spread. In some high-quality magazines, the list of contents is written by a journalist in order to make sure that the linguistic style is homogeneous. The page numbers themselves must be clearly laid out, either to the right or left of the subject matter; there's little room here for experimentation, because in its role as an instrument of navigation, the list's highest priorities should be clarity and ease of use.

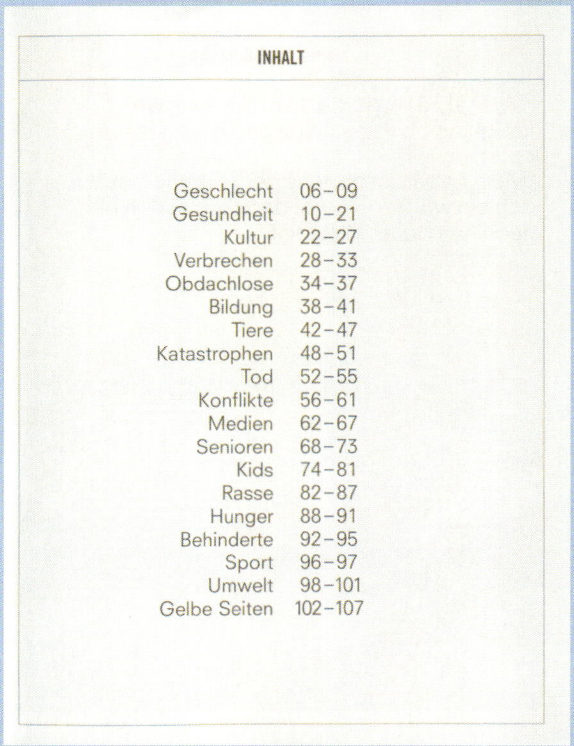

INHALT

Geschlecht	06–09
Gesundheit	10–21
Kultur	22–27
Verbrechen	28–33
Obdachlose	34–37
Bildung	38–41
Tiere	42–47
Katastrophen	48–51
Tod	52–55
Konflikte	56–61
Medien	62–67
Senioren	68–73
Kids	74–81
Rasse	82–87
Hunger	88–91
Behinderte	92–95
Sport	96–97
Umwelt	98–101
Gelbe Seiten	102–107

Colors, No. 46, 2001, Italy

RED HERRING

CONTENTS

26

FORWARD

TELECOM: As companies go bankrupt, buyout firms lick their chops 24

BIOTECH: Frankenforests cropping up. How genetic engineering of trees could boost productivity 25

ONE TO WATCH: Alpiri hopes to win the name game in e-commerce 26

POLICY: China prepares for a deregulated telco market ... 27

COMMERCE: The bar code's high-tech sibling. Radio frequency identification and the future of faster food ... 27

ENERGY: Coming soon to a roof over you: solar shingles 28

CAN THIS COMPANY BE SAVED?: Lucent angles for survival .. 28

VENTURE CAPITAL: Singapore gambles big with biotech payouts 34

EXCHANGES: Trading private equity publicly may not fly 36

OVER HERE: Paying the piper for Internet access 38

PROFILE: Anne Glover conquers the macho world of British venture capital 40

BOOK REVIEW: Follow the money 41

GRAPHITI 30
CASHFLOW 32
DEALFLOW 34
DEALFLOP 35

BRIEFING

STORAGE: With the dumb dot-com money gone, the space race begins in earnest 76

INTEROPERABILITY: Storage titans would rather fight than connect 78

EXPLAINED: iSCSI—SAN of the times 82

BUSINESS MODELS: SSPs adapt to market change 84

VC WHISPERS 86
PRIVATE COMPANY PROFILES 88
PUBLIC COMPANY PROFILES 90

INVESTOR

EMPIRE BUILDING: Here's how Microsoft should spend its huge pile of cash 92

MORE MONEY: Bankers focus on follow-ons 94

STAYING ALIVE: Lucent and Nortel raise some much-needed cash 94

NEWSREEL: IM rumor roils PeopleSoft 95

WEB RETAILING: The prodigal e-commerce sites return 96

STORAGE SHOWDOWN: Hitachi is now a big thorn in EMC's side 100

SPARE CHANGE 93
THE CONTRARIAN 98
TACTICS 102
THE RED HERRING PORTFOLIO 104

6 RED HERRING • SEPTEMBER 15, 2001

Red Herring, No. 104, 2001, USA

Tank, No. 1, 2000, Great Britain

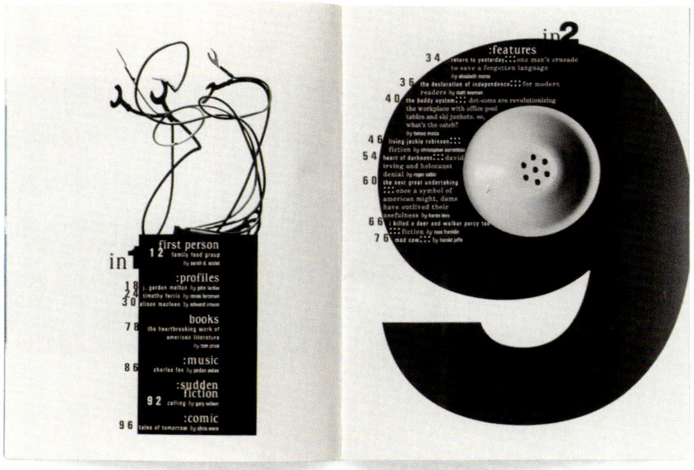

Speak, No. 2, 2000, USA

Eden, No. 1, 1999, Germany

Detnin Exclusief, No. 3, 2001, Netherlands

Tank, No. 4, 2001, Great Britain

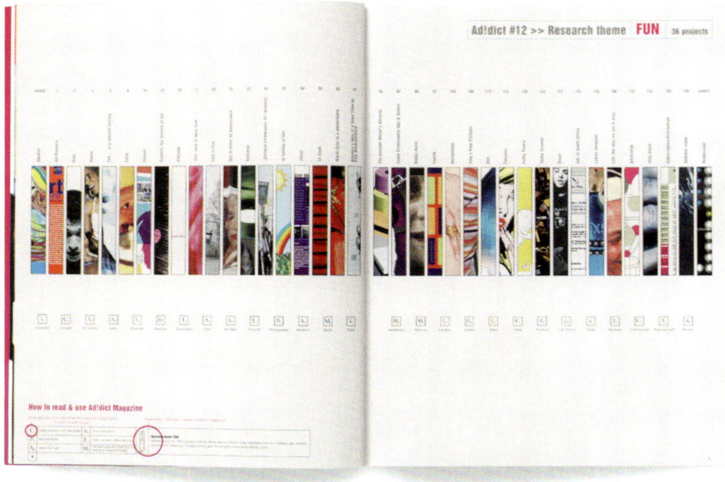

Ad!dict, Spring 2001, Belgium

11 Freunde, No. 12, 2002, Germany

2wice, November 1999, USA

Tank, No. 3, 2001, Great Britain

Aspects, No. 1, 2000, Germany

AM7, No. 7, 2001, Germany

Bloom, No. 5, 2000, France
Double page contents, photo by Anton Beeke

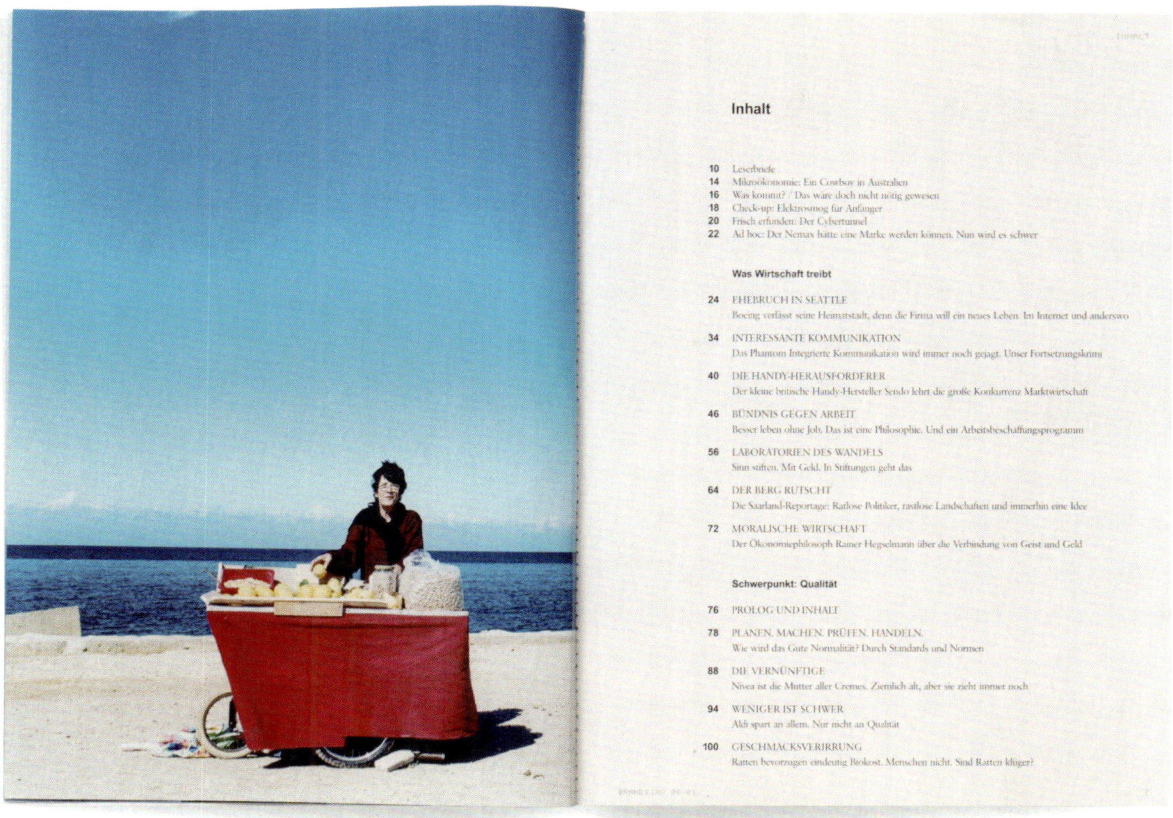

Inhalt

10 Leserbriefe
14 Mikroökonomie: Ein Cowboy in Australien
16 Was kommt? / Das wäre doch nicht nötig gewesen
18 Check-up: Elektrosmog für Anfänger
20 Frisch erfunden: Der Cybertunnel
22 Ad hoc: Der Nemax hätte eine Marke werden können. Nun wird es schwer

Was Wirtschaft treibt

24 EHEBRUCH IN SEATTLE
Boeing verlässt seine Heimatstadt, denn die Firma will ein neues Leben. Im Internet und anderswo

34 INTERESSANTE KOMMUNIKATION
Das Phantom Integrierte Kommunikation wird immer noch gejagt. Unser Fortsetzungskrimi

40 DIE HANDY-HERAUSFORDERER
Der kleine britische Handy-Hersteller Sendo lehrt die große Konkurrenz Marktwirtschaft

46 BÜNDNIS GEGEN ARBEIT
Besser leben ohne Job. Das ist eine Philosophie. Und ein Arbeitsbeschaffungsprogramm

56 LABORATORIEN DES WANDELS
Sinn stiften. Mit Geld. In Stiftungen geht das

64 DER BERG RUTSCHT
Die Saarland-Reportage: Ratlose Politiker, rastlose Landschaften und immerhin eine Idee

72 MORALISCHE WIRTSCHAFT
Der Ökonomiephilosoph Rainer Hegselmann über die Verbindung von Geist und Geld

Schwerpunkt: Qualität

76 PROLOG UND INHALT

78 PLANEN. MACHEN. PRÜFEN. HANDELN.
Wie wird das Gute Normalität? Durch Standards und Normen

88 DIE VERNÜNFTIGE
Nivea ist die Mutter aller Cremes. Ziemlich alt, aber sie zieht immer noch

94 WENIGER IST SCHWER
Aldi spart an allem. Nur nicht an Qualität

100 GESCHMACKSVERIRRUNG
Ratten bevorzugen eindeutig Biokost. Menschen nicht. Sind Ratten klüger?

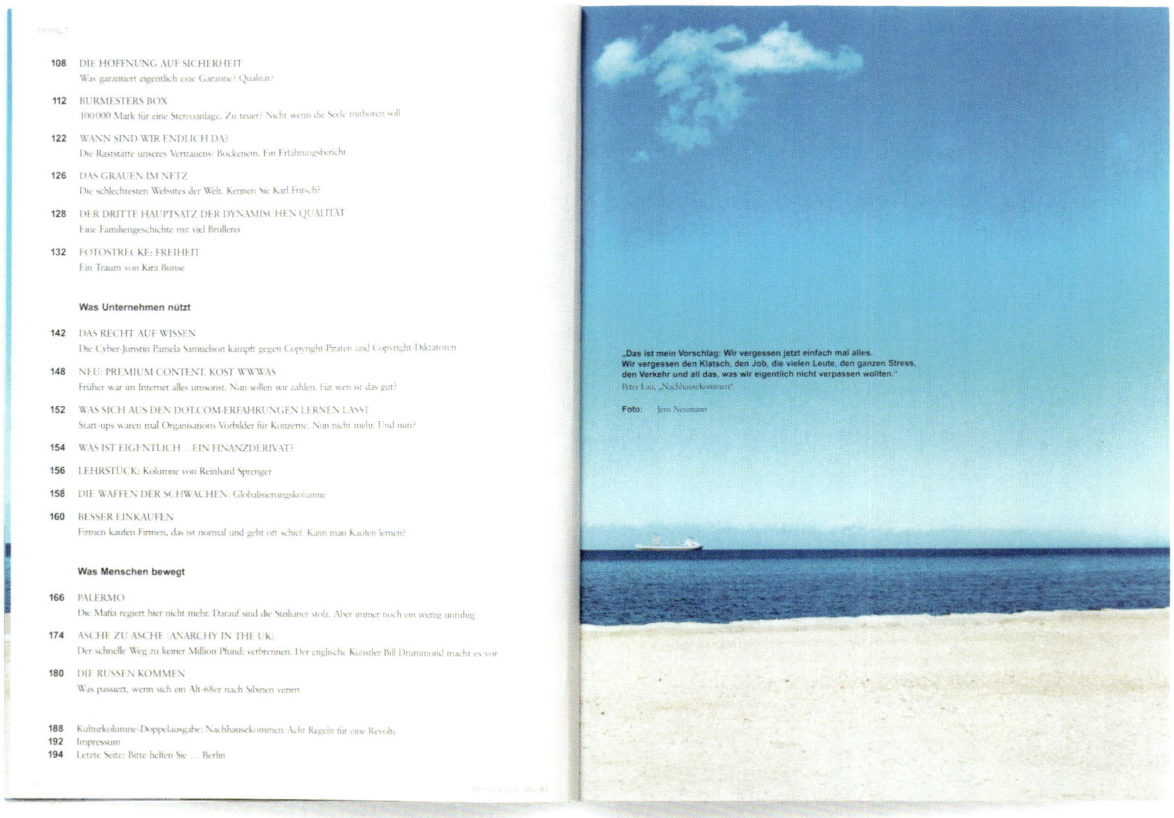

108 DIE HOFFNUNG AUF SICHERHEIT
Was garantiert eigentlich eine Garantie? Qualität?

112 BURMESTERS BOX
100 000 Mark für eine Stereoanlage. Zu teuer? Nicht wenn die Seele mithören soll

122 WANN SIND WIR ENDLICH DA?
Die Raststätte unseres Vertrauens: Bockenem. Ein Erfahrungsbericht

126 DAS GRAUEN IM NETZ
Die schlechtesten Websites der Welt. Kennen Sie Karl Fritsch?

128 DER DRITTE HAUPTSATZ DER DYNAMISCHEN QUALITÄT
Eine Familiengeschichte mit viel Brüllerei

132 FOTOSTRECKE: FREIHEIT
Ein Traum von Kira Bunse

Was Unternehmen nützt

142 DAS RECHT AUF WISSEN
Die Cyber-Juristin Pamela Samuelson kämpft gegen Copyright-Piraten und Copyright-Diktatoren

148 NEU: PREMIUM CONTENT. KOST WWWAS
Früher war im Internet alles umsonst. Nun sollen wir zahlen. Für wen ist das gut?

152 WAS SICH AUS DEN DOT.COM-ERFAHRUNGEN LERNEN LÄSST
Start-ups waren mal Organisations-Vorbilder für Konzerne. Nun nicht mehr. Und nun?

154 WAS IST EIGENTLICH … EIN FINANZDERIVAT?

156 LEHRSTÜCK: Kolumne von Reinhard Sprenger

158 DIE WAFFEN DER SCHWACHEN: Globalisierungskolumne

160 BESSER EINKAUFEN
Firmen kaufen Firmen, das ist normal und geht oft schief. Kann man Kaufen lernen?

Was Menschen bewegt

166 PALERMO
Die Mafia regiert hier nicht mehr. Darauf sind die Sizilianer stolz. Aber immer noch ein wenig unruhig

174 ASCHE ZU ASCHE (ANARCHY IN THE UK)
Der schnelle Weg zu keiner Million Pfund: verbrennen. Der englische Künstler Bill Drummond macht es vor

180 DIE RUSSEN KOMMEN
Was passiert, wenn sich ein Alt-68er nach Sibirien verirrt

188 Kulturkolumne-Doppelausgabe: Nachhausekommen/Acht Regeln für eine Revolte
192 Impressum
194 Letzte Seite: Bitte helfen Sie … Berlin

„Das ist mein Vorschlag: Wir vergessen jetzt einfach mal alles.
Wir vergessen den Klatsch, den Job, die vielen Leute, den ganzen Stress,
den Verkehr und all das, was wir eigentlich nicht verpassen wollten."
Peter Lau, „Nachhausekommen"

Foto: Jens Neumann

Brand eins, No. 6, 2001, Germany

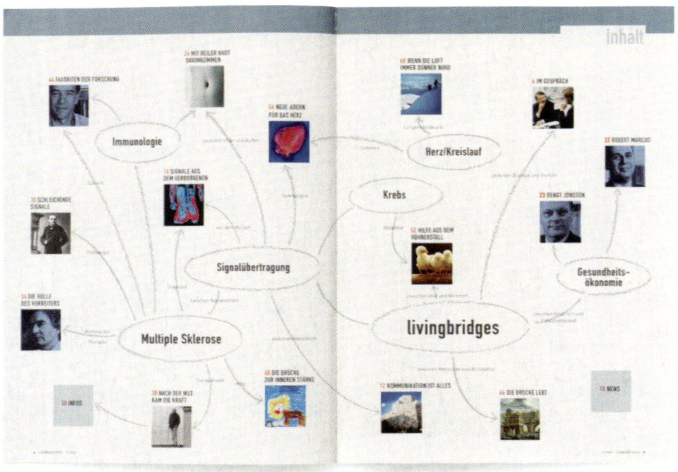

Living Bridges, No. 1, 2002, Germany

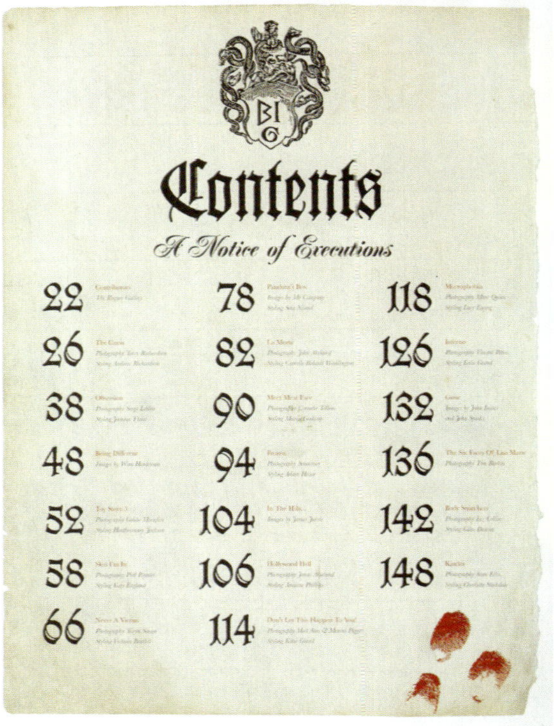

Big, No. 28, 2000, USA

Values, No. 2, 2002, Germany

Blue Inc., 2001, Germany

Raygun, No. 41, 1996, USA

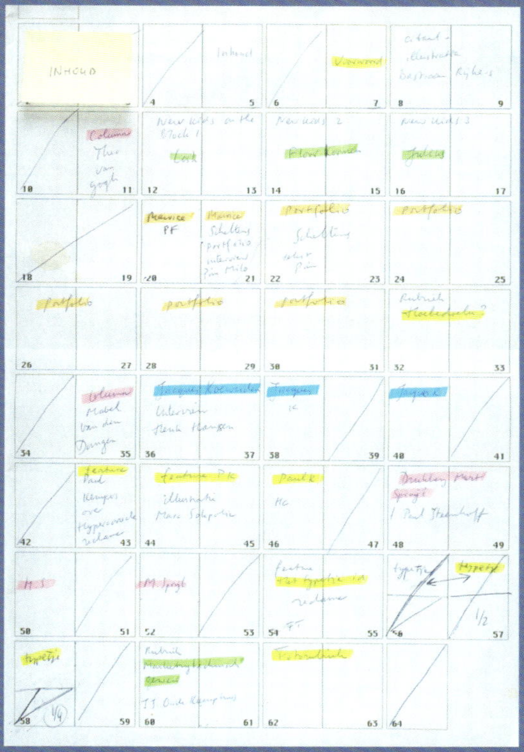

Credits, 1999, Netherlands

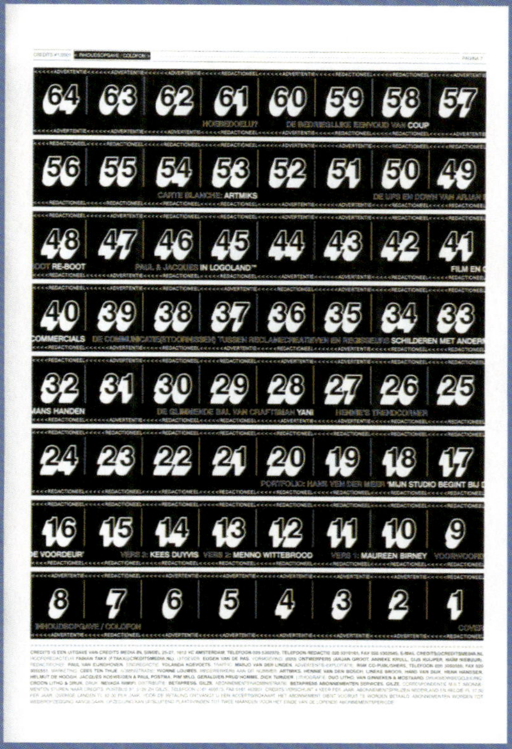

Credits, No. 1, 2001, Netherlands

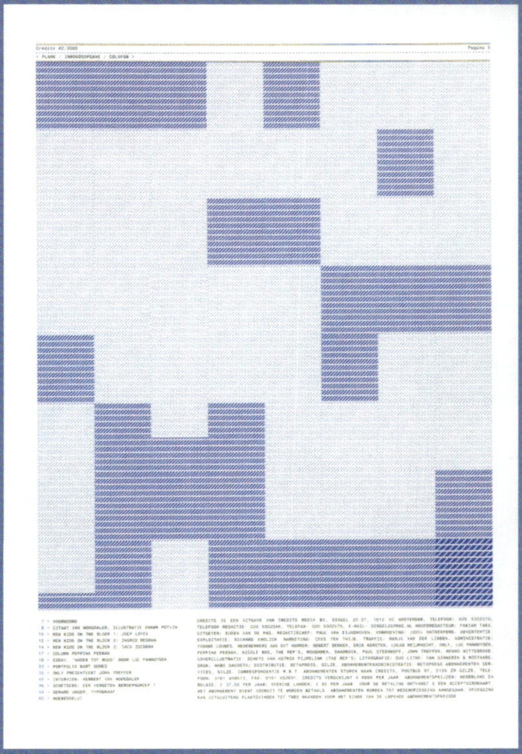

Credits, No. 2, 2000, Netherlands

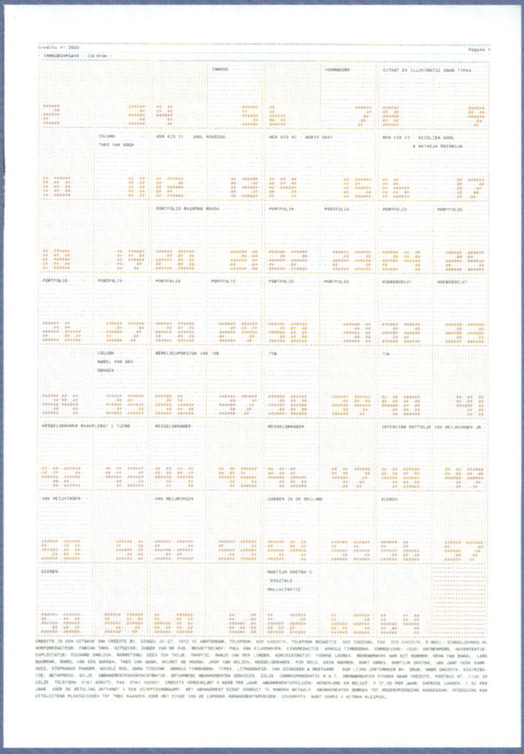

Credits, No. 1, 2000, Netherlands

Differentiating between ads and reports

In the classic magazine, there's a strict division between ads and editorial material. Most magazines cannot survive purely on sales, and so much of the cost is borne by ads. The division should be absolutely clear to the reader – who, after all, has a right to know what interests may lie behind a particular contribution – but this isn't always the case. One official hybrid form is the advertorial – a feature written by the editorial team but paid for by a commercial client. Such contributions should really come under the umbrella of public relations, and they often actually contain offers for the reader. But there are also features that describe or recommend selected products and are written quite independently of the firms concerned. It's only when sources and prices are quoted that the article becomes a promotional exercise. When products are recommended independently, the design should ensure that the feature is easily distinguishable from an ad.

Vogue, August 2001, Great Britain

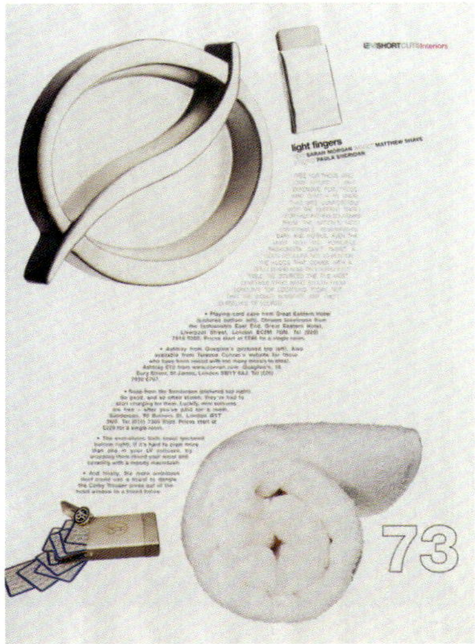

Loaded Fashion, Spring/Summer 2001, Great Britain

Bogey, June 2002, Great Britain

Home, July/August 2000, Germany

Vogue Paris, June/July 2000, France

Nova, No. 6, 2001, Germany

Ministry, August 2001, Austria

Esquire, April 2001, USA

Bare, January/February 2001, Great Britain

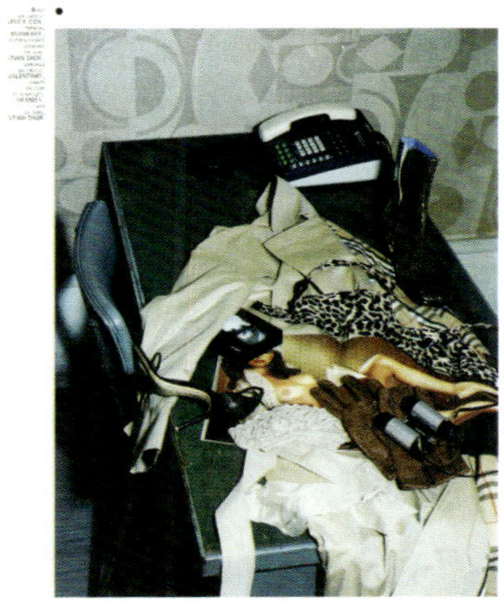

Mixt(e), September/October/November 2000, France

Harper's Bazaar, February 2002, USA

Ish, August 1999, Singapore

Vogue Pelle, September 2001, Italy

Ahead, No. 1, 2002, Austria

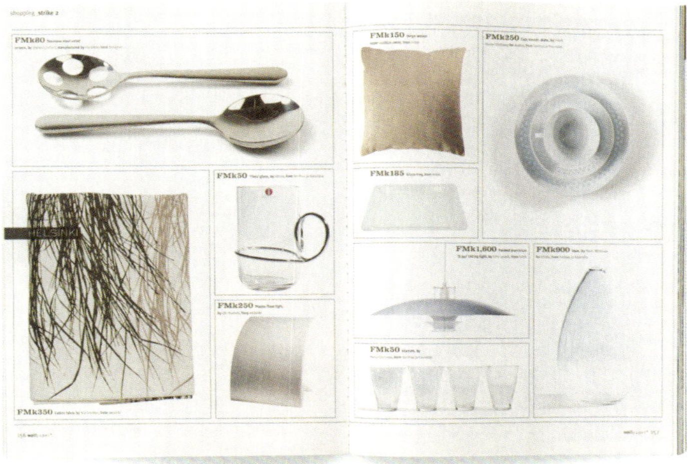

Wallpaper, July/August 2000, Great Britain

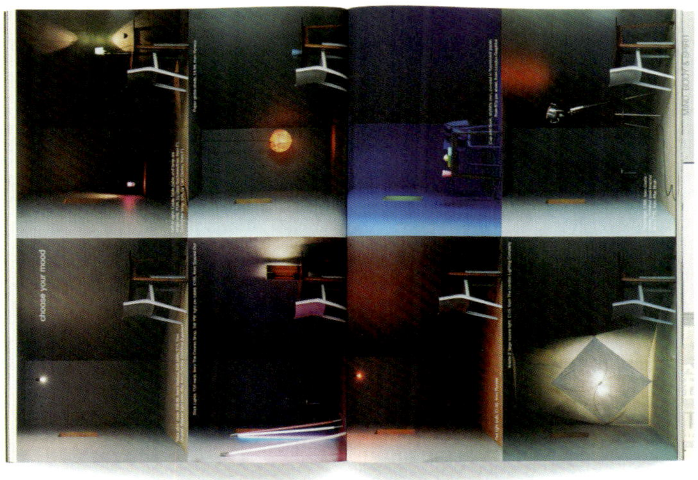

Bare, January/February 2001, Great Britain

Blond, No. 3, 2002, Germany

Snow, No. 2, 2002, Germany

Wallpaper, No. 3, 2000, Great Britain

Room, May/July 2001, Germany

Wired, December 2000, USA

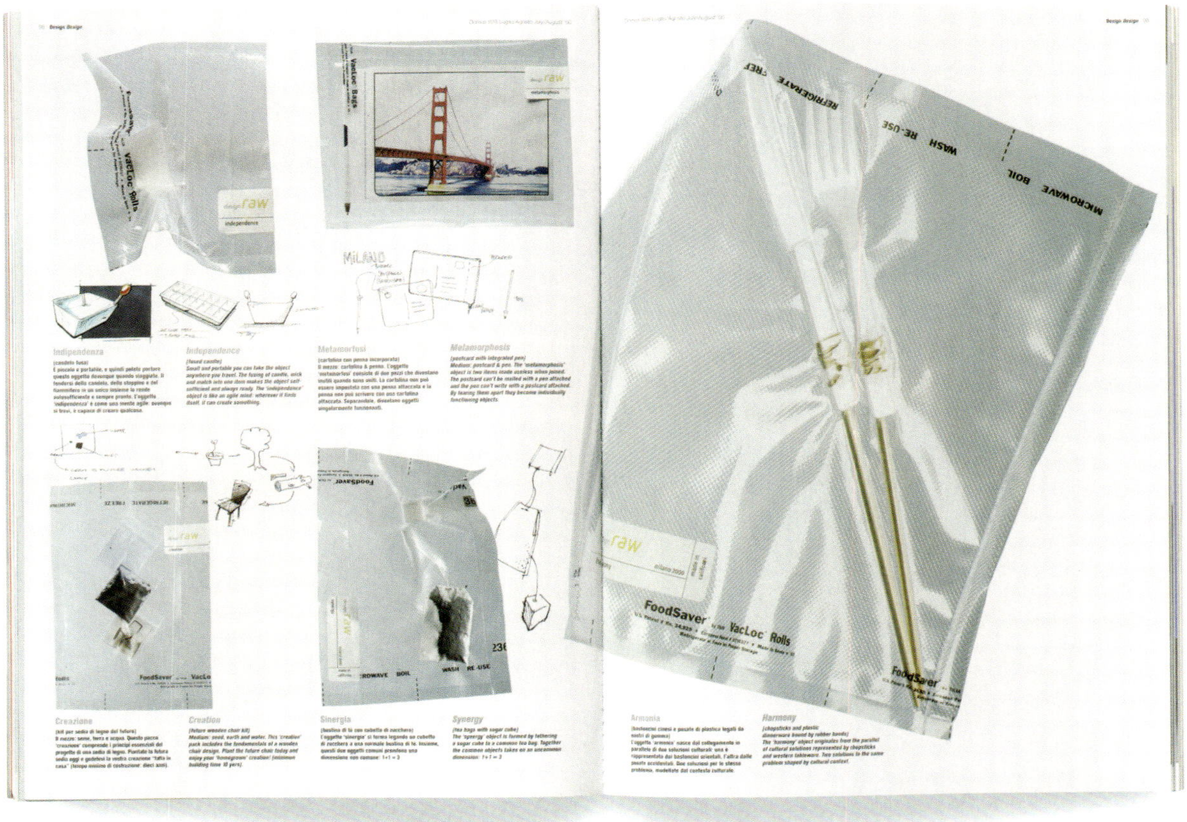

Domus, July/August 2000, Italy

TYPES OF PAGE. Columns

Distinguishing opinion pages from the editorial

Every feature in a magazine will add up to a general reflection of editorial opinion. With political magazines it's important for the reader to know the party line that's being followed, but many magazines also pride themselves on publishing articles that express views independent of, or even contrary to, those of the editors. Such contributions, along with readers' letters, appear as comments or columns on the opinion pages.

Again, the design should make them easily recognizable, and they're often combined with a photo or drawing of the author. As well as purely textual contributions, there may be columns that lay emphasis on pictorial comparisons. The various columns and comments may be one-off or regular, and obviously the former offers more freedom to the designer than the latter.

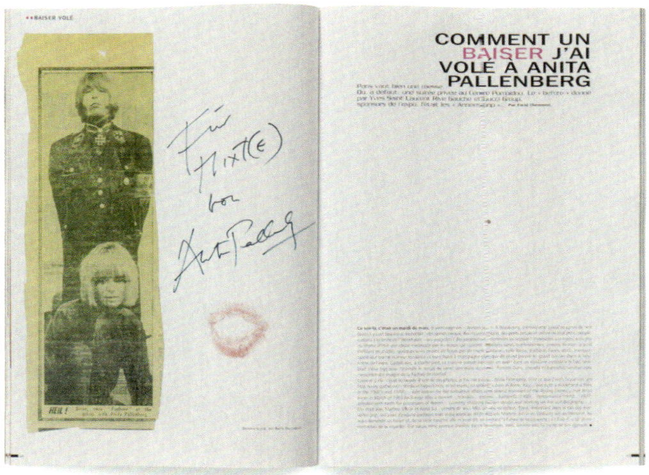

Mixt(e), June/July/August 2001, France

Mixt(e), October/November 2001, France

Mixt(e), September/October/November 2000, France

Hemisphere, No. 1, 2001, USA

Esquire, No. 4, 2001, USA

Surface, Spring 2000, USA

The Face, No. 9, 2001, Great Britain

TYPES OF PAGE. Imprint

From publisher's name and address to full-page list of credits

A publisher's imprint is required by law. Everyone responsible for content and ads must be named, and the imprint must also contain copyright details. All other information concerning the publishers and editorial staff is for the benefit of clients and readers.

Patron
Prof Tommy Koh

Advisor
Ong Pang Boon

Board of Directors
Mr Chew Kheng Chuan (Chairperson)
Prof Leo Tan
Dr Jennifer Lee
Mr Arun Mahizhnan
Prof Koh Tai Ann
Mr Lam Pin Foo
Mr Mok Wei Wei
Ms Tisa Ng
Mr Ong Peng Tsin
Dr Quah Sy Ren
Mr T. Sasitharan
Dr Mary Ann Tsao
Ms Yong Ying-I

Founder
Kuo Pao Kun

Artistic Co-Directors
Audrey Wong
Lee Weng Choy

General Manager
Seow Sher Yen

Marketing Manager
Juliana Chong

Programme Executive, Visual Arts
Aleksandar Obradovic

Programme Executive, Performing Arts
Glynisia Yeo

Programme Executive, New Media
Wahyuni Adiputri Hadi

Administrative Executive
Mazlinda Asmuni

Accounts Executive
Zhao Xin

Box Officer
Christopher Ong

Technicians
Patrick Wong

Honorary Legal Advisors
Robert W H Wang & Woo
Jan Tan & Chan

Honorary Company Secretary
June Tan

Auditor
Diong T P & Co

Editor
Wahyuni Adiputri Hadi

Creative
Design Asylum Pte Ltd

Printer
Capricorn Media Publication & Communication Services with MTM Printing Pte Ltd

The Substation is a beneficiary of the National Arts Council's Annual Grant Scheme

Cover
"Reactors As Vessel" by Joe Lewis

Substance, January/February 2001, Singapore

MIXT(E)
N°18 PRINTEMPS-ÉTÉ 2002 # 2

PUBLICITÉ ET SIÈGE SOCIAL
1, rue du Colonel-Pierre-Avia, 75503 Paris Cedex 15
Tél. : 01 46 48 48 48 Fax : 01 46 48 48 09
Edité par Excelsior Publications SA
Capital social 1 717 360 €

ÉDITEUR DELEGUÉ
Tiziano Humler-Rovero (01 46 48 19 95)

RÉDACTION
7, rue du Colonel-Pierre-Avia, 75503 Paris Cedex 15
Tél. : 01 46 48 47 74 Fax : 01 46 48 47 70
Adresses e-mail : prenom.nom@excelsior.fr

DIRECTEURS DE CRÉATION
Christian Rovera et Guy Guglieri
Tél. : 01 46 48 01 50
RÉDACTION EN CHEF
Sandrine Boury-Heyler (mode)
Farid Chenoune (magazine)
PRODUCTION
Véronique Chaubin
SECRÉTARIAT DE RÉDACTION
Yves Nespoulous
SERVICE ARTISTIQUE
Caroline Maillet
MODE
Carole Bellot, Karina Givargisoff, Samantha Hughes, Darryl Rodrigues, Joanna Thaw, Maria Virgin
ONT COLLABORÉ À CE NUMÉRO
Anne Bianchi, Margot Deponti, Vincent Dieutre, Anne-Marie Fèvre, Laurent Goumarre, Jérôme Hanover, Sarah de Haro, Mathieu Orléan, Axelle Roppert, Olivier Truc, Goran Vejvoda, Philippe Verzaro, Arnaud Viviant
PHOTOGRAPHIES
John Akehurst, Copai Barbieri, Bill Georgoussis, Patrick Ibanez, Maciek Kobielski, Thomas Lagrange, Antoine Le Grand, Jean-François Lepage, Magnus Mårding, Michel Momy, Serge Paulet, Patrick Pipard, Luis Sanchis, David Slijper, Goran Vejvoda
ILLUSTRATIONS
François Berthoud

DIRECTION – ADMINISTRATION
PRÉSIDENT-DIRECTEUR GÉNÉRAL : Paul Dupuy
DIRECTRICE GÉNÉRALE : Yveline Dupuy
DIRECTEUR GÉNÉRAL : Jean-Pierre Beauvalet
DIRECTEUR GÉNÉRAL ADJOINT : François Fahys
DIRECTEUR FINANCIER : Jacques Béhar
DIRECTEUR DE LA FABRICATION : Pascal Rémy
DIRECTRICE DU MARKETING : Marie-Hélène Arbus
DIRECTRICE DES VENTES : Chantal Contant
DIRECTEUR COMMERCIAL : Patrick-Alexandre Sarradeil
DÉPARTEMENT INTERNATIONAL : Marie-Ange Rouquet-Dezellus, directrice (01 46 48 47 26) Fax : 01 46 48 19 19/49 39
DIRECTEUR DES ÉTUDES : Roger Goldberger

PUBLICITÉ
Tél. : 01 46 48 19 70 Fax : 01 46 48 19 71
DIRECTRICE COMMERCIALE : Sophie Muller
DIRECTRICE DE LA PUBLICITÉ : Christine Desjardin
ASSISTANTES : Valérie Carimontrant, Véronique Alex
ITALIE : Cesanomedia Srl, Milan (00 39 02 84 40 441)
ROYAUME-UNI : MWA (Michael Waterhall), Londres
Adresses e-mail : prenom.nom@excelsior.fr

SERVICES COMMERCIAUX
CHEF DE PRODUIT : Capucine Jahan (01 46 48 47 30)
ABONNEMENTS ET MARKETING DIRECT : Patrick-Alexandre Sarradeil
COMMANDES D'ANCIENS NUMÉROS : Chantal Poirier (01 46 48 47 18)
VENTE AU NUMÉRO : Chantal Contant
BELGIQUE : AMP, 1, rue de la Petite-Isle, 1070 Bruxelles
RÉASSORTS ET MODIFICATIONS : Terminal E91
N° VERT : 0 800 43 42 08 (réservé aux dépositaires de presse)
RELATIONS EXTÉRIEURES : Michèle Hilling (01 46 48 47 28)
RELATIONS PRESSE : Chrystel More (01 46 48 48 43)

DIRECTEUR DE LA PUBLICATION : Paul Dupuy

© EXCELSIOR PUBLICATIONS
COMMISSION PARITAIRE : 0505 K 79699 – ISSN : 0994-4516
PHOTOGRAVURE : Dupont, Paris
IMPRIMERIE : Aubin Imprimeur, Poitiers

Mixt(e), No. 18, 2002, France

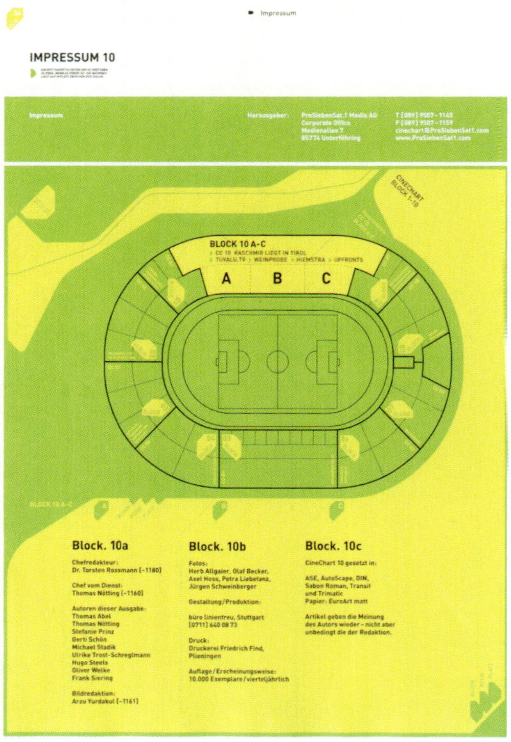

Impressum

IMPRESSUM 10

Impressum

Herausgeber: ProSiebenSat.1 Media AG
Corporate Office
Medienallee 7
85774 Unterföhring

T [089] 9507 - 1145
F [089] 9507 - 1159
cinechart1@ProSiebenSat1.com
www.ProSiebenSat1.com

Block. 10a

Chefredakteur:
Dr. Torsten Rossmann [-1180]

Chef vom Dienst:
Thomas Nötting [-1160]

Autoren dieser Ausgabe:
Thomas Abel
Thomas Nötting
Stefanie Prinz
Gerti Schön
Michael Stadik
Ulrike Trost-Schreglmann
Hugo Steels
Oliver Welke
Frank Siering

Bildredaktion:
Arzu Yurdakul [-1161]

Block. 10b

Fotos:
Herb Allgaier, Olaf Becker, Axel Hess, Petra Liebetanz, Jürgen Schweinberger

Gestaltung/Produktion:

büro linientreu, Stuttgart
[0711] 640 08 73

Druck:
Druckerei Friedrich Find, Plieningen

Auflage/Erscheinungsweise:
10.000 Exemplare/vierteljährlich

Block. 10c

CineChart 10 gesetzt in:

ASE, AutoScape, DIN, Sabon Roman, Transit und Trimatic
Papier: EuroArt matt

Artikel geben die Meinung des Autors wieder – nicht aber unbedingt die der Redaktion.

Cine Chart, No. 10, 2001, Germany

Material, No. 4, 2001, Switzerland

AM7, No. 7, 2001, Germany

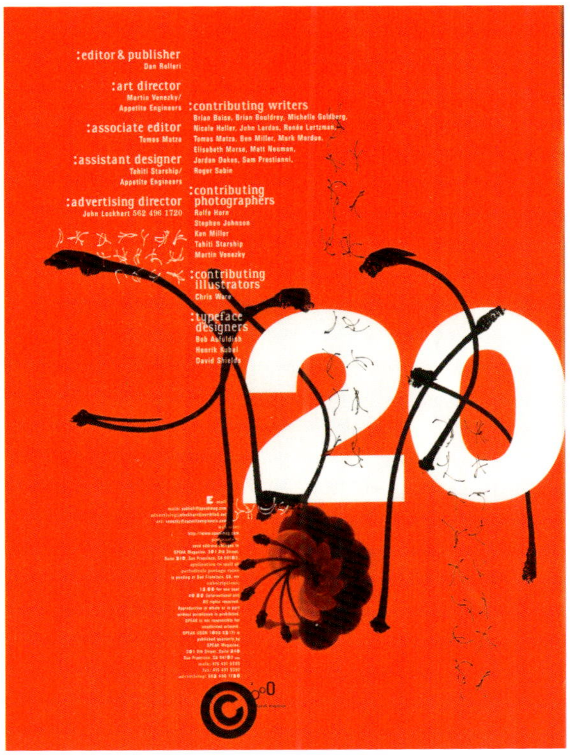

Speak, Spring 2000, USA

Ausdruck, Spring 1997, Germany

The title pages for separate sections within a magazine

For all kinds of reasons, it can sometimes be necessary to make a clear distinction between different sections of the same magazine. For example, there might be extended special features which, if not published in a separate supplement, have to be integrated into the issue as a whole – a sort of magazine within a magazine. In such cases, the special features are divided off from the rest of the issue and highlighted by a title page of their own. This will, of course, be secondary to the main cover. Another optical form of division is the page that introduces a particular section. These 'pseudocovers' are normally large-scale, with coloured areas and prominent section titles, but they can also be conceived as announcements. In fashion magazines, the first editorial page often has a dividing function – particularly in the thick, international publications that begin with fifty to a hundred pages of ads, leading eventually to the editorial section, which then proceeds uninterrupted. Fabien Baron's design for different issues of *Harper's Bazaar* consists of numerous colourful variations on the word 'Bazaar' to suit the time of year.

Harper's Bazaar, September 1992, USA

Harper's Bazaar, May 1994, USA

Harper's Bazaar, October 1992, USA

Harper's Bazaar, April 1994, USA

Harper's Bazaar, May 1998, USA

Harper's Bazaar, February 1999, USA

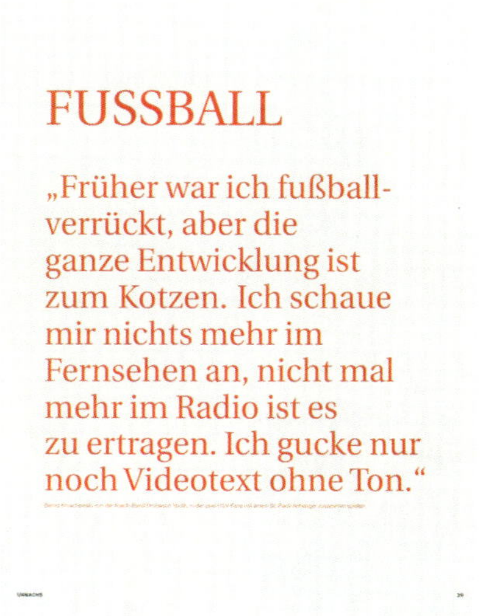

1/4 nach 5, No. 4, 2002, Germany

1/4 nach 5, No. 4, 2002, Germany

1/4 nach 5, No. 4, 2002, Germany

Copy, No. 10, 2001, Austria

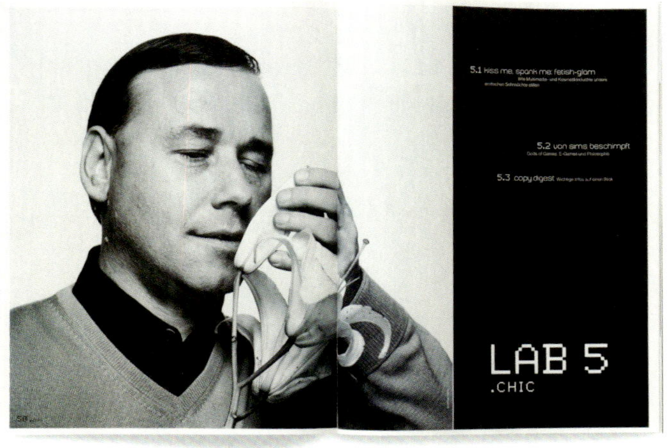

Copy, No. 12, 2001, Austria

Börse Online, No. 4, 2002, Germany

Börse Online, No. 4, 2002, Germany

Börse Online, No. 4, 2002, Germany

Examples of dividing pages: textual introduction in *1/4 bei 5*;
large-scale double pages in *Copy*; enlarged section titles in *Börse Online*.

Original layouts from different types of magazine

The preceding chapters dealt initially with the basics of magazine design, and then with typography and the different kinds of page. This chapter looks at original, creative examples of design related to individual themes. For the most part, these themes coincide with the broad range of special interest magazines. Those of general interest have become increasingly less important; there are now so many branches of each topic that a so-called general magazine is likely to be on a single theme like music, which then splits up into fifty special interest magazines on individual aspects of the field. Whenever there are particular rules for designing these themes, they will be dealt with as they appear.

A glance at the market reveals the striking fact that there's no magazine with a monopoly on any subject. There may be market leaders, though these will change from time to time, but in countries where there's a well-developed readership for magazines, there's always lively competition. Generally each special interest section of the market creates its own visual forms so that the type of magazine will be instantly recognizable. This is particularly noticeable with computer magazines, whose covers are almost indistinguishable from one another. What they all have in common is the purely typographical list of their various topics. The assumption is that the densely packed list of subjects will be the deciding factor in the reader's choice. There seems to be no end in sight to this 'arms race', and the fact that all these magazines look like ads for supermarkets or carpet shops doesn't seem to bother the publishers. The opportunity to create a magazine with an individual identity and to steal a march on the competition appears not to enter into their calculations. The guiding principle is 'me too', and the love of conformity continues on the inside. If a magazine does dare to come up with new ideas – tests, icons, tables, sections, tips, boxes – the others will shamelessly copy them anyway. Fashion magazines are not quite so uniform. Unlike computer magazines they manage to distinguish themselves mainly through the style and standard of their photography.

Independently of style and standard, though, it's photography that moulds the design of fashion magazines. The cover already sets the tone. In women's magazines the subject is usually female, and she usually makes eye contact with the reader. Sometimes the picture is of the face only, and sometimes it's the whole body, though close-ups are more popular. Techniques of lithography and print are now so sophisticated that they can reproduce the finest details of the skin to aesthetic perfection. During the great era of the fashion magazine, the 1940s, covers were far more varied than they are today, and often made use of illustrations. As regards typography, it's a striking fact that the classical Didot with its extremely fine lines still dominates. Didot is equipped with special fonts for different sizes, and these preserve the fineness of the lines even in enlargements.

FASHION AND THE ZEITGEIST

In order to make the editorial sections of a fashion magazine distinct from the ads, the two need to be kept separate. For this reason, the major international magazines begin with a long series of ads, deliberately embracing the principle that's shunned in most other magazines – namely, to set ad next to ad. Since both sections are devoted to current fashion, this is the only way they can be kept apart. Once the editorial section is underway, a sequence of ten to twenty pages of photos per subject – with no ads in between – is ideal. The different features and reports will then be separated by

FHM, July 2001, Germany

their particular subject matter and photographic style. For instance, sequences of colour photographs may be followed by black and white, outdoor scenes by indoor, classical by experimental and so on. Ideally, the pictorial language and the formal and technical elements should all complement the content, and there should be some overall direction to the alternation of different photographic styles. Fashion photography powerfully reflects the spirit of the age, and it offers an important showcase for the world's finest photographers. The fashions depicted are often an expression of a certain way of life, as well as an extension of the formal range of pictorial language. Of course there are also many visual quotations, analogous to fashion revivals. But by and large the evolution of photography has been significantly influenced by the great fashion magazines.

The subject matter of these magazines is not, of course, restricted to fashion. It covers the whole range of modern living with themes such as make-up, health, beauty, food and drink, travel, gardening, architecture, art, the home, and so on. But on each of these subjects there are also vast numbers of special interest magazines, some elitist, some mainstream, and all adapting their visual design to the theme and to the requirements of their own target group. This also applies to the technical composition – the paper, the type of binding, the quality of the print, and all the other refinements. The magazine's position in the market will even influence its categorisation. If it sets out to hit the mass market, it will call itself a women's rather than a fashion magazine – even if it deals with the same topics.

Its counterpart, the men's magazine, is by no means a mirror image. The main difference is the amount of space devoted to sex and erotica. In this field, the nature of the photography will vary considerably from one culture to another. Although this is perhaps something of an over-simplification, generally French erotic magazines tend to be staged voyeuristically. The man watches, the girl doesn't always know that he's watching, and so there's no eye contact. The setting is often from everyday life rather than in the artificial world of the studio, and in contrast to American magazines, for example, the focus is not always on the breasts. However, as the major men's magazines are produced under licence for a world market, for the most part there's not much difference. If you want to conquer the American market, you have to cater for American sexual predilections, and that means that in the post-*Playboy*

GQ, June 2001, Germany

Maxim, July 2001, Germany

Loaded, July 2001, Great Britain

generation of magazines – *Maxim*, *FHM*, *GQ*, *Loaded* – it's the American taste that's prevailed. A concrete example of this is the collection of 2001 covers (on page 175). They all follow the same pattern: the front view of a girl in a bikini looking straight at the potential buyer. In these posed photos, the girls never quite know what to do with their hands, and so they tend to go up into their hair or down into their underwear. The background is calm and neutral – either monochrome or vaguely suggestive of a watery seaside scene. The text is in two colours (one of which is white), and the bright one is always the same as the logo. The barcode is on the right-hand side, and the only decision left to the creativity of the designer is where to put it.

PICTURE QUALITY

By comparison with other magazines that specialize in naked women, the covers mentioned above are pretty modest. Even the cover of *Playboy* is basically not all that different to some covers of the Italian *Capital*, the German *Stern*, or other picture magazines. In general the design of these magazines is greatly influenced by the quality of the picture material, and if the photos and photographers are top class, it would be a bad mistake to detract from them through clumsy use of frames, cutting, excessive text, or the addition of more photos. Here the designer must take a back seat and allow the power of the picture to speak for itself. Magazines on fashion, architecture, food, living, erotica, art, design and – for some time now – gardening as well have all become increasingly dependent on the quality of their pictures. In such publications rhythm and alternation play an essential role, giving full aesthetic value to each sequence of beautiful pictures without overdoing it. The situation is not the same with computer or business magazines, which have a different function to perform. They may require a degree of subtlety in their design, especially in the use of micro- and tabular typography, but they are not meant to catch the eye with sequences of gorgeous photos. With the relatively dry subject of business, designers will make their mark through intelligent ways of giving accessible, visual form to complex factual or abstract themes. There were plenty of good examples during the boom years at the end of the twentieth century – *Fast Company*, *Brand eins*, *Business 2.0*, *Quote*, and *Red Herring*, to name just a few. Illustration plays a vital part here, because it can stimulate the imagination and add a personal touch that gives the feature a certain amount of colour.

TECHNOLOGY AND EMOTION

Other major players in the field are magazines on technology. Some of the most popular subjects are cars, planes, boats, bikes and cameras. There are conceptual problems here because different readers will have different interests. One group will want to focus almost exclusively on the technical side and will want immensely detailed information. The other – generally the minority – is not concerned with the technology itself, but with all the fascinating experiences connected with cars, boats, and so on, or in the case of camera enthusiasts, the main focus may be the artistic side. Some magazines strive for a compromise and combine construction with emotion. With travel magazines there are no such conflicts of interests, since the subject matter is nearly always geared to giving the reader ideas for indulging their wanderlust. The problem here is to establish a level, because there are marked differences between the potential target groups, as there are with all magazines that deal with lifestyles. What may interest the ordinary tourist may be irrelevant for the business traveller or adventurer, and vice versa. The designer must be able to use visual means in order to depict these different worlds convincingly and appropriately. The overall design of the magazine has to create a visual atmosphere individually tailored to each facet, so that the level can be identified before the reader turns to the text. When the content of a magazine is restricted to a single subject – gourmet food, for example – there's always a danger of monotony. In this case it would be a good idea not to automatically end every article with a photo of the finished dish, but to look for ways of varying the presentation. The chef at work could be shown, for instance, or the ingredients in their raw state. Food photography can also make use of different perspectives – diners seen from an angle, a meal seen from above. The essence of variety is close attention to detail.

REPORTAGE AND PORTRAITS

During the last few decades, photojournalism has undergone a major transformation. As a primary means of conveying information, it has disappeared almost totally into the background. Gone are the days of the great photo-reportages like the coronation of Queen Elizabeth II in the 1950s, when *Life* magazine rented extra accommodation in order to take photographs from all the different angles, and even chartered a plane to get the pictures back to head office as quickly as possible. Such reports clearly followed cinematic technique, using sequences of stills, but not long afterwards this kind of operation was made redundant by the mass medium of moving pictures in the form of global television. We now expect to receive our pictures live and instant. The magazine *Life* has disappeared, along with most other illustrated magazines on current affairs. War reporting as a branch of photojournalism has managed to survive, but only because there are still a few daredevil photographers who are prepared to venture deeper into the danger zones than some camera teams. Photojournalism has therefore had to change direction and seek out other subjects. This is clear from the various competitions. Photographers with artistic ambitions pick their own themes, and imprint them with their own personality. Magazines are no longer an adequate showplace for such work, and so it's often collected together and published in the more appropriate form of books. And then the magazines in turn report on the books. Meanwhile, the techniques of photojournalism have inspired other branches such as fashion and sports photography. Some photo magazines do include reports as part of a complete portfolio, but of course in this form they lose their immediacy and function only as exhibition pieces.

Portraits are an important branch of photography. It would be very unusual for a magazine, regardless of its subject matter, to appear without a portrait, no matter what the context. There is therefore a constant demand and supply. Still, you have to look long and hard for a really good specimen, as the majority of these pictures are not specially commissioned but in most cases are taken from archives. Many of them are utterly mediocre and are not worthy of closer attention. Even ambitious photographers often suffer from the lack of time available because their star subjects are too busy. No doubt there are some excellent portraits taken even when time is short, but for the most part it's impossible for a photographer to capture the essence of someone's character in a ten-minute or even thirty-minute session, while in turn the subject cannot break free from the pressures of the engagement calendar and relax sufficiently to reveal the person beneath. Most of these sessions will end in some kind of cliché pose, with the subject pretending to be hard at work, or leaning casually somewhere in the glass entrance hall of their company. Stars from the art, music or film world are usually more at ease with photographers than people from other fields, but still you can rarely glimpse anything beyond their superficial, professional poses. To increase the chances of getting a really top quality portrait, you need plenty of time, an open approach, sensitivity, and a sharp eye.

Vogue Pelle, July 2001, Italy

Style, No. 1, 2001, Germany

'Holiday on Ice'. Photo sequence by Astrid Grosser for *Style*.

Style, March 2001, Germany

'He wants to wear'. Fashion sequence by Claude Closky for *Big*. These are simply portraits of models – what they want to wear is described in the captions.

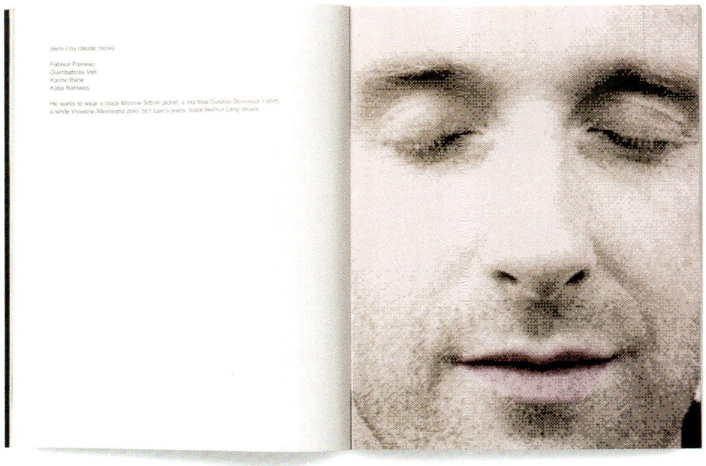

Big, No. 38, 2001, USA

'Artistic License' – from Botticelli to Koons.
Patrick Demarchelier translates art into fashion for *Harper's Bazaar*.

Harper's Bazaar, February 2002, USA

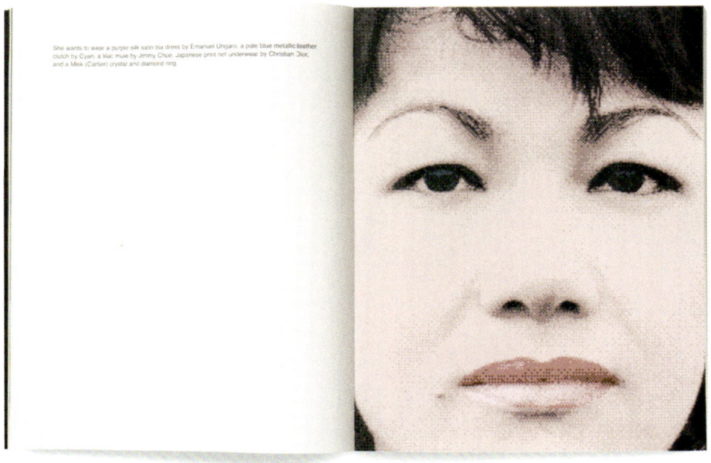

BARBIE STOPS TRAFFIC WITH DAZZLING HEART- AND FLOWER-SHAPED DIAMONDS
Platinum and diamond Fancy Victoria necklace, *on floor*, £42,800, at Tiffany. White-gold, pavé-diamond, heart-shaped necklace, *in boot*, with matching bracelet, *on car door*, £26,600, at Chatila. White-gold flower necklace with marquise-cut and round diamonds, *in boot*, £65,000. White-gold pointed necklace with marquise-cut and brilliant-cut diamonds, *in boot*, £114,000. Both at Dianoor. White-gold and diamond Sunbeam necklace, *on roof*, £16,995, at Wempe. White-gold full pavé-set diamond Love pendant and chain, £17,290, at Chopard. Digital artwork by Rob Taylor and Allan Finamore at Metro Imaging, London. Fashion editor: Kate Phelan

Vogue, July 2001, Great Britain

For kids and grown-ups. Mark Mattock sets the scene with jewelry and toys in English *Vogue*.

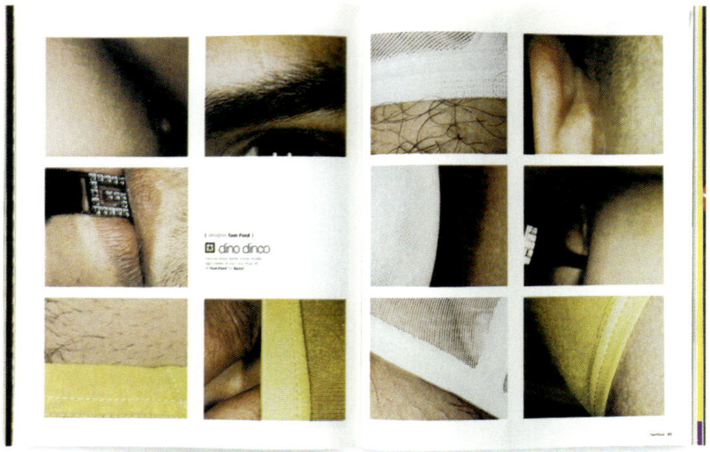

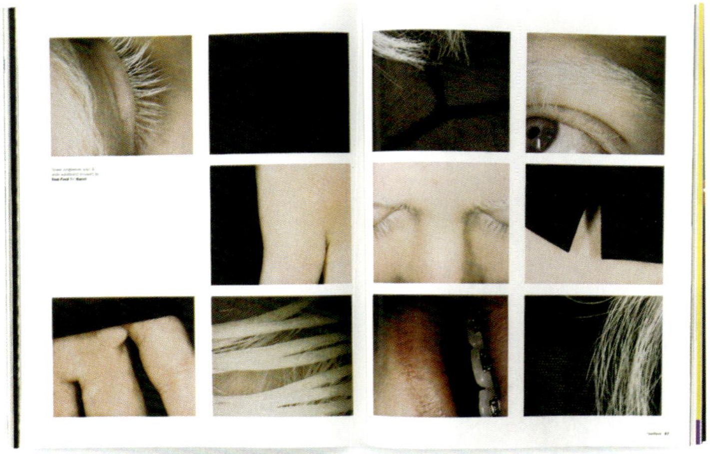

Surface, No. 15, 1998, USA

Harper's Bazaar, May 2002, USA

Vogue, February 2001, Italy

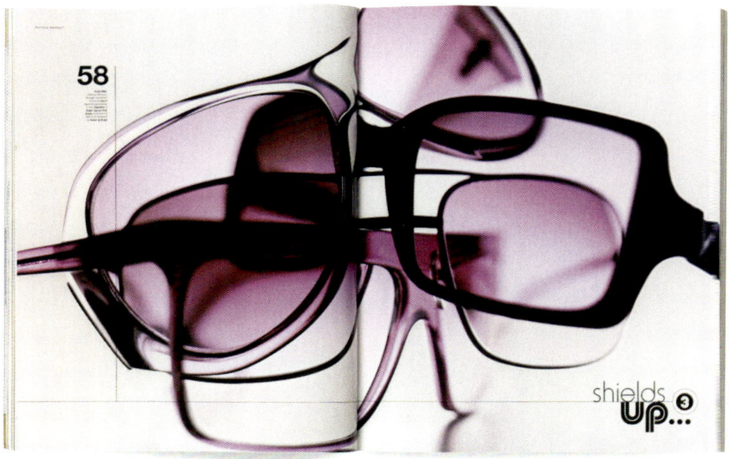

Surface, No. 29, 2001, USA

Biba, May 2002, Spain

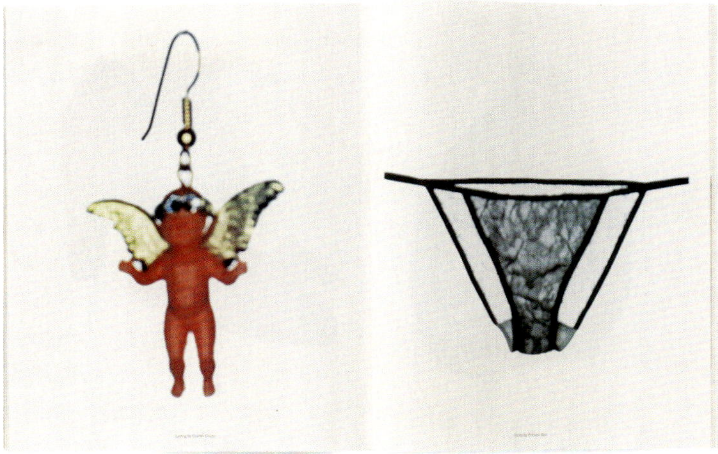

Nylon, September 2000, USA

Vogue, March 2001, Italy

The Fader, No. 9, 2001, USA

Dutch, July/August 2001, Nether.ands

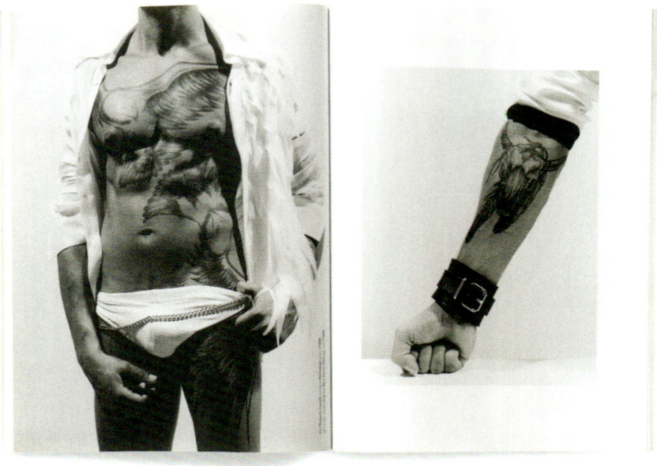

Dutch, January 2001, Netherlands

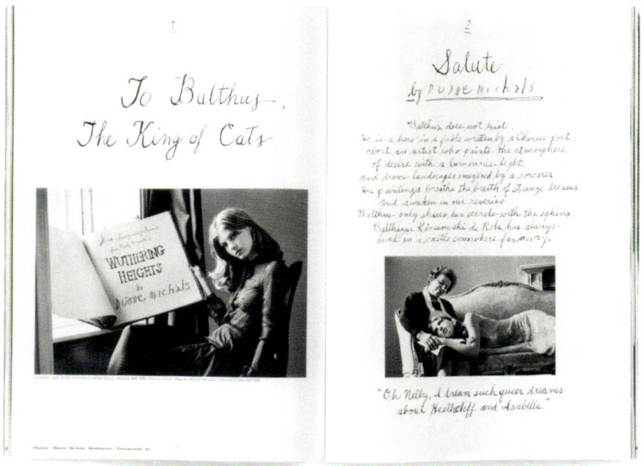

Mixt(e), No. 9, 2000, France

Vogue, December 2000, Italy

'Thunderbirds'. Photo sequence by Alan Scrymgeour for *Dutch*.

'Salute' by Duane Michals. Photo sequence based on scenes from Emily Brontë's *Wuthering Heights* for *Mixt[e]*.

Photo sequence on red, the new trendy colour, by Anna Piaggi for Italian *Vogue*.

Süddeutsche Zeitung Magazin, No. 50, 2001, Germany

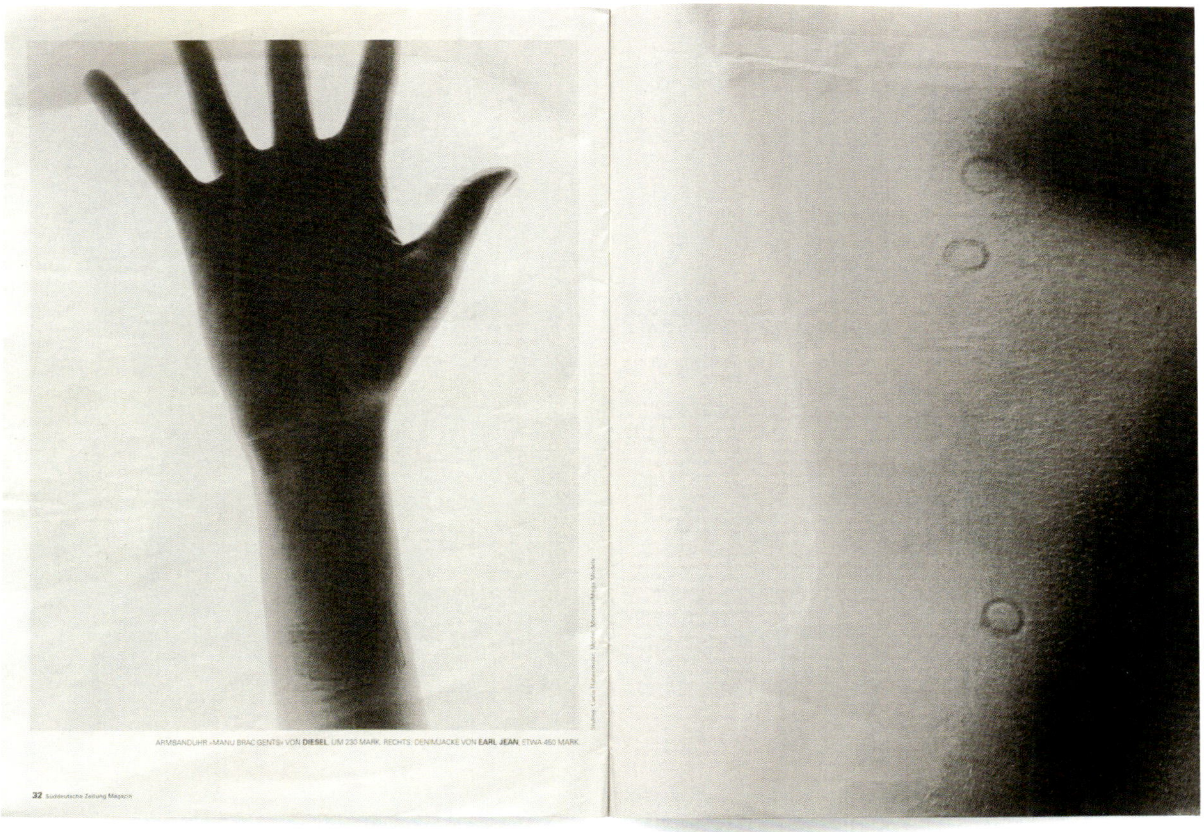

'Model Courage'. The models are wearing nothing but the marks left by their clothes.
Photographed by Joachim Baldauf for *Süddeutsche Zeitung Magazin*.

Selfservice, No. 14, 2001, France

Nylon, March 2000, USA

Top: Illustration by Julie Verhoven for *Selfservice*.

Bottom: Illustration by Tanya Ling for *Nylon*.

The Face, September 2000, Great Britain

Blvd., March 2001, Netherlands

Top: New Wave style in *The Face*. Styling by Simon Robbins, photographed by Sølve Sundsbø.

Bottom: One letter is sprayed onto the dress, the rest of the message is set in the layout by the designer. Concept by Netty Nanta, photographed by Joakim Bloström for *Blvd.*

Nova, January 2001, Great Britain

Photos: Andy Snow, Stencils: Bernie Reid, for *Nova*.

Vanidad, March 2002, Spain

Photos: David Dunan for *Vanidad*.

Quest, Autumn 2001, Germany

Illustration: Alexander Gnädiger for *Quest*.

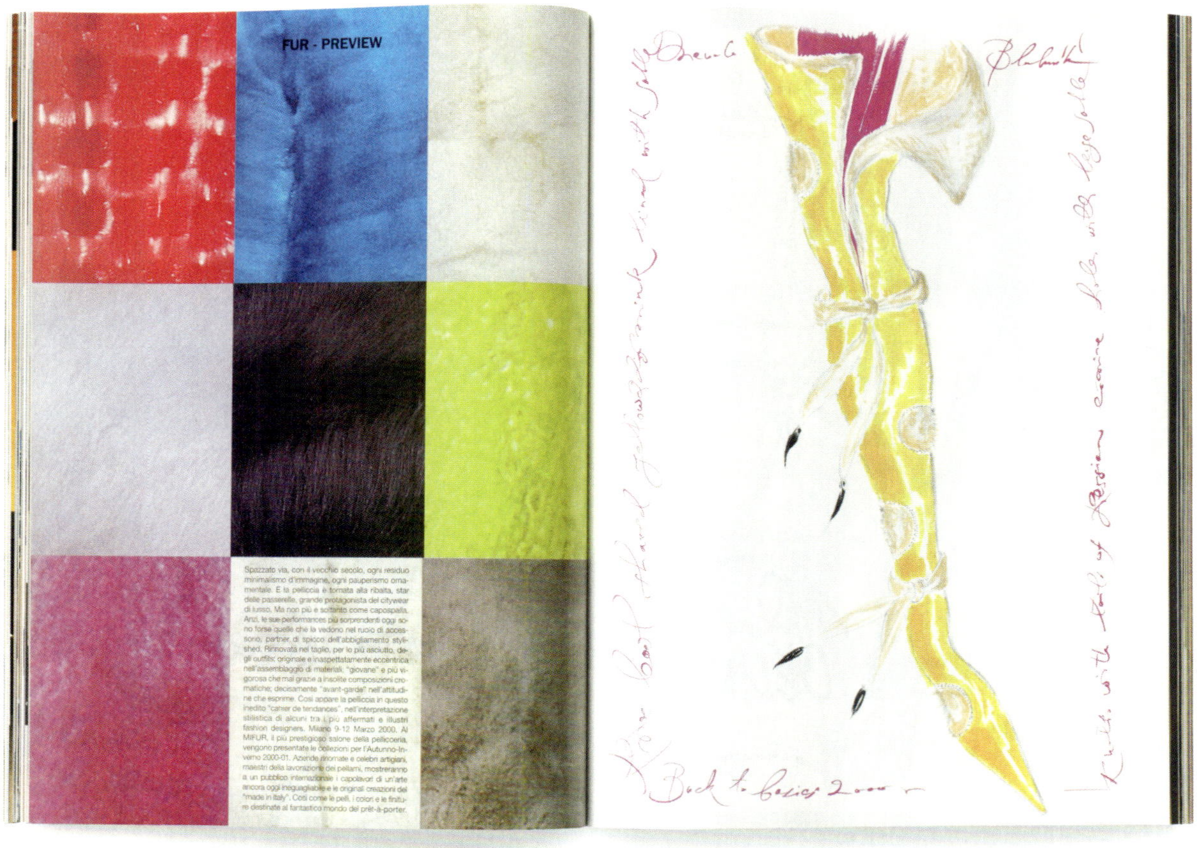

Vogue, No. 2, 2000, Italy

Current fashions in fur: different designers display drawings of their collections in Italian *Vogue*.

Deliciae Vitae, No. 1, 2001, Great Britain

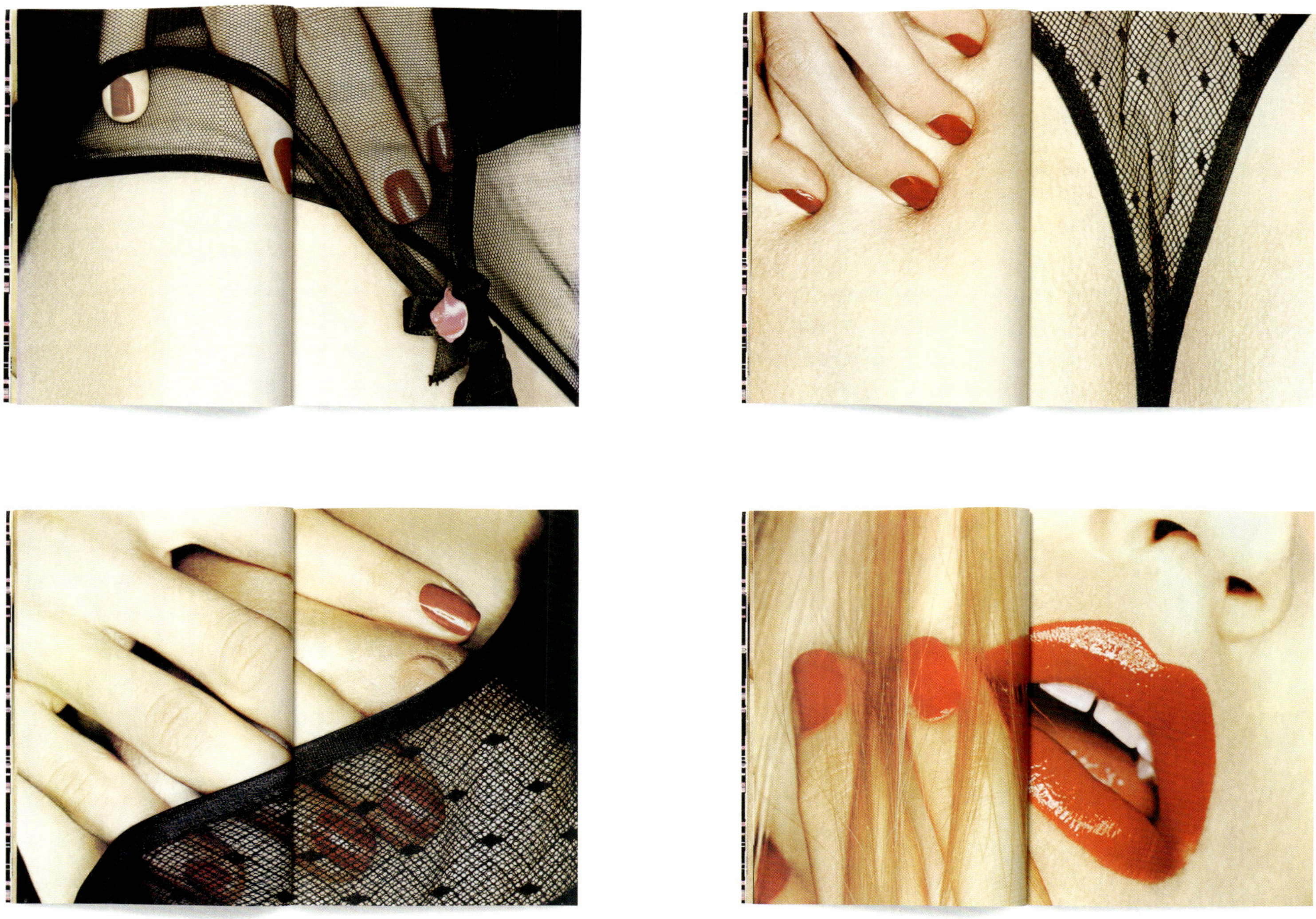

You can hardly get closer – photo sequence by Robin Derrick for *Deliciae Vitae*.

Deliciae Vitae, No. 1, 2001, Great Britain

Deliciae Vitae, No. 1, 2001, Great Britain

Fashion show, computer generated by Faiyaz Jafri for *Deliciae Vitae*.

Likewise for *Deliciae Vitae*, this time illustrated by Jasper Godall.

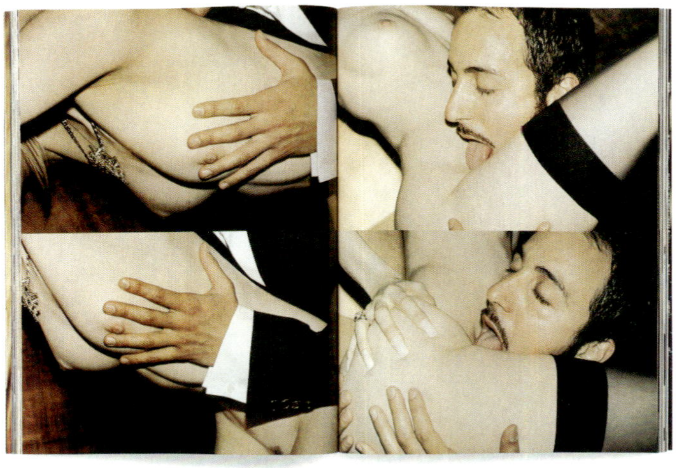

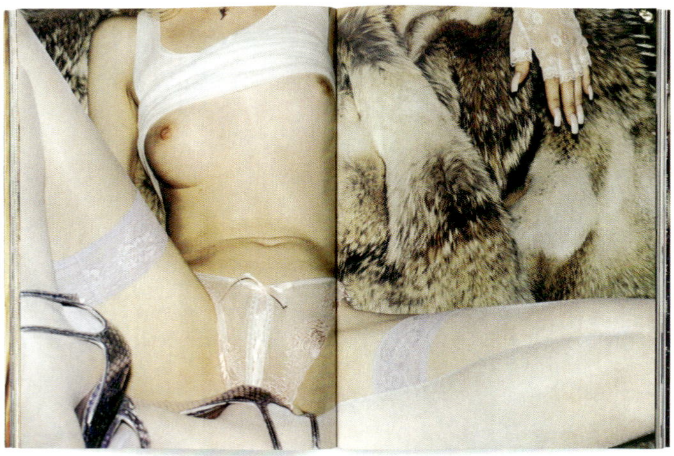

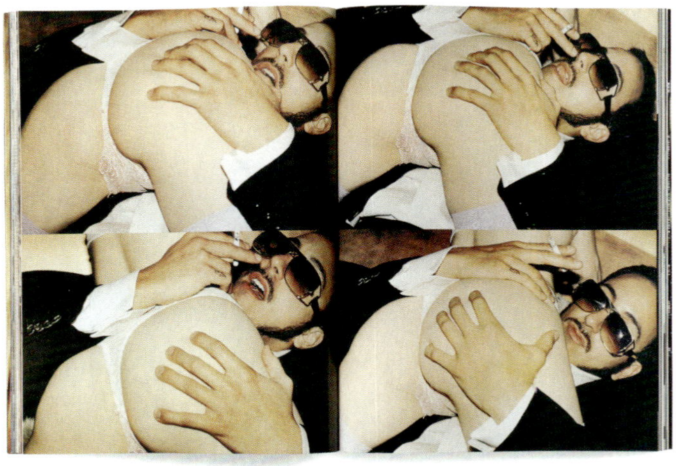

Deliciae Vitae, No. 1, 2001, Great Britain

'Lover'. Photo sequence by Matthias Vriens for *Deliciae Vitae*.

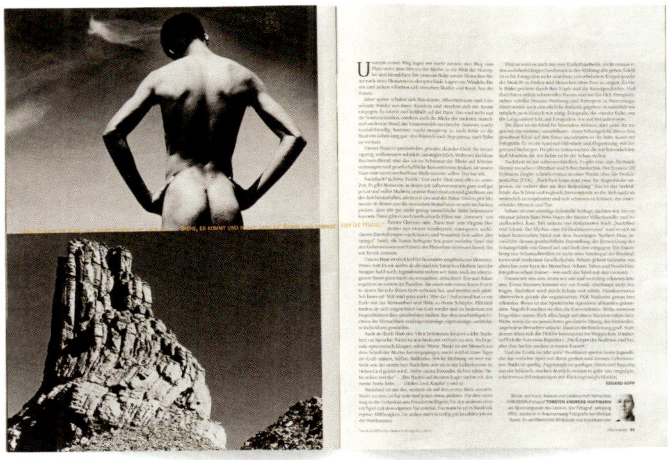

Chrismon, August 2001, Germany

The human body and its counterpart in nature: Thorsten Andreas Hoffmann for *Chrismon*.

«Je suis un voyeur qui passe son temps à regarder les femmes. J'essaie de capter des mouvements intimes et naturels, des gestes de tous les jours, familiers, féminins et sensuels.»

Quand Photo lui avait demandé d'élire sa photo du siècle, il avait choisi celle-ci : Tunisie, 1950. Photo : Rudolf Lehnert et Ernst Landrock.

NU Jonvelle

«Une femme qui se sent belle est la plus belle femme du monde !» disait-il et devant son objectif le miracle s'accomplissait

«Je me sens photographe par passion et je ressens plus spécialement une passion irrésistible pour la femme»... «Je suis de plus en plus amoureux» disait-il. «Femmes, je vous aime» aurait-il pu chanter avec Julien Clerc.

Avec la photographie de nu, qu'il ne faisait qu'en noir et blanc, Jonvelle nous montre l'intimité. L'intimité des femmes, ou plutôt, il en capte les moments fugitifs, les gestes, les attitudes. Le charme qu'elles déploient, même à leur insu, pour séduire les hommes. Parce qu'il aime les femmes qui aiment les hommes, bien sûr. Il a besoin de leur complicité pour traduire le «langage» de la séduction. Comme il fonctionnait à l'instinct, et qu'il aimait rire, il faisait le pitre sans arrêt. C'était sa façon de mettre à l'aise les filles qu'il allait photographier mais les gens en général aussi, parce qu'il aimait les gens. Il aimait la vie. Autant d'hommes que de femmes ont adoré son premier livre «Celles que j'aime». Les femmes ne rêvaient que d'être prises en photo par lui, elles savaient qu'il les aurait rendues belles et sexy. Quant aux hommes, ils réalisaient tout d'un coup que leur petite amie pouvait être sublime alors qu'*a priori* elles n'avaient rien d'un mannequin justement.

Bernard Chapuis, un de ses amis, journaliste, a écrit comme introduction de ce livre épuisé sorti aux éditions Filipacchi en 1983 : «A demi vêtues d'un tee-shirt, d'une culotte, de chaussettes, de draps de lit, de chaussures, d'une serviette sur la tête... On imagine chacune de ces femmes marchant dans la rue, sortant du métro, descendant d'un taxi, achetant des cigarettes au tabac, écoutant les nouvelles à la radio...». Il nous fait vivre l'érotisme au quotidien. Sans maquillage outrancier, ni garde-robes de princesse.

Ses photos de nus ressemblent à ses photos de mode, ou plutôt, il traite la mode comme le nu, car ce sont toujours ces gestes, ces attitudes naturelles qui comptent pour lui, plus que les poses. Il préférait ne pas travailler avec des mannequins professionnels qui à ses yeux avaient perdu toute spontanéité. Quand il ne pouvait pas faire autrement, il devait leur dire tout ce qu'il attendait d'elles, parce qu'elles ont totalement oublié ce que naturel veut dire. Bien qu'elles soient nues, les femmes, qu'il a photographiées, sont restées pudiques. Il n'y a jamais ni voyeurisme, ni indécence. «Ce que j'aime chez une femme, ce n'est pas tant ses charmes que son charme» disait-il. «La femme représente mon travail et ma vie.» Jonvelle était trop amoureux et respectueux des femmes. Il avait besoin de leur complicité pour les rendre belles. Et il savait les rendre belles, désirables même, car il savait qu'«une femme qui se sent belle est vraiment la plus belle femme du monde.» Alors Jean-François Jonvelle faisait tout pour arriver à cela, et il parvenait plutôt bien. Il charmait à sa façon, en les faisant rire, bien sûr !

Image illustrant la préface du livre «Celles que j'aime».

31

SERGE MOATTI
Son ami

A ses amis, il savait donner son cœur. Dans ses photos, il savait mettre son âme. Sous son regard, les hommes se sentaient plus courageux, les femmes plus belles. Un photographe de génie nous a quittés. Jean-François, nous te pleurons tous.

ALAIN PANCRAZI
Producteur

Lors d'une soirée complice, Jean-François m'a confié un secret. Lorsqu'il partira pour le grand voyage, il en profitera pour compter les étoiles. Et quand il les aura toutes comptées, il reviendra parmi nous. Dépêche-toi, Jean-François, on t'attend.

DIDIER POUPARD
Son agent

Lorsqu'il y a deux ans, Jean-François Jonvelle entra dans mon bureau, je connaissais l'artiste mais c'est l'homme que je découvris au fil des jours. Son extrême gentillesse, sa grande disponibilité et son charme en faisaient un interlocuteur idéal. Aussi son absence s'en ressent-elle d'autant plus, maintenant qu'il n'est plus là.

PASCAL BRIARD
Ami et Directeur du marketing chez Canon

La passion de l'image avait déclenché notre rencontre un jour de l'année 1991. Par la suite, la fidélité, la générosité et la simplicité qui caractérisaient la personnalité de Jean-François n'avaient jamais cessé de consolider les fondations d'une très profonde amitié. Si Jean-François était «fou d'elles», j'appartenais pour ma part à la grande famille de ceux qui étaient «fous» de l'homme et de son immense talent. Il me manque terriblement...

PATRICK DEMARCHELIER
Photographe

Jonvelle, c'est mes débuts de photographe, et j'y pense toujours avec plaisir. C'était notre Jardin (des modes) à nous avec tout ce que ça comporte comme souvenirs délectables et indélébiles, bien plus forts que la mort. C'était un photographe de talent !

«Les femmes qu'aiment Jonvelle sont rarement toutes nues, elles sont presque toujours «à demi-vêtues d'un tee-shirt, d'une culotte, de chaussettes... Il s'agit là d'un érotisme domestique, non d'un érotisme de palace avec tout le bataclan des désirs incertains.»

Que ce soit le lavabo, le bidet, l'évier, le divan ou le réfrigérateur, c'est dans l'environnement familier que Jonvelle crée la surprise érotique.

Photo, March 2002, France
Jean-François Jonvelle for *Photo*.

BENOÎT DEVARRIEUX
Coprésident de l'agence DevarrieuxVillaret
CATHERINE BERGAUD
Une amie
Cher Jean-François,
PUBLIMOD' PHOTO
Son laboratoire

ALBANE NAVIZET
Photographe
FRÉDÉRIC BEIGBEDER
Journaliste, écrivain et ami
MARYLINE BELLIEUD-VIGOUROUX
Directrice du musée de la mode à Marseille
ANDRÉ CARARA
Photographe
BRUNO SUTER
Publicitaire

Wellfit, March 2001, Germany

Blvd., March 2001, Netherlands

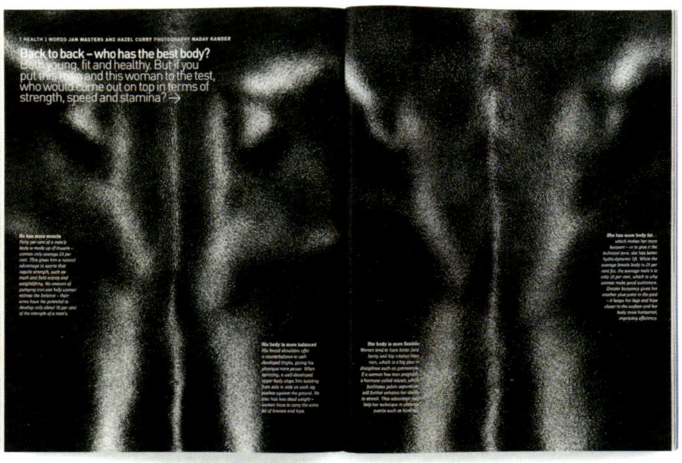

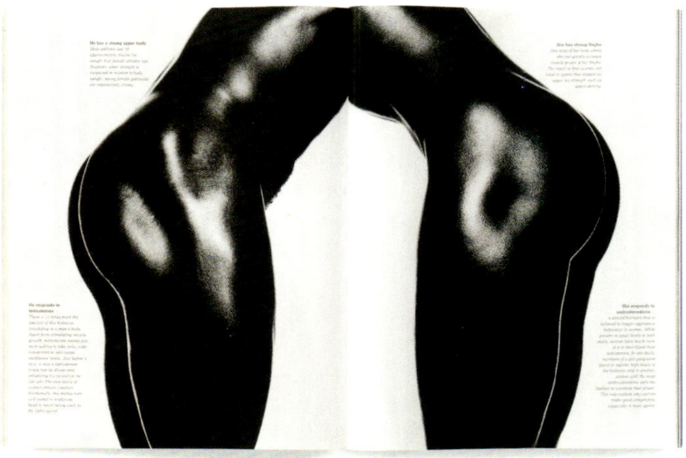

Collezioni Edge, Spring 2002, Italy

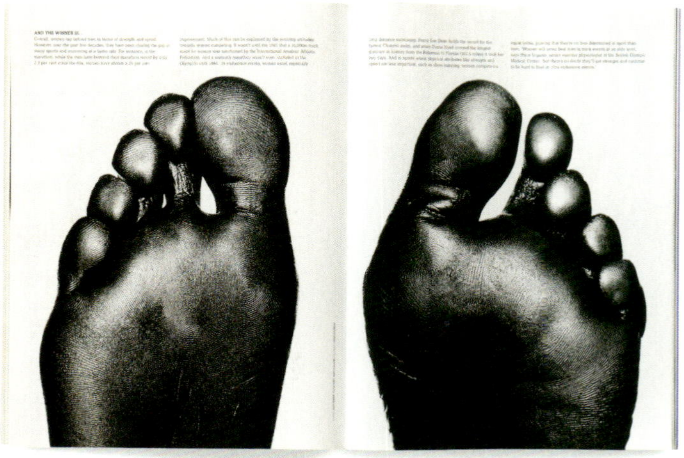

Nova, September 2000, Great Britain

Citizen K, Summer 2000, France

Style, March 2001, Germany

The Face, July 2001, Great Britain

Vanity Fair, May 2002, USA

A very different view of make-up:
photographed by Tobias Zarius for *Style*.

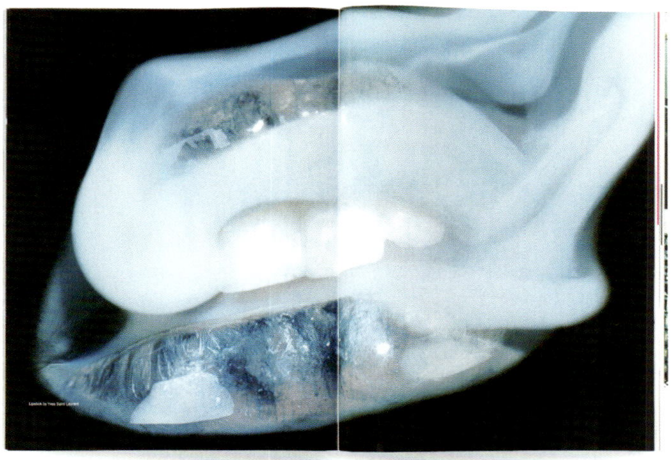

'Hot mouths for hot nights'.
Lipstick as seen by Miles Aldridge for *The Face*.

Perfume underwater:
arranged by Susan Irvine and Gavin Shaw for *Vanity Fair*.

COAST 2 COAST

From the streets to your feets, local heroes demonstrate the look.

D.C.

In Washington D.C., where the big men roam at nearby Georgetown, they wear long socks, 'cause they're supposed to make you look taller. D.C. players copped it from notable area players Walt Williams, now of the Sacramento Kings, and Sherman Douglas, now of the Celtics. There are variations: Williams takes the sock almost over the knee; Douglas wears it three quarter, covering most of his calf. Lawrence Moten of Syracuse and Jerry Stackhouse of North Carolina are leading the way in the NCAA. And black sneakers, like these Nike Air Solo Flights (left) well, you gotta look bad in Bullet-town, USA.

Maybe all that sock gives a nice backdrop to D.C.'s famed "devastating dribble," 'cause if you don't have D.C.'s two crossover moves, you don't take the court. There's the below the knee, below the curb crossover—where only your shoes see your moves, shoes like these Nike Diamond Turf (above left). And then there's the high dribble, almost over the shoulder crossover. Local heroes Tyjuan Campbell, 14, Chris Turner, 14, Greg Lomax, 13, and Harris Hill, 14 mastered the moves on the hard streets, and if you don't believe it, try 'em.

N.Y.C.

In New York City, the shorts are baggy, the socks are low and the ethic is work, work, work. You won't find flashy T-shirts here, old tourney shirts are worn like badges of honor. Which they are, 'cause in New Jack City, they save the flashy stuff for the move to the hoop. If you can't take it strong to the hoop, you take it somewhere else. Here at the Gauchos gym in Da Bronks, Chitunder Weeks, 14, Vohn Hunter 14, Ernest Brown, 14 (yes, boys and girls, Junior is 6' 8"), Sirah Turner, 12, and Wakim Banks, 13, show that the only style is studying the game.

Parish DeBerry, 12, has a move or two of his own, zipping the ball between his Reebok Above the Rim's (below right). And those Nike Haurache's belong to Marcus Ferrer, 12. And they're black 'cause they're beautiful.

Slam, No. 5, 1994, USA

Crunch, Winter/Spring 2002, USA

Snow, No. 2, 2002, Germany

'Lines' by Arcu Sedwag, Jancsi Hadiç and Bertrand Boone
with text by Vera Schröder for *Snow*.

Snow, No. 2, 2001, Germany

Photo sequence on snowboarding in a 'new dimension' – photographed by Richard Walsh in 3D for *Snow*; the requisite glasses were also provided.

Wired, April 2002, USA

1/4 nach 5, March 2002, Germany

Line, Spring/Summer 2001, Great Britain

Report on kite surfing in Hawaii –
photographed by Stephen C. Whitesell for *Wired*.

The youth team of FC St Pauli –
portraits by Stefan Schmid for *1/4 nach 5*.

Sporting fashion – staged on the beach in Rio
by photographer Sesse Lind for *Line*.

Wallpaper, May 2000, Great Britain

Dynamically staged: international helicopters, photographed by Christopher Griffith for *Wallpaper*.

6580
DANGER
KEEP AWAY

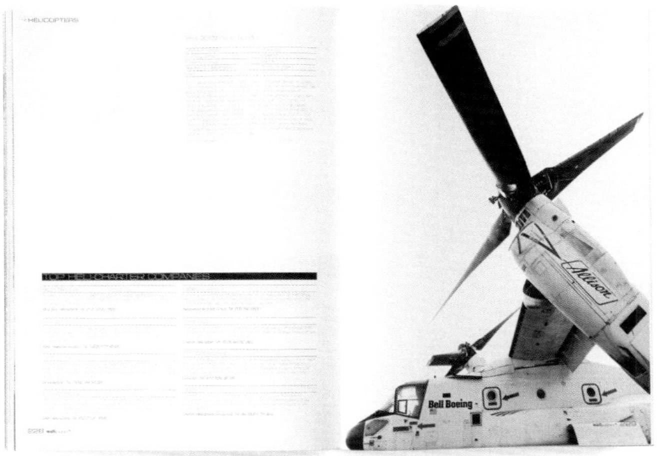
Allison
Bell Boeing

Below: Report on the Jaguar company.
Photos by Wilbert Weigend for *Premium*.

Right : The new Mini in Kapstadt.
Photos by Edgar Rodtmann, car illlustration by Mustafa Malika for *Mini International*.

Middle and bottom right: BMW design study.
Photos by Simon Puschmann for *BMW Magazin*.

Premium, No. 1, 2001, Germany

Mini International, No. 1, 2002, Germany

BMW Magazin, No. 1, 2002, Germany

wie gedruckt

Gut 550 Jahre nach Erfindung des Buchdrucks durch Johannes Gutenberg plant Xerox wieder ein Projekt von historischen Ausmaßen: elektronisches Papier

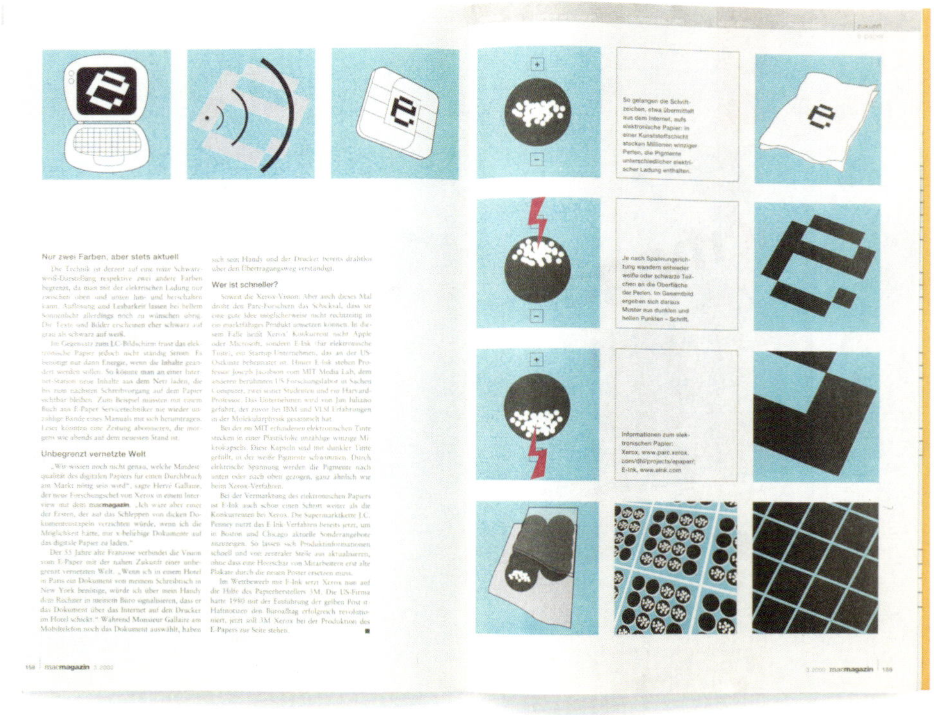

Mac Magazin, No. 3, 2000, Germany

'Like print'. Report on Xerox's 'electronic paper' in *Mac Magazin*.
Illustration: Boogie Entertainment.

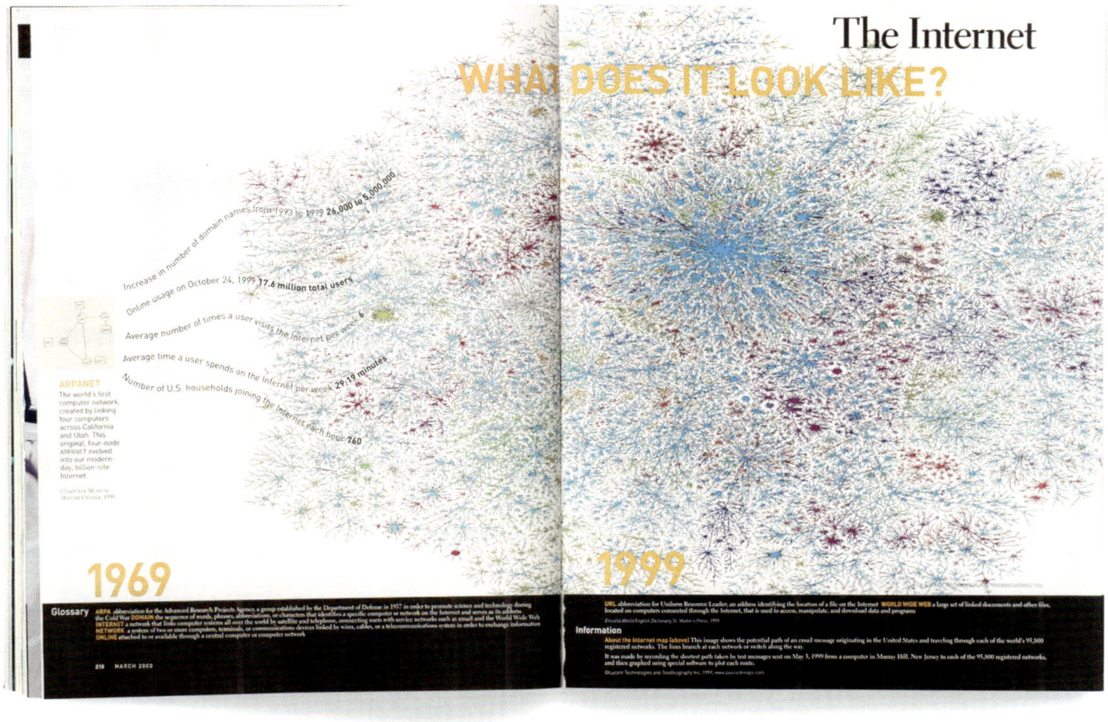

Fast Company, No. 3, 2000, USA

'Information as if understanding mattered'. Report in *Fast Company* on Richard Saul Wurmans' book *Understanding USA*.
Illustrations from the same book by Michael Donovan and Nancye Green.

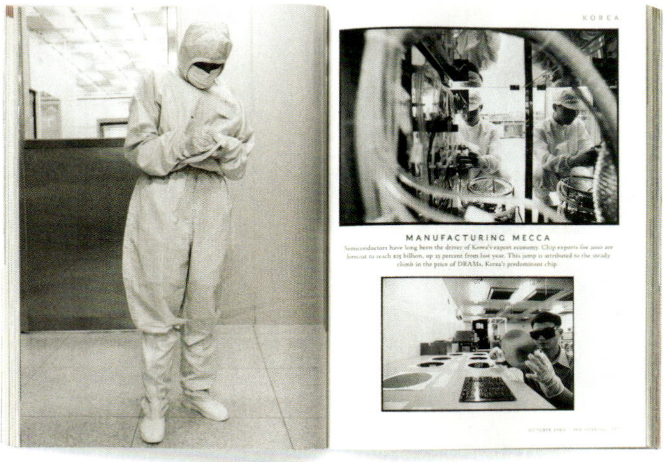

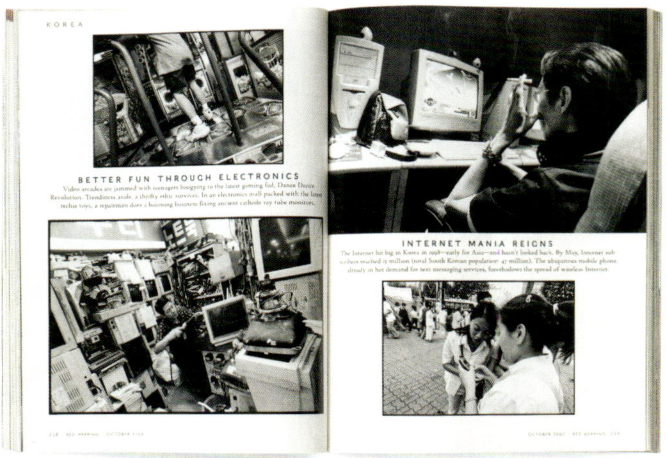

Red Herring, No. 10, 2000, Great Britain

'Seoul Salvation'. Photo sequence by Graham Uden for *Red Herring* on the production of microchips.

HP Omnibook, No. 3, 2001, Germany

Report on the company Echtzeit Ltd.
Maurice Weiss/Ostkreuz for *HP Omnibook Ready, Steady, GO!*

Right: 'Attack from Cyberspace'.
Illustration by 'Linientreu' for *Cine Chart*.

Cine Chart, No. 12, 2001, Germany

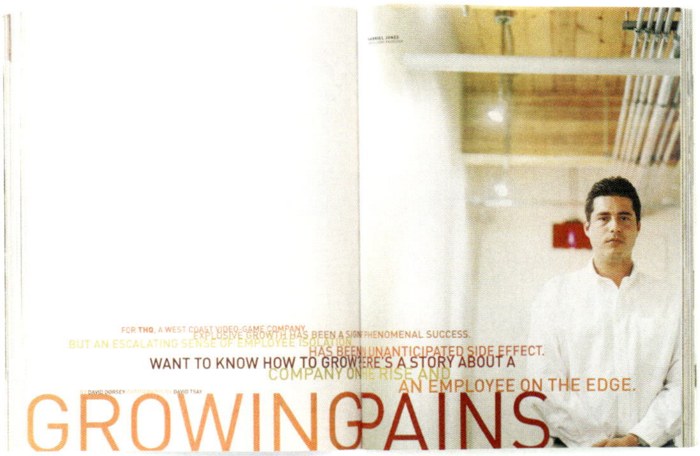

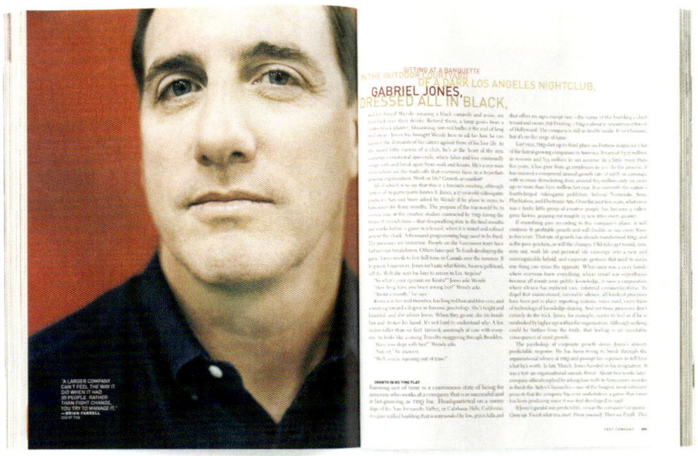

'Growing Pains'. Portrait of the American firm THQ for *Fast Company*. Photos: David Tsay.

Fast Company, No. 10, 2000, USA

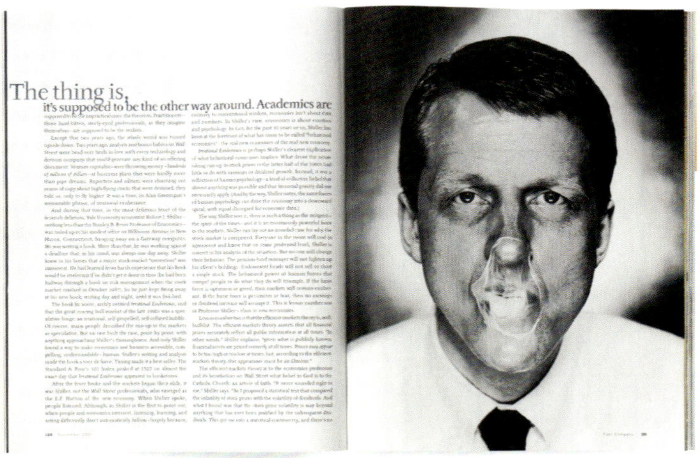

Fast Company, No. 9, 2001, USA

The bubble has burst. Report on the New Economy.
Photos: Len Irish for *Fast Company*.

'A star is born'. Report on the Euro.
Illustration: Michalke/Zaribaf for *Anleger*.

Anleger, No. 3, 2001, Germany

Brand eins, No. 3, 2002, Germany

Fast Company, No. 1, 2001, USA

Quote, No. 3, 1998, Netherlands

'People – Worlds'.
Photos by Janin Stötzner of people in the Altai Mountains in *Brand eins*.

'Man with a (talent) plan'.
Photographed by Debra McClinton of 'Electronic Arts' for *Fast Company*.

'De Pietje Bell bank'.
Photos: Bert Teunissen for *Quote*.

LUSTMORD

Ein Bilderzyklus von Jenny Holzer
für das Magazin der
Süddeutschen Zeitung

Süddeutsche Zeitung
No. 46 — MAGAZIN — 19.11.93

»Da, wo Frauen sterben, bin ich hellwach«, dieser Satz auf der Titelseite des *SZ-Magazins* wurde nicht mit normaler Farbe gedruckt. Wenn Sie die Schrift berühren, dann berühren Sie Blut, das Blut von Frauen.
Mit diesem symbolischen Akt will die amerikanische Künstlerin Jenny Holzer das Thema ihres Zyklus zuspitzen: Gewalt gegen Frauen.
Erinnern wir uns an die Nachrichten aus dem ehemaligen Jugoslawien, die diesem Thema eine neue, unvorstellbare Dimension gegeben haben: Frauen wurden systematisch vergewaltigt (man spricht von 60 000 Opfern), zwangsgeschwängert, gequält, verstümmelt, ermordet.
Diese Nachrichten erreichten uns, wurden zu Schlagzeilen – und schnell wieder vergessen.
Jenny Holzer ist eine politische Künstlerin, sie gilt als das moralische Gewissen der Gegenwartskunst. Im *SZ-Magazin* zerstört sie unsere Distanz zu diesen Greueltaten, rekonstruiert die entsetzliche Atmosphäre, in der sie geschahen – und weiter geschehen: »Ich krieche in die Seelen der Täter, der Opfer und der Angehörigen.«
Mit Jenny Holzer gestaltet zum vierten Mal ein Künstler von Weltrang die »Edition No. 46« des *SZ-Magazins*. Ihre Vorgänger:
Anselm Kiefer (1990), Francesco Clemente (1991), Jeff Koons (1992).

32 **»Der Tod ist keine hygienische Angelegenheit«**
Ein Werkstattgespräch mit Jenny Holzer über ihren Zyklus für das *SZ-Magazin* und die Frage: Darf ein Magazin mit Menschenblut drucken?
VON CHRISTIAN KÄMMERLING UND ASHKAN SAHIHI (PHOTOS)

44 **Visca la Revolució!**
Andorra, der Winzling zwischen Frankreich und Spanien, erlebt große Zeiten: Nach siebenhundert Jahren Feudalismus herrscht nun Demokratie. Eitel Freude? Das Volk ist eher irritiert.
VON JÖRG-UWE ALBIG

56 **Mode der Neunziger**
Unsere Models tragen Entwürfe der internationalen Designer. Sie haben Namen wie Melissa, Anne und John – und sie sind alle um die neunzig Jahre alt.
VON KURT MARKUS (PHOTOS)

66 **Der Kamikaze des Kinos**
Bisher war es, als ob Harvey Keitel seine Karriere gezielt verhindern wollte: Mal spielte er gute Rollen in schlechten Filmen, mal schlechte Rollen in guten Filmen. Doch nach *Das Piano* bleibt selbst Keitel nicht vom Erfolg verschont.
VON NICK TOSCHES

74 **Es war einmal**
Wie sah der Alltag der Menschen zu Anfang des Jahrhunderts aus? Ein Archiv in Paris zeigt auf 72 000 Photos das ganz normale Leben der Leute. Wir präsentieren eine Auswahl: Bilder von Kindern aus aller Welt.
VON KLAUS KLEINSCHMIDT

Rubriken
86 Ehegeschichten
88 Cartoon
90 Rätsel
92 Impressum
94 Lassen Sie uns über Geld reden

MAGAZIN Süddeutsche Zeitung 3

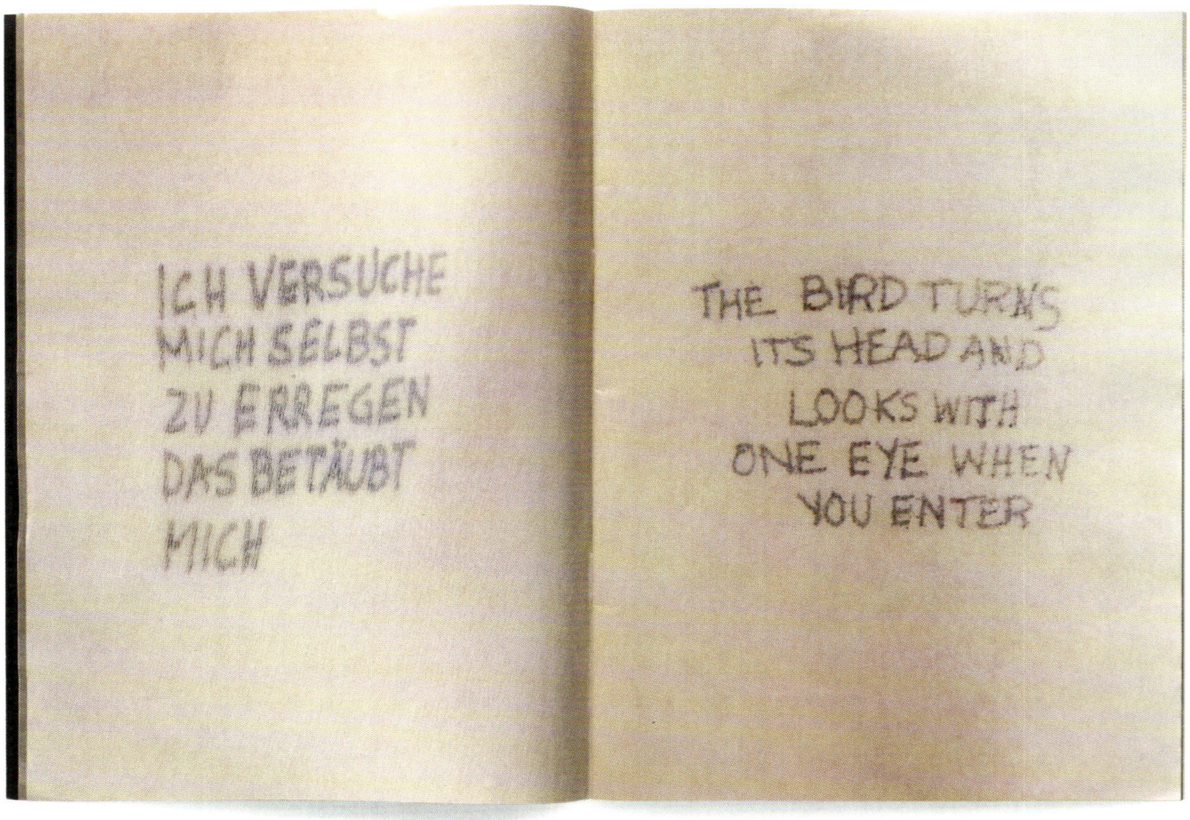

Süddeutsche Zeitung Magazin, November 1992, Germany

'Sex Murder'. Picture cycle by Jenny Holzer for *Süddeutsche Zeitung Magazin*.

DAE, 2001, Great Britain

Photos by Peter Morton and text by Gly Davis Marshall for *DAE*.

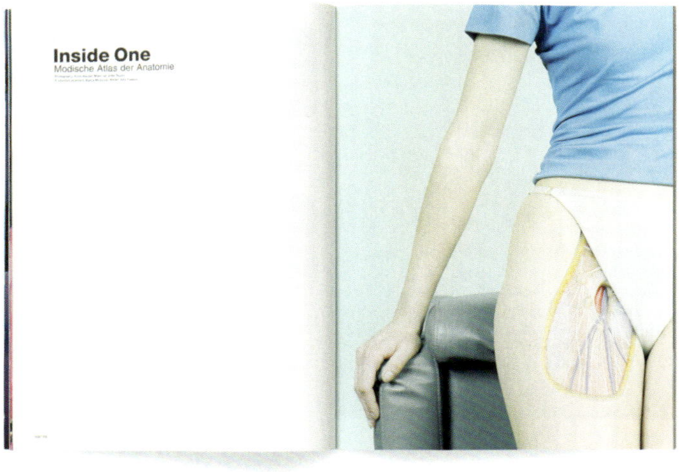

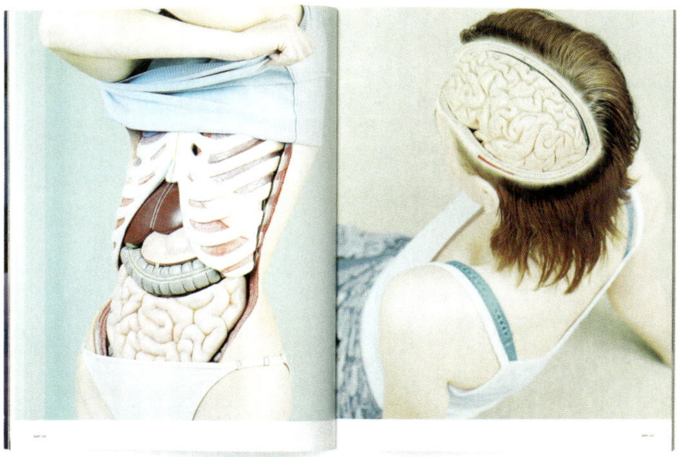

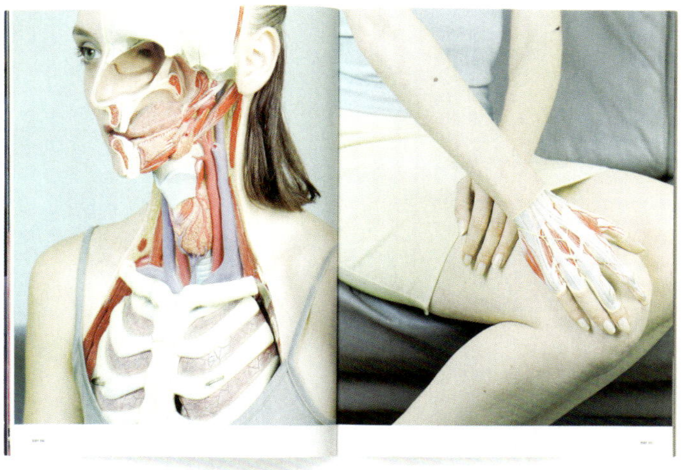

Baby, 2001, Netherlands

'Fashion Atlas of Anatomy'. Photographed by Koen Hanser for *Baby*.

Domus, July/August 2000, Italy

'Objects and concepts design' by Marti Guixé, photographed by Inga Knölke, accompanying text by Juli Capella.

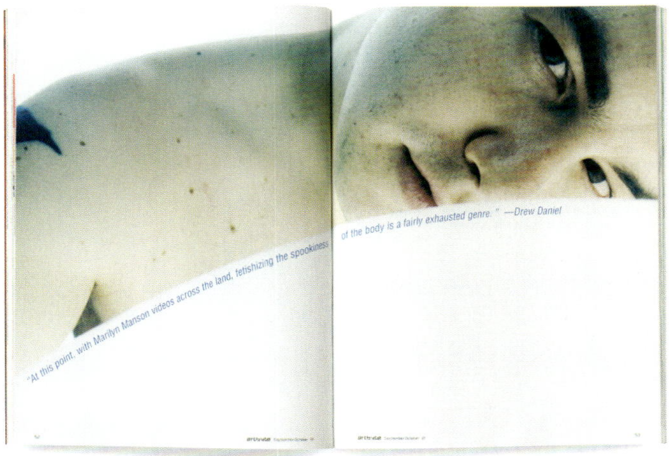

Artbyte, September/October 2001, USA

'Aural surgeons'. Report on the Californian sound specialists 'Matmos' who, among other things, incorporate hospital sounds into their music. Photos: Tim Knox for Artbyte.

Baby, Spring 2002, Netherlands

'One minute sculptures' by Erwin Wurm, photos by Galerie Krinzinger, Vienna, text by Sharifa Jamaldin.

Das Magazin, March 2002, Germany

'Earthlings'. Interplay of pictures and poems in *Das Magazin – Die Lust zu lesen*.
Lyric poetry: Artur Becker. Photos: Patrick Becker.

Soda, No. 17, 2001, Switzerland

Goethe meets candy colours – 'Stella' staged by Yoki van de Cream for *Soda*.

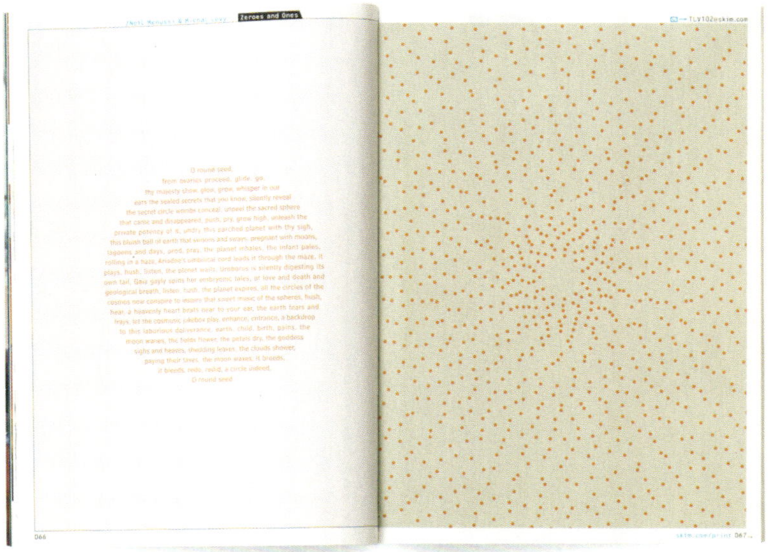

Slam Poetry transposed into pictures by Neil Menussi and Michael Levy for *Skim.com*.

Skim.com, No. 2, 2000, Switzerland

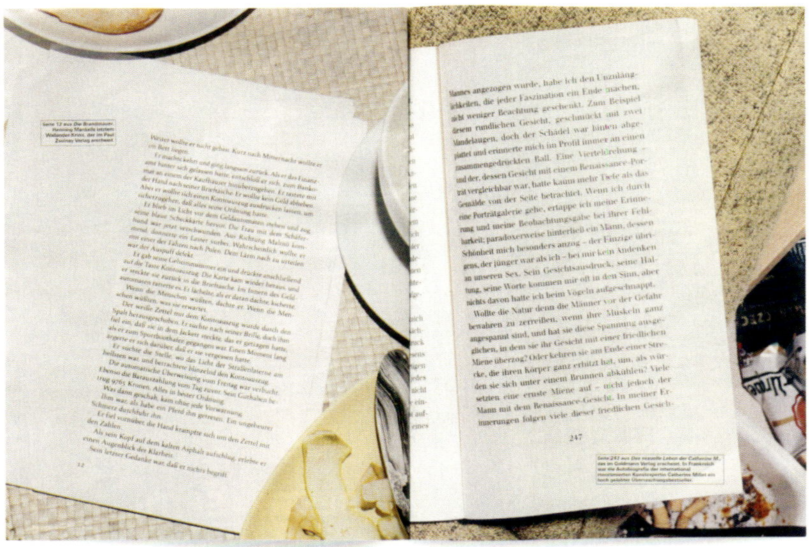

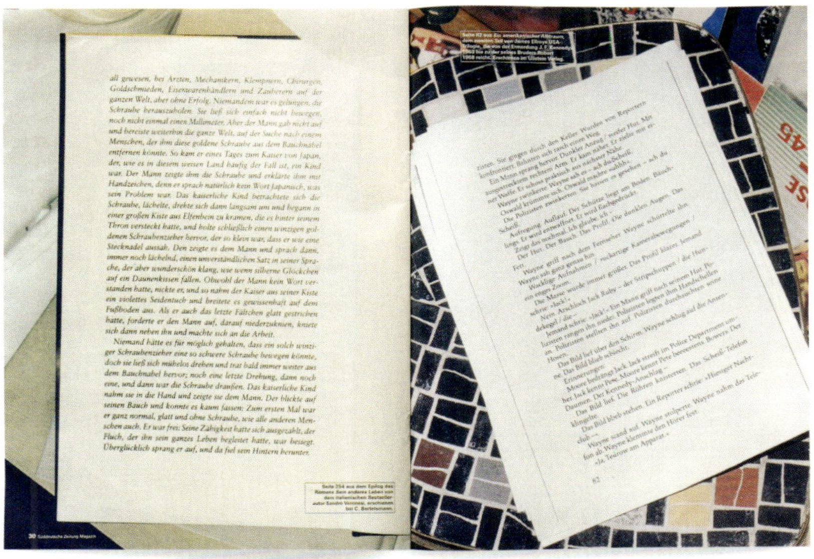

Süddeutsche Zeitung Magazin, No. 40, 2001, Germany

Little appetizers – individual pages from newly published books to start you reading. Photos: André Mühling for *Süddeutsche Zeitung Magazin*.

Nahsicht, Fernsicht

> Die Welt wächst zusammen. Wirklich? Für die Antwort machten sich drei Fotografen in drei Kontinenten auf, um die jeweilige Spielart von Leben, Wohnen, Arbeiten zu dokumentieren. Daraus sollte ein Bild entstehen, das zeigt — ja, was? Wird nun alles immer ähnlicher? Oder bleibt es doch unterschiedlich? Sehen Sie selbst.

USA

Foto:

Asien

Foto:

Brand eins, No. 6, 2001, Germany

'Short Sight, Long Sight'. A documentary on life, home and work in three continents for *Brand eins*.
Photos: USA, Imke Loss (top); Asia, Jan Siefke (bottom).

ADAC Reisemagazin, May/June 2001, Germany

'Faces of a Region'. Report on Southern Italy. Ralf Kreuels for *ADAC Reisemagazin*.

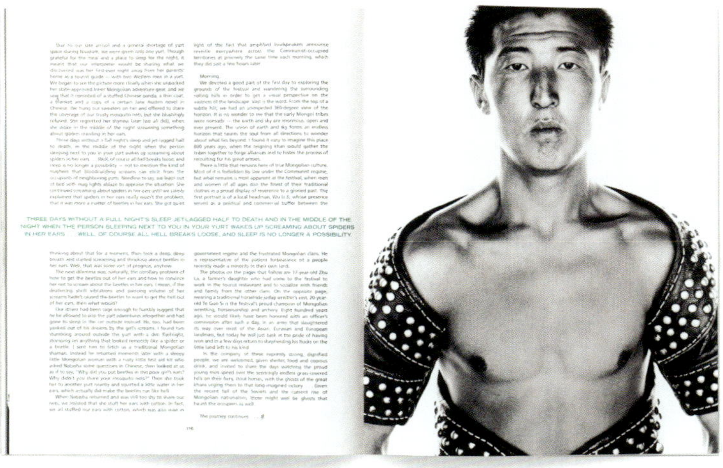

Madison, No. 1, 2000, USA

Report on Inner Mongolia for *Madison*, with text by Anthony Smith and photos by Gerald Foster.

Top: 'Tradition'. Illustration by François Berthoud for *Big*.

Bottom: 'In Search of Lost Time'. Travel report on the Mexican highlands with photos by Klaus Schoenwiese for *BMW Magazin*.

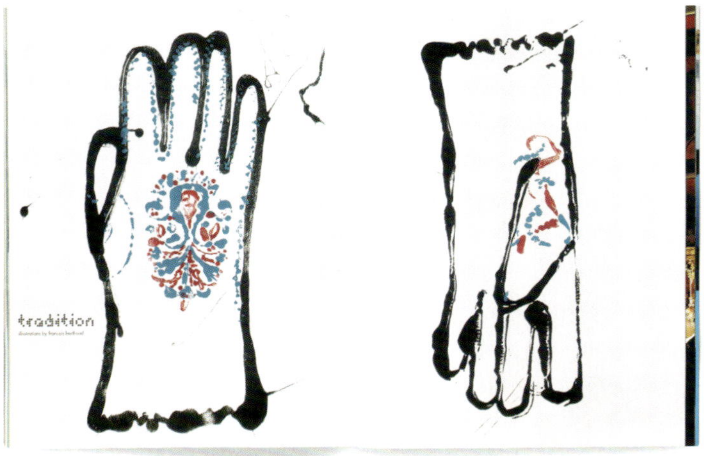

Big, No. 33, 2000, USA

BMW Magazin, No. 1, 2002, Germany

Blond, No. 3, 2002, Germany

Blvd., No. 4, 2001, Netherlands

Top: Report on a different kind of Japan in *Blond*, with illustrations by Imme Böhme and text by Gregor Wildermann.

Bottom: Declaration of love for Holland in *Blvd* with photos by Paul D. Scott and text by Lucas Mei.

NOTIONS OF NATURE

Dress yourself as you would your garden... Dress your garden as you would dress yourself: making your own design. Choose seasonal or perennial varieties as you would choose cottons, silks or velvets, and contemplate groves, flowerbeds, terraces or vistas like you would ponder over buttons, beads, frills, straps and ribbons.

photos Julie Chloe Degueldre styling Delphine Chailloux

Mix shades and textures until you've created your own personal statement: you won't be inspired by what a garden should be by other's standards, but by your own preferences for shiny details, frivolous extras, obscure finds and personal highlights. Nature becomes a little shop of wonders full of surprises, where you bend over crates, rummage through open drawers and climb shaky stairs to reach the highest shelves, tempting with frivolous glimpses of satin straps or strings of coloured glass beads.

Bloom, December 2000, France
Inside pages 'Notions of nature'. Photos by Julie Chloe Degueidre.

Gardens Illustrated, December 2001, Great Britain

Martha Stewart Living, March 2001, USA

Martha Stewart Living, March 2000, USA

DIANTHUS

Martha Stewart Living, March 2000, USA

bougainvillea

Martha Stewart Living, February 2002, USA

tulpen

Ein Königreich für eine Zwiebel

Eden, January 1999, Germany

Industrial Units. Photos by Frank Breuer, awarded the Peter Keetman Volkswagen Art Foundation Prize for Industrial Photography, reproduced in *Brand eins*.

Brand eins, No. 3, 2002, Germany

Audi Magazin, No. 1, 2002, Germany

'Temples of the Modern Age'. Report on football stadiums. Photos: Bongartz/imago for *Audi Magazin*.

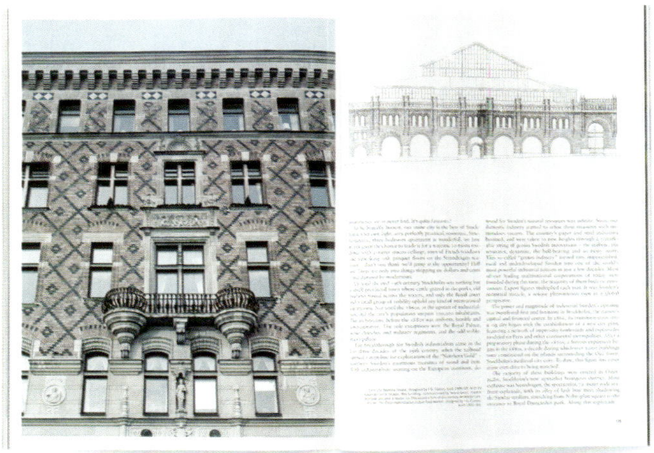

Stockholm New, No. 12, 2002, Sweden

'Stockholm stone city'. Photos: Åke E, Son Lindman for *Stockholm New*.

Fast Company, May 2000, USA

'Museums with a mission'. Photos: Anders Overgaard for *Fast Company*.

CORNING MUSEUM OF GLASS
Location Corning, New York
Year Opened 1951 Renovated 1997–2000
Mission To engage, educate, and inspire visitors and the community through the art, history, and science of glass
"We've rewritten the script for the Hot Glass Show dozens of times, each time adding more detail and information in response to visitors' questions."
—Rob Cassetti, Corning Museum
FAST COMPANY 223

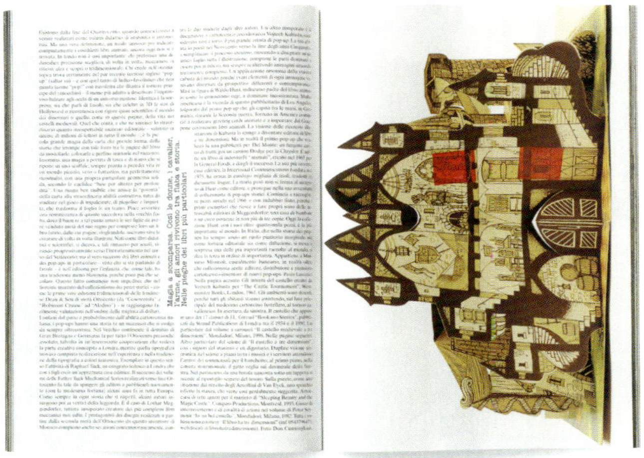

Casa Vogue, December 2001, Italy

Brand eins, No. 3, 2001, Germany

Maison Française, May/June 2001, France

Visualizing medieval buildings through modern pop-up pictures.
Photos: Don Cunningham for *Casa Vogue*.

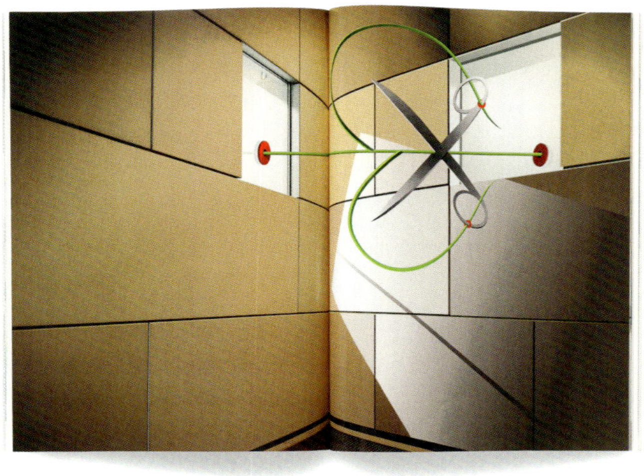

Photography and illustration combine to produce new realities.
Photos: Hartmut Nägele,
Illustration: Yves Netzhammer for *Brand eins*.

Report on 'Future Systems' furniture by Amanda Levete and Jan Kaplicky
for *Maison Française*. Photos: Richard Davies.

Room, No. 2, 2002, Germany

Wallpaper, March 2000, Great Britain

Stockholm New, No. 11, 2001, Sweden

Madison, January/February 2000, USA

Martha Stewart Living, January 2001, USA

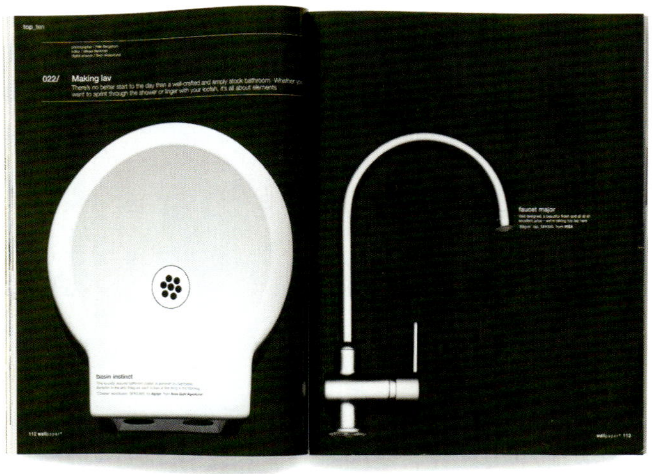

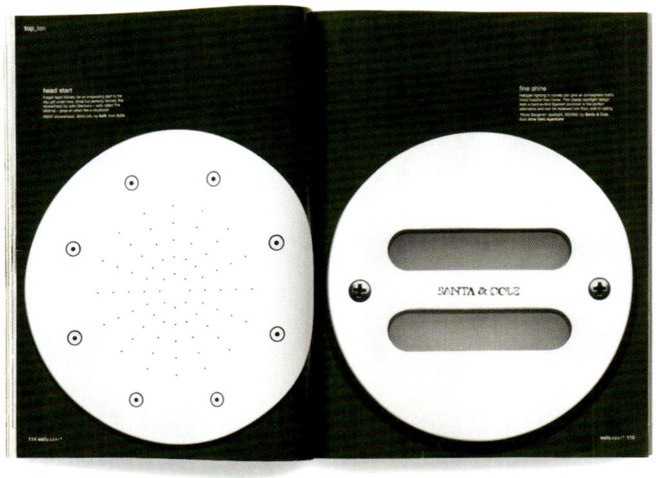

Wallpaper, December 2000, Great Britain

AD, April/May 2002, Germany

EUROPA IST ... WENN
DEUTSCHE NONCHALANCE
SICH MIT ITALIENISCHER
GRÜNDLICHKEIT VERBINDET.

EUROPA IST ...
SPANISCHEN WEIN
IN KRISTALL
AUS FRANKREICH
ZU SERVIEREN.

Martha Stewart Living, April 2000, USA

1. Making the Pom-Poms
2. Shaping the Body
3. Sewing the Head to the Body
4. Making Wire Feet
5. Assembling the Parts
HOW TO MAKE A BLUE JAY Make two wool and mohair pom-poms: one large, the other small. 1. Wrap large templates with one third white and two-thirds blue wool; add black wool in the center of one side. For the small ball, use half blue, half white wool. 2. Trim the large ball closer on the back than on the breast, making a plump oval. Have black and blue felt ready for the tail and beak. 3. Sew the pieces together. 4. Cut 8½ inches of black cloth-covered wire (30 gauge); fold so that one side is about ¾ inch longer. Crimp the wire into an approximate "M" shape as shown. Use needle-nose pliers to twist the three front claws into shape. Now shape that extra length of wire into back foot. Twist the remaining wire tightly for strong legs. 5. Cut two triangles of black felt for the beak and a notched banner of blue felt for the tail. Attach them to the body with white craft glue. Pull a needle threaded with knotted black cord though the small pom-pom to make eyes.
Perched on branches of flowering quince, this pageant of pom-pom BIRDS can be used as a springtime centerpiece. Add new species to the mix, and make enough birds so that each guest can take one home.
241

242
OPPOSITE: Loopy white yarn best captures the curly coat of the LAMB. Make his long face stand out by closely trimming the wool on the front of the top pom-pom. The legs are felt-covered pipe cleaners, adhered with craft glue. THIS PAGE: The humorous CATERPILLAR provides as much fascination as a creeper found on the stem of a milkweed. Yours doesn't have to be green; some caterpillars are brightly colored—orange, yellow, and black, for instance—to ward off hungry birds.
CREATED BY CLAUDIA BRUNO, MEGEN LEE, AND LAURA NORMANDIN
243

lifestyle

ES IST NOCH SUPPE DA!

GEMEINSAM ETWAS LECKERES KOCHEN SORGT GLEICH FÜR GUTE PARTYLAUNE. LASSEN SIE SICH VON FRANK BUCHHOLZ INSPIRIEREN

Ein Duft, der auf wunderbare Weise an Kindheit, Weihnachten und kuschelige Abende erinnert, erlebt in diesem Winter ein Revival: Die raffiniert einfache Küche hat die Crème brûlée wieder entdeckt. Kürzlich habe ich Freunde zum gemeinsamen Kochen zu mir nach Hause eingeladen. Die Zutaten hatte ich alle besorgt, beim Schnippeln, Waschen und Putzen musste jeder mithelfen. Lebhafter Smalltalk schon beim Prosecco. Nach den ersten Happen Parmaschinken und Grissini kommt allgemeiner Appetit auf. Dann haben wir uns alle um meinen großen runden Tisch in der Küche versammelt und bis weit nach Mitternacht gegessen und diskutiert und so manche Flasche Rotwein geleert. Als Vorspeise: pikantes Chutney vom Kürbis mit Jakobsmuscheln im Tempurateig, anschließend saftig-zarten Spanferkelrücken mit Lasagne vom Wirsing und Paprika. Nur meine Crème brûlée zum Dessert hatte ich mir als Überraschung aufgehoben. Denn diesmal gab es eine Variante des französischen Klassikers: Crème brûlée mit Mascarpone. Als ich die kleinen Schälchen auf den Tisch stellte, war ich angenehm überrascht, dass eine so schlichte Nachspeise so gut ankommen konnte. Crème brûlée ist wirklich das Einfachste der Welt, aber der Duft von Vanille entlockt unseren Sinnen Erinnerungen, die bis in die Kindheit reichen. Erinnerungen an Großmutters Küche und Garten, in dem wir uns als Kind die reifen Kirschen und Pflaumen, Birnen und Äpfel von den Bäumen pflückten und heimlich die verführerisch prallen Brombeeren in den Mund stopften. Weihnachten roch es in Omas Küche so, wie es im Paradies riechen müsste, wenn Köche das Sagen hätten: nach Lebkuchen, Orangen und Nüssen, Geflügel und Wild.

Genau das ist der Trend: Back to the roots – zurück zu Großmutters Küche. Zurück zu Milch und Mehl, Eiern und Salz, Butter und Schmalz? Nicht ganz – Omas Gerichte sind moderner, leichter, kalorienärmer geworden. Eine Küche, die reduziert ist, aber nicht asketisch. Olivenöl anstatt Butter, viel Knoblauch, frisches Gemüse.
Heimische Produkte, nach Manier der Mittelmeerländer zubereitet, haben Konjunktur, seitdem Wissenschaftler festgestellt haben, dass Italiener und Südfranzosen weniger herzinfarktgefährdet sind als Deutsche. Das berühmte Glas Rotwein soll dazu einen nicht unwesentlichen Beitrag leisten. Mäßiger Alkoholkonsum scheint besser zu sein als gar keiner. Möglichst als Begleiter zu einem gemütlichen Essen.

Denn auch das haben unsere Nachbarn uns voraus: Mittelmeer-Anrainer gönnen sich einfach längere Essenszeiten. Aber die Deutschen holen auf. Der Slow-Food-Trend – Italiens Antwort auf Fastfood – hat inzwischen auch in Deutschland eine Menge Anhänger, ▸

28

die sich dafür einsetzen, dass regionale kulinarische Kulturen neu belebt und Nahrungsmittel ökologisch sinnvoll erzeugt werden. Naturschonende Produktionsweisen sind damit gemeint, genauso wie artgerechte Tierhaltung.

Trends erzeugen Gegentrends. Der kulinarische Purismus der letzten Jahre ließ zeitgleich die gutbürgerliche Küche mit ordentlichen Portionen wieder auferstehen. Die deutsche Hausmannskost ist global geworden. Aufregende Impulse aus Asien und Indien, Kalifornien und Mexiko, Italien und Frankreich haben ihre Spuren hinterlassen. Und geben regionalen Gerichten eine neue Würze. Herzhafte Suppen werden mit Ingwer gewürzt, zur geschmorten Rehkeule wird Polenta gereicht und Crème brûlée wird mit Mascarpone angerichtet. Vielfalt ist Trumpf. Der Trend: Crossover-Cusine. Eine neue Generation von kulinarischen Kosmopoliten will aus allen Töpfen dieser Erde naschen. Sushi trifft Salami, Sauerkraut-Pizza mit Eisbein, Lasagne vom Wirsing, Jakobsmuscheln im Tempurateig – alles keine Seltenheit mehr. Eine Küche für den Bauch, nicht für den Kopf. So sollen auch meine winterlichen Rezepte alle Sinne berühren. Weihnachten ist die Zeit der Besinnung. Seltsamerweise gestalten sich aber gerade die Festtage für manche alles andere als vergnüglich. Das Leben wird zum Stress. Aber nix da, ich möchte, dass Sie die Weihnachtszeit entspannt erleben. Deshalb sind meine Gerichte einfach vor- und zuzubereiten und bewirken gleichzeitig den wünschenswerten Aha-Effekt bei den Gästen.

Kulinarisch gesehen ist der Herbst die schönste Jahreszeit: Das Angebot ist überwältigend, und das kühlere Wetter lockt, den Abend mit Freunden zu verbringen.

Den Garten vor dem Haus gibt es heute nur noch sehr selten. Stattdessen schnappt man sich den Korb und fährt zum Markt. Achten Sie auf die prallen Kürbisse, unter deren Last die Marktstände zusammenzubrechen drohen. Noch nie gab es eine so überwältigende Auswahl dieser „Dickmänner" mit den barocken Formen. Alles an den etwa 800 Sorten lässt sich verwerten: das Fruchtfleisch für Suppen und Gemüsegerichte, die Kerne zum Knabbern, die Schalen romantisch als Kerzenbehälter oder gruselig an Halloween.

Der Winter lockt mit Kohl: Wirsing- und Grünkohl, Weißkraut und Brokkoli sind ganz und gar nicht bieder und erleben in diesem Jahr ihr Comeback. Der Herbstwirsing muß dunkle, kräftige Blätter haben und einen makellosen Strunk. In den USA zum Beispiel greifen figurbewusste Hollywood-Schönheiten deshalb immer öfter zu kalorienarmen Kohlbrühen. Wer den Winter von seiner süßen Seite erleben will, der backt heiße Maroni und serviert sie seinen Gästen als Fingerfood in kleinen Papiertüten.

Denn nicht nur was auf den Tisch kommt, ist wichtig, sondern auch, wie es präsentiert wird. Ein stimmungsvoller Rahmen, eine dekorative Inszenierung wirkt manchmal Wunder.

Eine neue Art von Cocooning ist angesagt. Man bleibt nicht mehr allein zu Hause, nein, man öffnet alle Türen, holt sich Freunde ins Haus. Das Zuhause wird Treffpunkt der Genießer und Lebenskünstler. Bei Kerzenlicht an großen Tischen sitzen und über den besten Rotwein der Welt diskutieren und einfach nur gut essen. Die Küche ▸

lifestyle

30

Room, November/December 2001, Germany

DS, No. 10, 2001, France

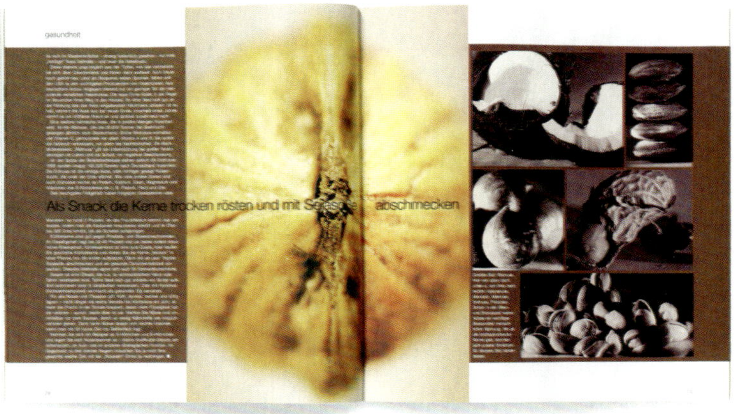

Room, No. 4, 2001, Germany

Big, No. 29, 2000, USA

Martha Stewart Living, February 2002, USA

Elle Bistro, February 2002, Germany

the_dish

roque and roll

Blue cheese dip

120ml sour cream . 120ml mayonnaise . 150g Roquefort cheese, crumbled . 1/2 small white onion, very finely chopped or grated . 1 tbsp lemon juice . a few drops Tabasco

METHOD Place all the ingredients in a bowl and combine them very gently. Do not beat the cheese or the dip will take on a grey appearance.

Glass bowl, £20, from Retro Home

154 wallpaper*

stink pink

Roasted garlic and beetroot

2 whole heads garlic . 2 raw beetroot . 1 tbsp olive oil . 200g cream cheese . 150ml sour cream . 1/2 tsp salt . freshly ground black pepper to taste

METHOD Break the bulbs of garlic into cloves but don't remove their papery skins. Scrub the beetroot and quarter them, then place in a roasting tin with the garlic. Drizzle with the olive oil and place in a hot oven at 375°F/190°C. Roast for 1 to 1 1/2 hours or until the beetroot and garlic are tender. (Check after one hour, and if the garlic cloves are soft before the beetroot, remove them and reserve.) When the beetroot is tender allow to cool then trim the beet pieces and remove their skins with a sharp knife. Remove the roasted garlic cloves from their papery cases and place in a food processor with the beetroot, cream cheese and sour cream. Blend until smooth then season to taste before serving.

Cocoa bowl, £2.50, from Habitat

For stockists, see Resources, page 224

wallpaper* 155

the_dish

fishing for condiments

Smoked salmon and dill

200g smoked salmon, roughly chopped . 350ml crème fraîche . juice of half a lemon . 3 tbsp fresh dill, chopped . freshly ground black pepper

METHOD Place the salmon, crème fraîche and lemon juice in a food processor and pulse until just creamy. Remove to a bowl and fold in the dill, then season with black pepper to taste and serve with Wasa bread.

Glass bowl, £7.50, from John Lewis

deeplydippy

This summer, home entertaining should extend no further than a cupboard full of crackers, a crisper full of crudités and six dips on permanent standby. *Wallpaper** dips its stick into something soft, rich and saucy

choc therapy

Chocolate ganache

METHOD

Glass plate, £17, by LSA, from The Conran Shop

wallpaper* 151

Wallpaper, June 2000, Great Britain

Wallpaper, January 2001, Great Britain

Big, No. 37, 2001, USA

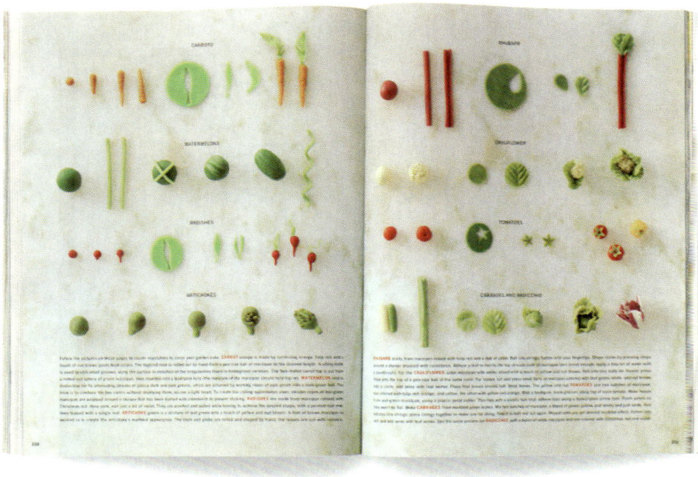

Martha Stewart Living, March 2000, USA

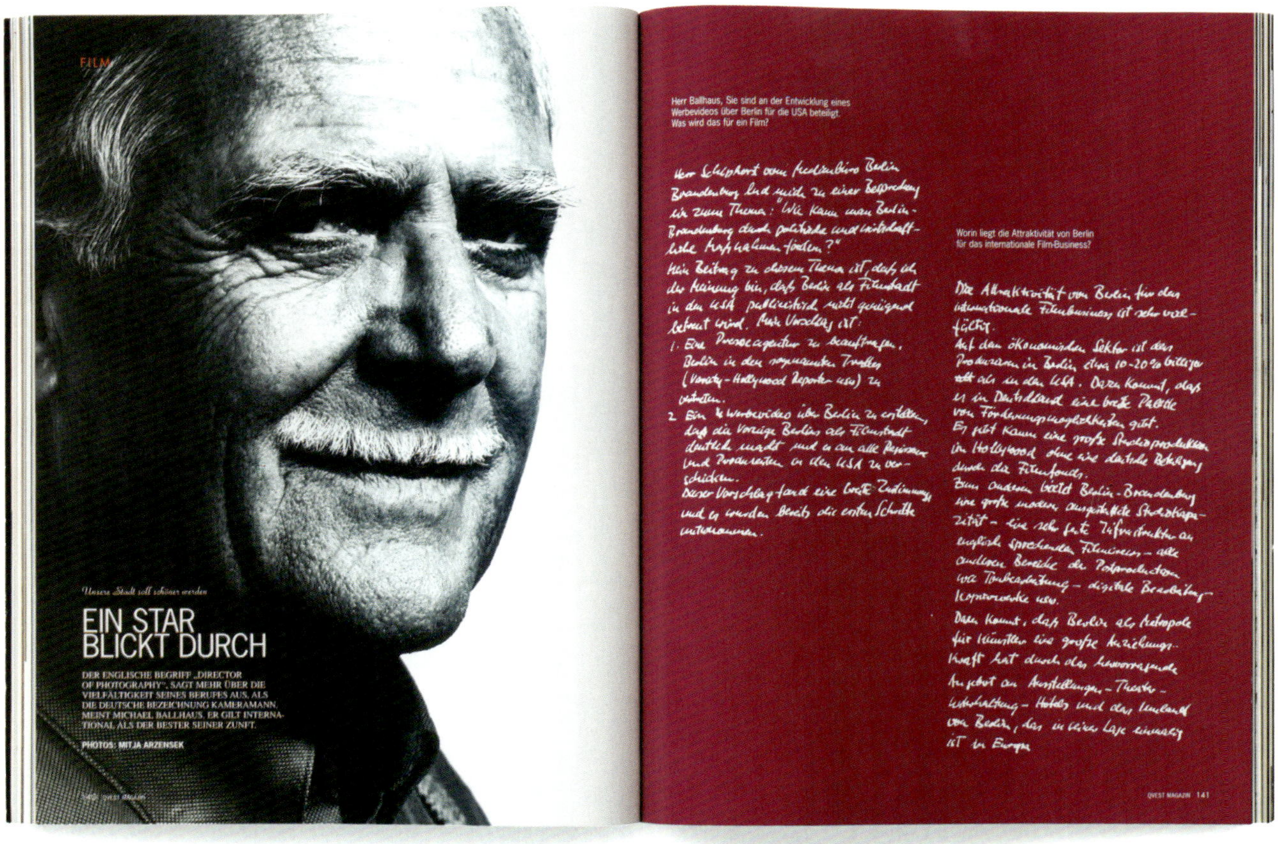
FILM

Unsere Stadt soll schöner werden

EIN STAR
BLICKT DURCH

DER ENGLISCHE BEGRIFF „DIRECTOR OF PHOTOGRAPHY", SAGT MEHR ÜBER DIE VIELFÄLTIGKEIT SEINES BERUFES AUS, ALS DIE DEUTSCHE BEZEICHNUNG KAMERAMANN, MEINT MICHAEL BALLHAUS. ER GILT INTERNATIONAL ALS DER BESTER SEINER ZUNFT.

PHOTOS: MITJA ARZENSEK

Herr Ballhaus, Sie sind an der Entwicklung eines Werbevideos über Berlin für die USA beteiligt. Was wird das für ein Film?

Worin liegt die Attraktivität von Berlin für das internationale Film-Business?

QUEST MAGAZIN 141

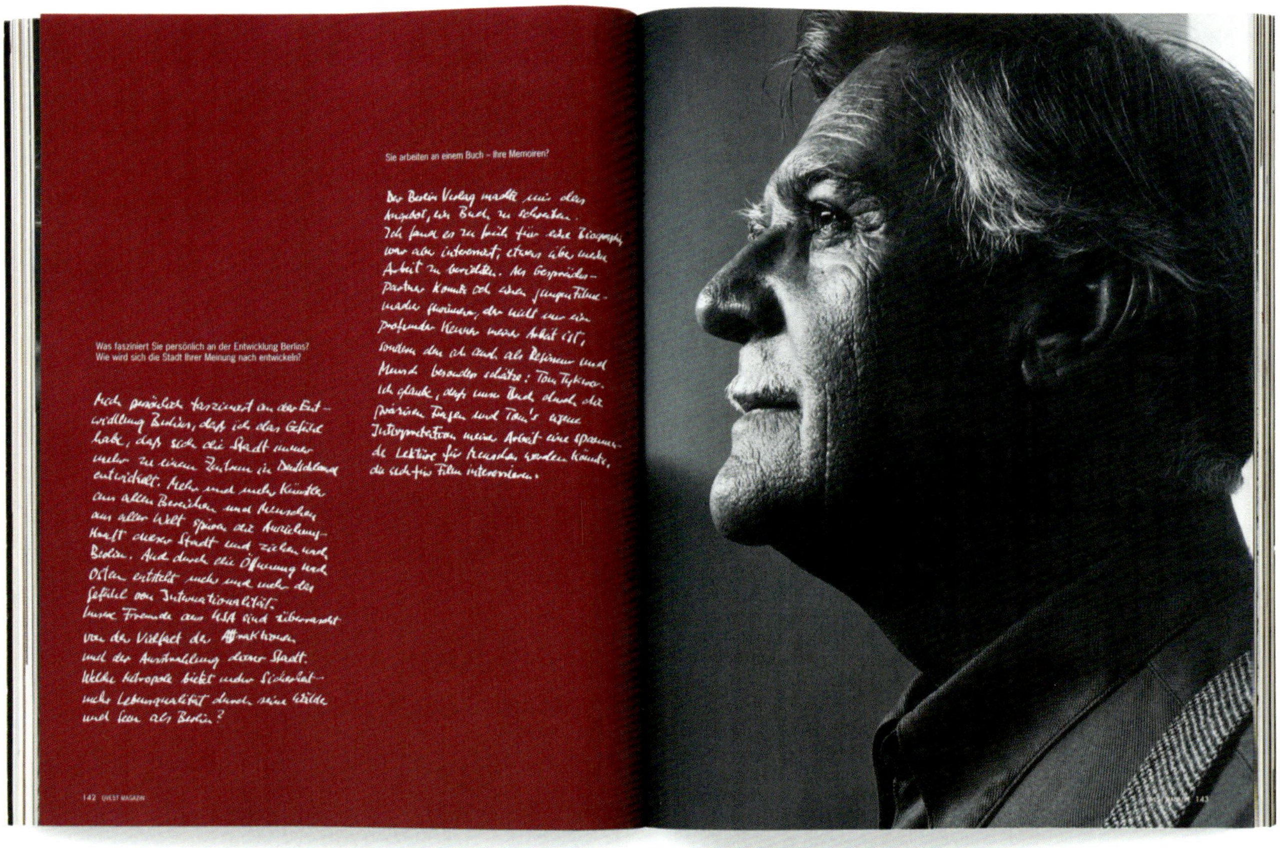
Was fasziniert Sie persönlich an der Entwicklung Berlins? Wie wird sich die Stadt Ihrer Meinung nach entwickeln?

Sie arbeiten an einem Buch – Ihre Memoiren?

142 QUEST MAGAZIN

Quest, February 2001, Germany

Marathonman

Met zijn eigen atletiekcarrière was het te snel afgelopen. Nu organiseert hij marathons en behartigt de belangen van 160 atleten. De voormalig wereldrecordhouder wil hen vooral behoeden voor de fouten die hij zelf maakte. De marathon van Jos Hermens.

door **Dylan van Eijkeren**

Marathonman

Zijn haar is zilvergrijs, net als de kleur van zijn Volvo. En het is kort. Terwijl de wilde haardos van Jos Hermens, nu eenenvijftig, vroeger een begrip was en de hardstlopende activist zelf een fenomeen. Een kleurrijke, keihard trainende sporter waarop moderne marketeers gek zouden zijn. Hermens profileerde zich met boude, linkse uitspraken én met verbluffende wereldrecords op het werelduurrecord en de twintig kilometer. Hij deed mee aan de Olympische Spelen van 1972 en 1976 en hij was de aanstaande wereldrecordhouder op de marathon. Maar hij werd het nooit, want ineens had hij geen achillespezen meer. Ze waren domweg opgelost door de cortisoneninjecties die hem waren toegediend. Dat was het einde van Jos Hermens, atleet.

Zijn achillespezen mochten dan verdwenen zijn, de passie voor het langeafstandslopen bleef. Hermens ging aan de slag bij Nike, een beginnend sportschoenenfirmaatje. Hij verkocht de schoenen letterlijk vanuit de achterbak van zijn auto en in de vroege jaren tachtig werd hij hoofd van de promotieafdeling. Tot 1985, toen hij voor zichzelf een eenmansfirma begon onder de niet van optimisme gespeende naam Global Sports Communications. Vanaf een even spreekwoordelijke als bestaande zolderkamer diende hij atleten van advies dat hij zelf moest ontberen in zijn sportieve gloriedagen: train niet te veel, loop jezelf niet kapot, pas op je lichaam. Ook nu zegt hij: 'Bij ons staat de atleet op de eerste plaats.'

Zijn aanpak sloeg aan onder atleten, bij uitstek solisten. Hermens bouwde een stal op die in omvang en kwaliteit kan wedijveren met de gerenommeerdste ter wereld. Inmiddels heeft Global Sports Communications tien werknemers in vaste dienst, wat fors is voor een sport die niet bepaald bekendstaat om de miljoenenomzetten. Daarnaast startte Hermens begin 1994 Global Sports Marketing, een bedrijf dat wedstrijdorganisaties de public relations, marketing en sponsorwerving uit handen neemt. In 1996 werd Hermens' imperiumpje tot een trias via Global Sports Events. Die tak organiseert hele wedstrijden, zoals de Amsterdam Marathon. Dat hoofdstedelijke evenement stond vroeger bekend om de gammele organisatie, maar sinds een paar jaar is 'Amsterdam' vermaard om zijn snelle tijden.

Wereldrecord

Het idee hele wedstrijden op touw te zetten, is vooral voortgekomen uit de internationale successen die Hermens al twintig jaar boekt als mede-organisator van de Rotterdam Marathon. Ooit begonnen met het budget voor één wereldtopper, heeft 'Rotterdam' het inmiddels niet alleen geschopt tot het 'grootste eendaagse sportevenement van Nederland'; de marathon geniet over de hele wereld aanzien. Aanzien dat is ontstaan door snelle tijden, jaar in jaar uit, met als hoogtepunt de Ethiopiër Densamo, die in 1988 in Rotterdam een wereldrecord liep dat tien jaar lang niet gebroken zou worden.

De week die voorafgaat aan de Rotterdam Marathon van afgelopen 16 april is voor Hermens een drukke. De stal, met inmiddels een kleine honderdzestig atleten uit zesentwintig landen, vereist de gebruikelijke aandacht, en dan zijn er nog de besognes die de organisatie van een race met zich meebrengt. Hermens: 'We hebben meer afzeggingen dan normaal. Ik ga nog proberen andere lopers te regelen, maar dat mislukt vaak. Daarbij zijn er de Afrikanen die vergeten hun visum op te halen, te laat komen, niet op de persconferentie verschijnen, dat soort grappen.'

De drukte impliceert dat zijn mobiele telefoon met gekmakende regelmaat weerklinkt, dat er lawines e-mail op zijn laptop verschijnen en dat zijn aanwezigheid op twaalf plaatsen tegelijk vereist lijkt. Hermens: 'Ik werk altijd, tachtig uur per week. Ik begin 's ochtends rond negen uur en ga vaak door tot een uur of elf. Ik ben vijfenveertig weekeinden per jaar in het buitenland om races te bekijken en atleten te zien en te ontmoeten. Noem dat gerust acquisitie. Maar in zo'n week voor Rotterdam of Amsterdam ben ik vooral op kantoor te vinden, dan houd ik mijn agenda zoveel mogelijk leeg. Ik wil direct kunnen reageren als het nodig is.'

Ondanks de groei van het bedrijf houdt Hermens zich nog altijd met de details bezig. 'Het leukst aan mijn werk vind ik carrièreplanning. Heel belangrijk, want dat is eigenlijk de marketing van de atleet. Wat zijn z'n sterke en zwakke punten, hoe zet je hem in de markt? Dat kan ik natuurlijk niet bijhouden van honderdvijftig man, maar van de toptwintig doe ik dat wel. Ik bezoek veel wedstrijden, en daar zie ik ook de nieuwe talenten. Ik overleg alles met de mensen hier: hoe gaan we het aanpakken, hoe komt de atleet over bij de mensen en hoe komt hij over bij de pers? Maar het allerleukst is jonge mensen van achttien, negentien jaar te begeleiden tot hun dertigste, vijfendertigste. Dan zie je niet alleen hoe ze zich ontwikkelen als atleet, maar ook als mens. Ze slurpen kennis op en groeien uit van jochies uit kleine Afrikaanse dorpen tot echte wereldburgers.'

'Laat Gebrselassie maar lekker eerst in Londen lopen. Dan loopt hij dat wereldrecord later wel in Rotterdam'

Balans

Hermens' kantoor staat in een Nijmeegse buitenwijk, na jarenlang in een landelijke, uiterst moeilijk te vinden boerderij in het Brabantse Boekel te hebben geresideerd. Het nieuwgebouwde kantoor biedt niet alleen onderdak aan Hermens' staf, onder wie oud-toplopers als Getano Tessema en Ellen van Langen, maar herbergt op de eerste en tweede verdieping ook een sporthotel. Hermens: 'Daar kunnen onze atleten voor vijftien dollar per dag verblijven. Veel atleten kunnen niet na elke wedstrijd naar huis. Ze komen uit Ethiopië, Zuid-Afrika of Rusland, en verdienen niet genoeg om na elke wedstrijd terug te vliegen. Dus lopen ze drie à vier wedstrijden in één maand, en verblijven in de tussentijd hier.'

Gevolg is dat de oud-atleet, nog altijd met een wee gevoel in het hart, vanuit zijn kantoorraam wereldtoppers in vrijwel iedere atletiekdiscipline richting bos of sintelbaan ziet draven. 'Doordat ze hier verblijven, kunnen we ervoor zorgen dat ze altijd wat geld mee naar huis nemen. Want vaak is het zo dat een heel dorp afhankelijk is van de inkomsten van de atleet. Ons streven is hen niet met lege handen naar hun land terug te laten keren, hoe weinig ze ook verdienen.'

Hermens gaat vrij ver in dat streven: vanwege de luttele inkomsten die vooral startende atleten hebben, betaalt Global Sports Communications veel retourtickets Addis Abeba-Schiphol. En wie echt weinig verdient, hoeft ook die vijftien dollar per dag niet aan Her-

110 QUOTE juni 2000

Quote, June 2000, Netherlands

Gwen Stefani and Terry Hall –
staged by Lizzi Finn (Artwork) for *Dazed & Confused*.

Dazed & Confused, No. 89, 2002, Great Britain,

Lenny Kravitz –
cool and simple by Christopher Witkin for *Surface*.

Surface, No. 15, 1998, USA

Drew Barrymore –
as seen by Mark Seliger for *Rolling Stone*.

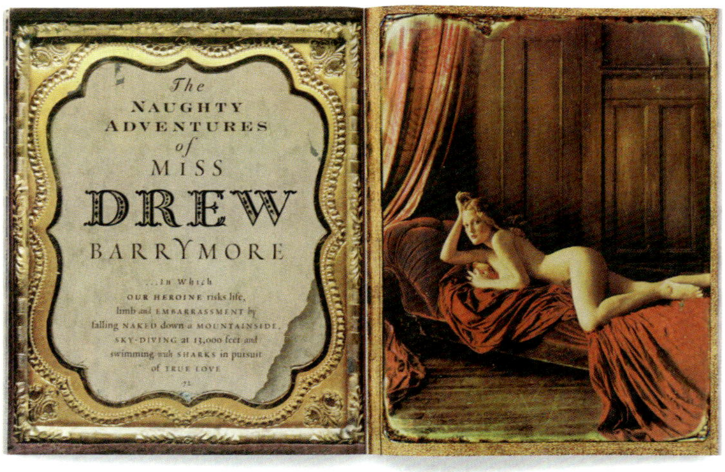

Rolling Stone, November 2000, USA

"It was hard to imagine what it was like for you back in the day"

GWEN STEFANI

"We wanted to change the world... but it was too big"

TERRY HALL

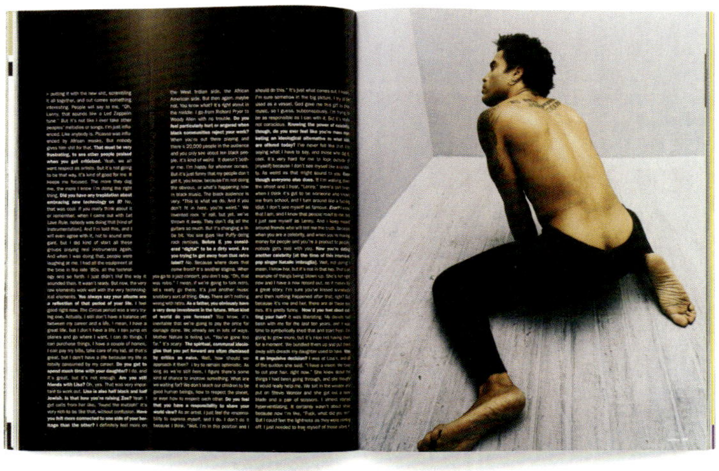

By CHRIS HEATH

Photography by MARK SELIGER

TO MARK the new millennium, Drew Barrymore went to a small Hawaiian island with friends. At midnight, after cooking food on a secluded beach, they privately wrote down the resolutions they wished to make on pieces of paper, which they then rolled up and set on fire. They dug a hole in the sand, a few feet above the waterline, and buried the ashes.

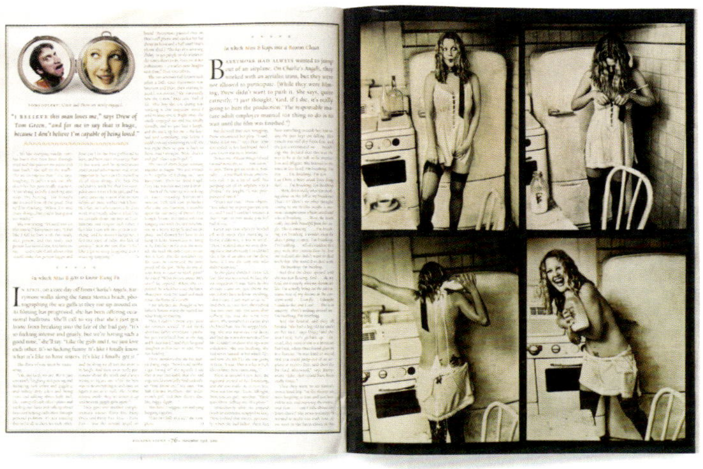

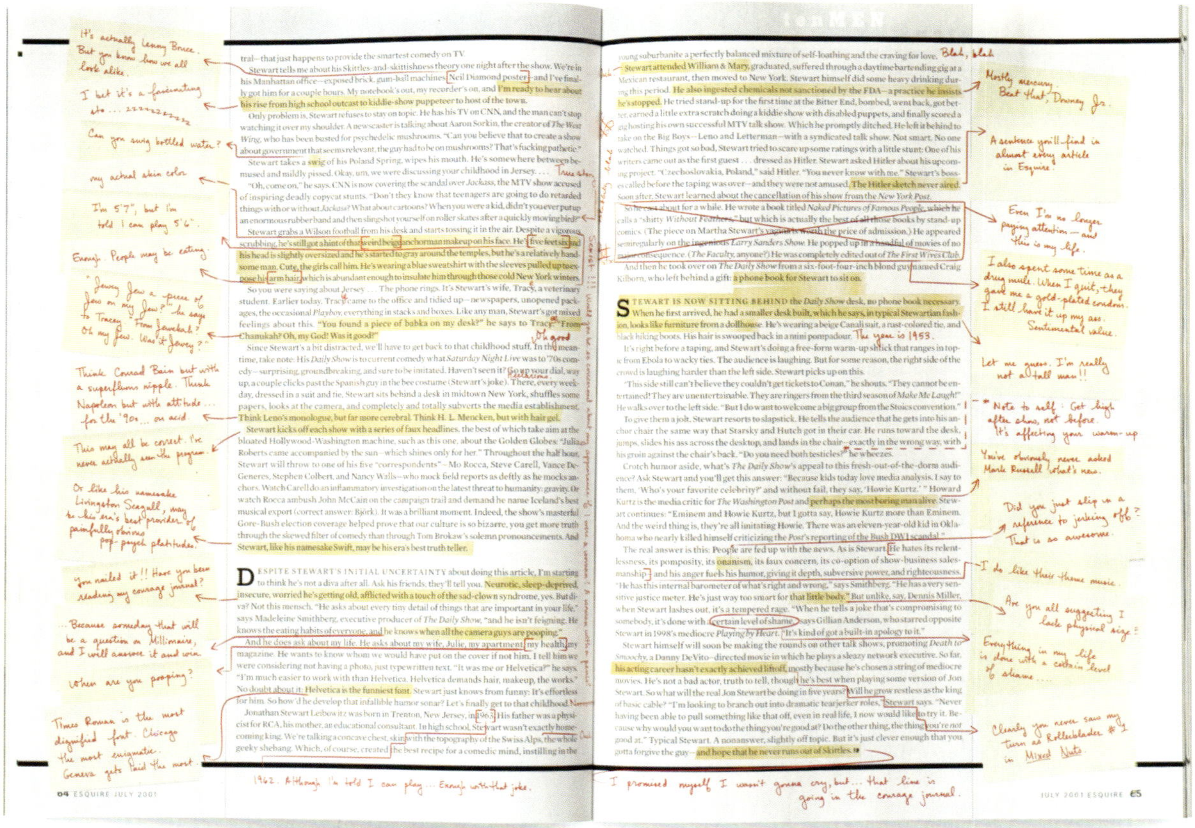

Esquire, No. 136, 2001, USA

Trace, No. 34, 2001, USA

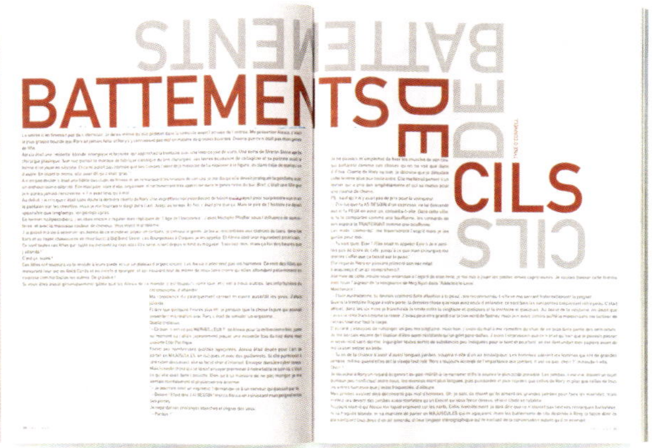

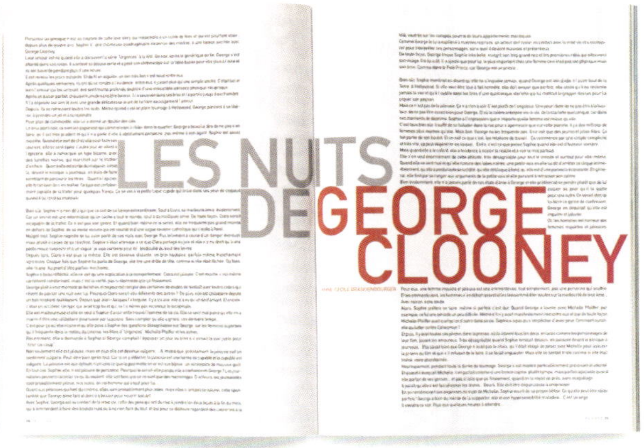

Jalouse, No. 35, 2000, France

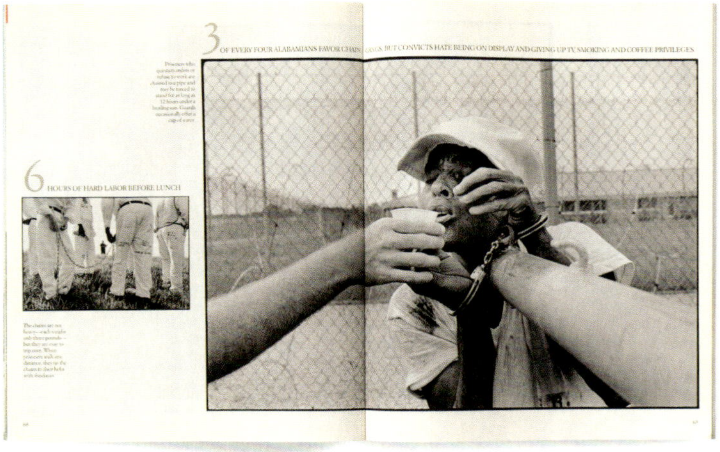

Life, No. 10, 1995, USA

Top: Report on a labour camp in Huntsville, Alabama. Photos: James Nachtwey for *Life*.

Right: 'A hole in the city'. Photos: Joel Meyerowitz for *The New Yorker*.

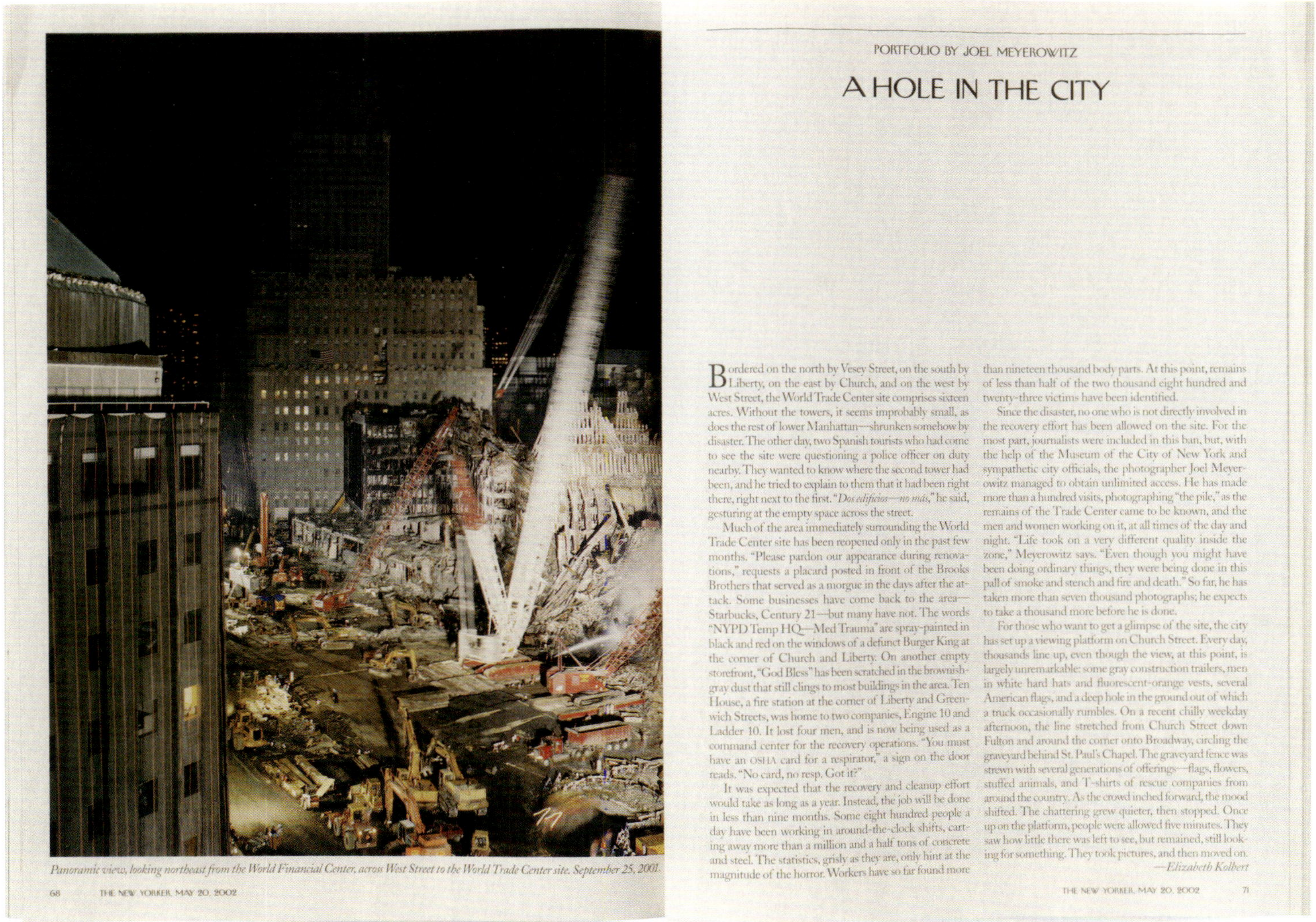

PORTFOLIO BY JOEL MEYEROWITZ

A HOLE IN THE CITY

Bordered on the north by Vesey Street, on the south by Liberty, on the east by Church, and on the west by West Street, the World Trade Center site comprises sixteen acres. Without the towers, it seems improbably small, as does the rest of lower Manhattan—shrunken somehow by disaster. The other day, two Spanish tourists who had come to see the site were questioning a police officer on duty nearby. They wanted to know where the second tower had been, and he tried to explain to them that it had been right there, right next to the first. "*Dos edificios—no más,*" he said, gesturing at the empty space across the street.

Much of the area immediately surrounding the World Trade Center site has been reopened only in the past few months. "Please pardon our appearance during renovations," requests a placard posted in front of the Brooks Brothers that served as a morgue in the days after the attack. Some businesses have come back to the area—Starbucks, Century 21—but many have not. The words "NYPD Temp HQ—Med Trauma" are spray-painted in black and red on the windows of a defunct Burger King at the corner of Church and Liberty. On another empty storefront, "God Bless" has been scratched in the brownish-gray dust that still clings to most buildings in the area. Ten House, a fire station at the corner of Liberty and Greenwich Streets, was home to two companies, Engine 10 and Ladder 10. It lost four men, and is now being used as a command center for the recovery operations. "You must have an OSHA card for a respirator," a sign on the door reads. "No card, no resp. Got it?"

It was expected that the recovery and cleanup effort would take as long as a year. Instead, the job will be done in less than nine months. Some eight hundred people a day have been working in around-the-clock shifts, carting away more than a million and a half tons of concrete and steel. The statistics, grisly as they are, only hint at the magnitude of the horror. Workers have so far found more than nineteen thousand body parts. At this point, remains of less than half of the two thousand eight hundred and twenty-three victims have been identified.

Since the disaster, no one who is not directly involved in the recovery effort has been allowed on the site. For the most part, journalists were included in this ban, but, with the help of the Museum of the City of New York and sympathetic city officials, the photographer Joel Meyerowitz managed to obtain unlimited access. He has made more than a hundred visits, photographing "the pile," as the remains of the Trade Center came to be known, and the men and women working on it, at all times of the day and night. "Life took on a very different quality inside the zone," Meyerowitz says. "Even though you might have been doing ordinary things, they were being done in this pall of smoke and stench and fire and death." So far, he has taken more than seven thousand photographs; he expects to take a thousand more before he is done.

For those who want to get a glimpse of the site, the city has set up a viewing platform on Church Street. Every day, thousands line up, even though the view, at this point, is largely unremarkable: some gray construction trailers, men in white hard hats and fluorescent-orange vests, several American flags, and a deep hole in the ground out of which a truck occasionally rumbles. On a recent chilly weekday afternoon, the line stretched from Church Street down Fulton and around the corner onto Broadway, circling the graveyard behind St. Paul's Chapel. The graveyard fence was strewn with several generations of offerings—flags, flowers, stuffed animals, and T-shirts of rescue companies from around the country. As the crowd inched forward, the mood shifted. The chattering grew quieter, then stopped. Once up on the platform, people were allowed five minutes. They saw how little there was left to see, but remained, still looking for something. They took pictures, and then moved on.

—Elizabeth Kolbert

Panoramic view, looking northeast from the World Financial Center, across West Street to the World Trade Center site. September 25, 2001.

68 THE NEW YORKER, MAY 20, 2002

THE NEW YORKER, MAY 20, 2002 71

The New Yorker, May 2002, USA

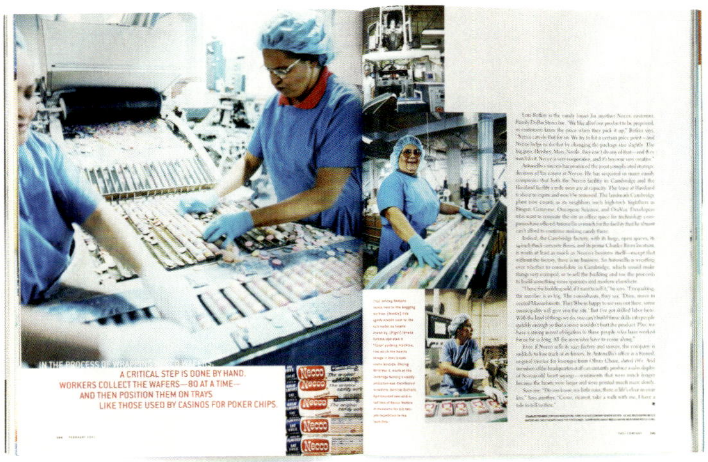

Fast Company, No. 2, 2001, USA

Dutch, March/April 2001, Netherlands

Top: 'Sweet Company' – Visit to Necco's. Photos: Michael McLaughlin for *Fast Company*.

Bottom: 'Chrome Cowboys' – Biker life in Brooklyn. Captured by Martin Dixon for *Dutch*.

Right: 'The world from my front porch'. Larry Towell shows his Ontario world in *Life*.

THE WAY WE LIVE

THE WORLD FROM MY FRONT PORCH

WHEN I was an adolescent, my father once scolded me for wanting to drive to Florida with a friend. It was too far from home, and I would be corrupted by the distance. I was 16. I'd been brought up on a small farm in Ontario and barely had been beyond 100 miles from home. Neither had he, at least not more than once or twice. He hated travel. He was rooted in the ground he stood on. The world for him was his front porch; it made him who he was.

Ten years after Ann and I were married, when we were expecting our third child, we bought a 75-acre farm at 40 percent of the owner's asking price. Its six small fields, severed by roads, gulleys and a river, made it awkward for modern machinery, and much of the land was unproductive. Once I had my own front porch, however, I felt positioned in the world.

PHOTOGRAPHY AND TEXT BY LARRY TOWELL

62

Ann holds Isaac on the front porch of their farmhouse in southern Ontario, as Moses looks on.

THE WORLD FROM MY FRONT PORCH

Most of these photographs were taken within 100 yards of the house. Although I travel extensively now, it is still with a sense of exile. From Hanoi to Managua, from San Salvador to East Jerusalem and the Occupied Territories, the longing for home persists. A photojournalist must work in the arena of international events. But when I am not traveling, I turn the camera inward.

Buying into a rural community demands an investigation of its history and a commitment to its past. One must treat the past as though it were the present. Many of my new neighbors could trace their ancestries to the first Scottish settlers of what was then Upper Canada. The first porch and original section of our house were built by pioneer surveyor Samuel Smith, who bought the farm in 1825 from the British Crown.

Ann and Moses (left) stop to eat a pear in the family's 1951 Chevy pickup, painted metallic orange.

Caught on one of the photographer's first rolls of film, in 1974: his two sisters, in an abandoned farmhouse

63

Life, No. 9, 1997, USA

MTC, No. 1, 2001, Netherlands

Photo, No. 3, 2002, France

Mare, No. 18, 2000, Germany

Top: Morocco is green – as seen by Bernard Touillon for *MTC – More than classic*.

Middle: 'Vietnam Inc.' Philip Jones Griffiths for *Photo*.

Bottom: 'The Magic Sailors'. Report on the building of an East African dhow. Photos by Jack Picone, text by Alison Campell for *Mare*.

KLEPPERENDE EZELHOEVEN, HET GEROEP VAN DE MUEZZIN
HET RUMOER VAN KOOPLUI - DE GELUIDEN VAN MAROKKO

VEEL VAN DE OOSTERSE PRACHT
EN PRAAL GAAT SCHUIL ACHTER
VOOR WESTERLINGEN GESLOTEN DEUREN

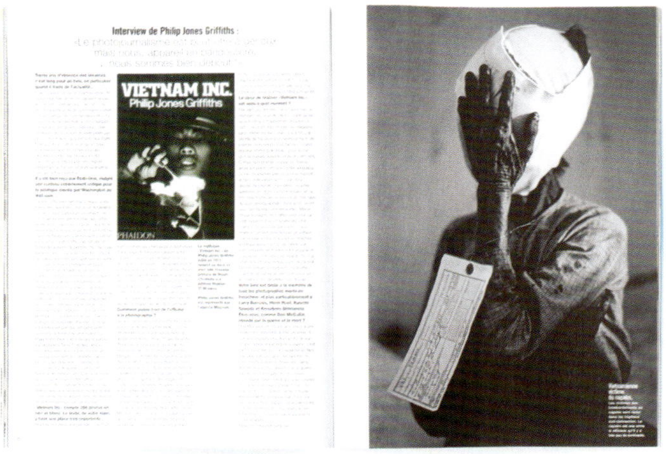
Interview de Philip Jones Griffiths
VIETNAM INC.
Philip Jones Griffiths
PHAIDON

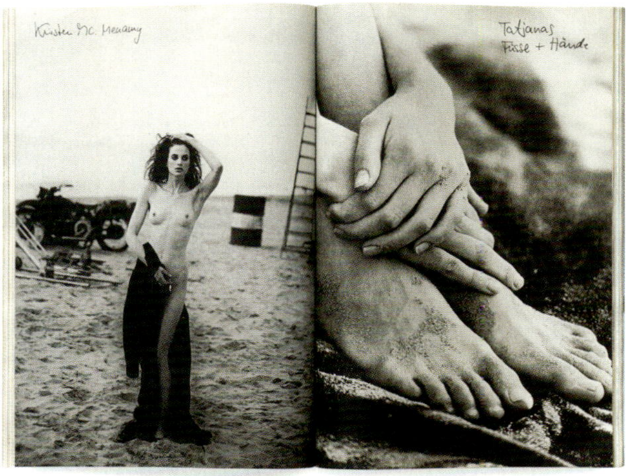

Max, December 1992, Germany

Max, November 1994, Germany

Top: Peter Lindbergh portfolio in *Max*.

Bottom: Richard Avedon portfolio in *Max*.

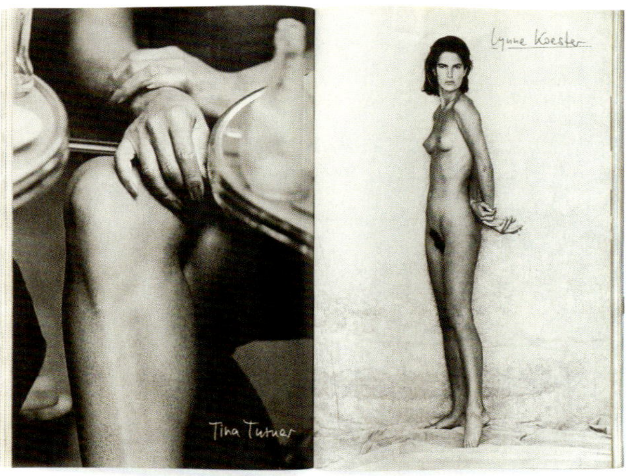
Lynne Koester
Tina Turner

Lynne Koester
Estelle
Halliday

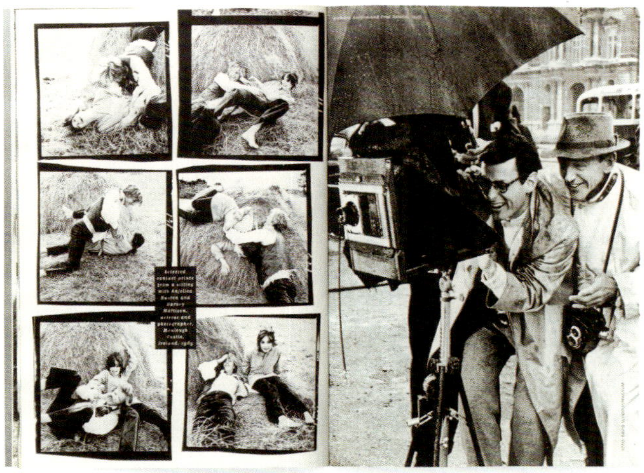

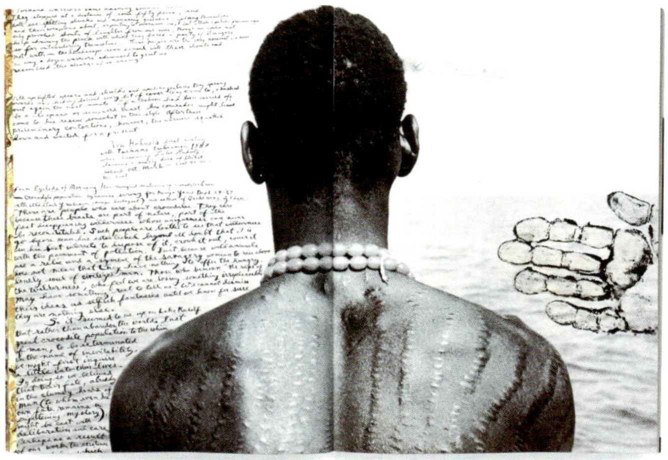

Matador, D, 1999, Spain

Peter Beard portfolio in *Matador*.

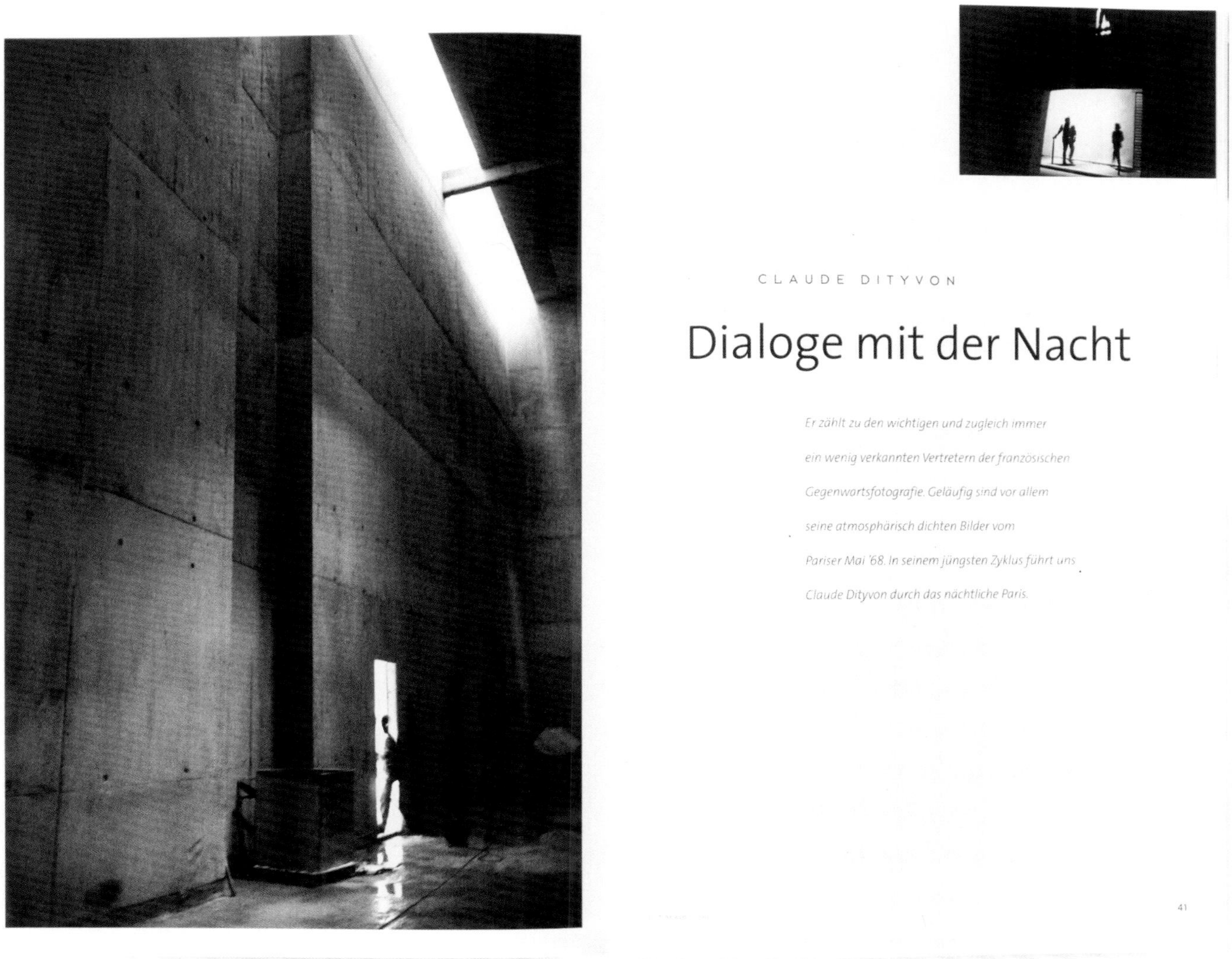

CLAUDE DITYVON

Dialoge mit der Nacht

Er zählt zu den wichtigen und zugleich immer ein wenig verkannten Vertretern der französischen Gegenwartsfotografie. Geläufig sind vor allem seine atmosphärisch dichten Bilder vom Pariser Mai '68. In seinem jüngsten Zyklus führt uns Claude Dityvon durch das nächtliche Paris.

41

Leica World, No. 1, 2001, Germany

Claude Dityvon portfolio in *Leica World*.

Original magazine spines, and a design for the year

The binding of magazines varies according to the thickness. A thin one will be stapled through the spine, whereas thicker ones will be glued. The latter usually have a spine that's several millimetres wide, and many publishers like to fill it with the name, date and various themes of the magazine. But there are also designers who incorporate the spine into their design, either individually for each issue, or as a continuation throughout the year. In some magazines, there are even complete pictures or texts formed when all the issues of one year are placed together in the correct order. *Avenue*, a Dutch magazine, was one of the first to experiment with this idea, and it achieved some fine effects. Other magazines use the spine to display different colour codes. Which is the best direction for the text remains an open question; it really depends on how the magazine is likely to be stored – upright or lying flat – as well as on personal preferences.

Ad!dict, No. 15, No. 13, June 1998, No. 8, No. 10, Belgium

Arena, Winter 1988/1989, Spring 1989, Spring/Summer 1989, Summer 1989, Summer/Autumn 1989, Great Britain

Designers Digest, Nos. 65, 72, 70, 69, 76, Germany

Page, Nos. 1 – 12, 1997, Germany

Business 2.0, February 2001, April – June 2001, June – September 2000, November – December 2000, Great Britain/Germany

Hightech, Nos. 1 – 12, 1988, Germany

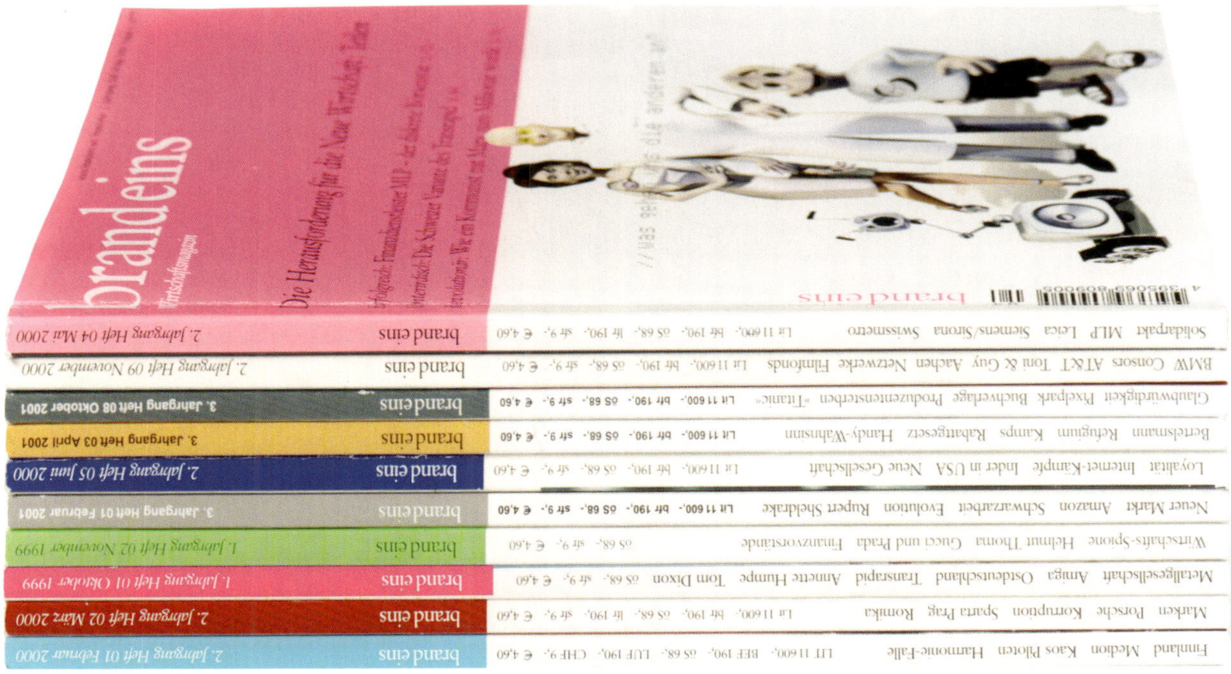

Brand eins, February – March 2000, October – November 1999, February 2001, June 2000, April 2001, October 2001, November 2000, May 2000, Germany

Spex, Nos. 1, 1999; 3 – 9, 1999; 11, 1999, Germany

Wired, January 2000; January, April – June, November 2001; January – February 2002; May 2002, USA

High Quality, 20, 1991; 15, 1989; 12, 1988; 30, 1994; 19, 1991; 16, 1990; 26, 1993; 25 – 27, 1993, Germany

Avenue, January – December 1991, Netherlands

Avenue, January – December 1986, Netherlands

Avenue, January – December 1988, Netherlands

Avenue, January – December 1992, Netherlands

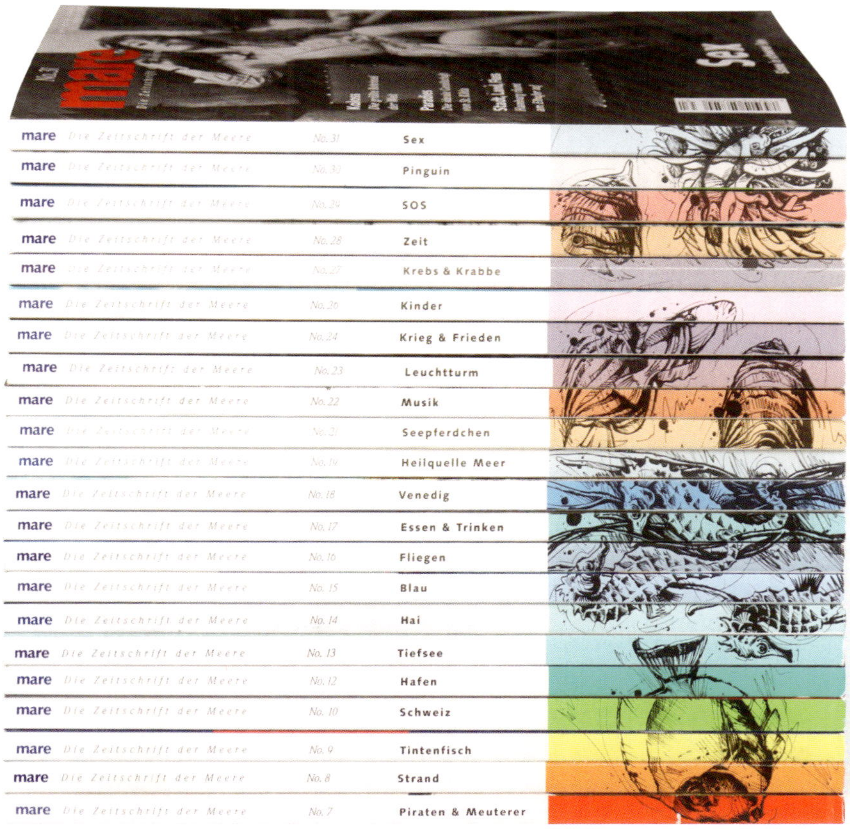

Mare, Nos. 7–10, 1998; Nos. 12–17, 1999; No. 19, 2000; Nos. 21–22, 2000; No. 24, 2001; Nos. 26–29, 2001; Nos. 30–31, 2002, Germany

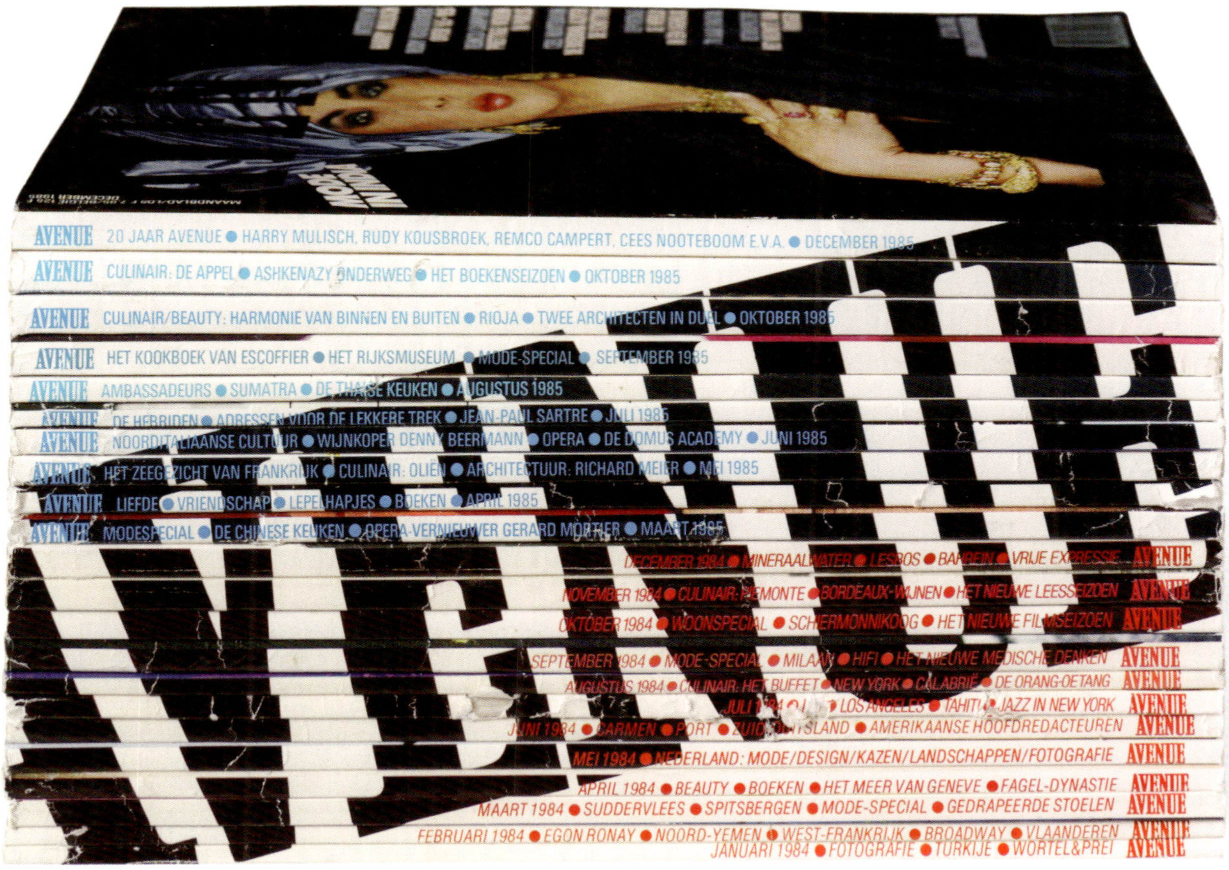

Avenue, January – November 1984; June – December 1985, Netherlands

INDEXES

INDEX OF MAGAZINES

Numbers in *italics* refer to mention within the text.

INDEX OF NAMES

Surprise Me
Editorial Design

This book is typeset in FF DIN and was designed by Independent Medien-Design, Munich, Germany.

Text by Ilse Moser and Horst Moser in collaboration with Stephanie Wiesner
Thanks to Stefanie Steiger

Translated from the German by David H. Wilson

First published in the United States of America in 2003 by
Mark Batty Publisher, LLC,
6050 Boulevard East, Suite 2H, West New York, New Jersey 07093

www.MarkBattyPublisher.com

Library of Congress Cataloging-in-Publication data:
Moser, Horst.
[Surprise me. English]
Surprise me! : editorial design / Horst Moser;
[translated from the German by David H. Wilson]. – 1st ed. in the U.S.A.
p. cm.
Includes indexes.
ISBN 0-9725636-0-1
1. Magazine design. 2. Graphic design (Typography) I. Title.
Z246.M9313 2003
741.6'52--dc21
2003004941

ISBN 0-9725636-0-1

Printed and bound in Germany

Y
NUMMERSECHS
JUNI 1991
FÜNF MARK
versieren. Moeilijk maar mogelijk: zeggen wat je l
vindt in bed. Doen: met je depressie naar de dokter
zij aan zij
Power ohne Ende:
Auf den Inha